PROBLEMS OF THE MODERN ECONOMY

Changing Patterns in Foreign Trade and Payments

Third Edition

PROBLEMS OF THE MODERN ECONOMY

General Editor: EDMUND S. PHELPS, *Columbia University*

Each volume in this series presents
prominent positions in the debate of
an important issue of economic policy

Changing Patterns in Foreign Trade and Payments

Edited with an introduction by
BELA BALASSA
THE JOHNS HOPKINS UNIVERSITY

THIRD EDITION

NEW YORK
W · W · NORTON & COMPANY · INC ·

Library of Congress Cataloging in Publication Data
Balassa, Bela A   ed.
    Changing patterns in foreign trade and payments.
    (Problems of the modern economy)
    Bibliography: p.
    1. Balance of payments—United States—Addresses, essays, lectures. 2. International
economic relations—Addresses, essays, lectures. 3. International finance—Addresses,
essays, lectures. 4. International business enterprises—Addresses, essays, lectures. 5.
Investments, Foreign—Addresses, essays, lectures. I. Title.   HG3883.U7B25 1978
332.4'5   77-11985
ISBN 0-393-05662-7
ISBN 0-393-09138-4 pbk.

1 2 3 4 5 6 7 8 9 0

Contents

v

PART FOUR: International Economic Interdependence
and Monetary Reform

Introduction

A NUMBER OF important developments have occurred during the six years that have elapsed since the last edition of this book of readings appeared. This has necessitated a complete overhaul of the volume and, with two exceptions, this edition contains only new selections. The new edition has also been enlarged in order to enable the reader to get a better appreciation of the increasingly complex problems of international trade, investment, and finance.

In the international trade field, major developments have been the completion of the Kennedy Round of tariff reductions and the undertaking of the Tokyo Round of negotiations that aims at reducing tariff as well as nontariff barriers. In the United States, the protectionist Burke-Hartke Act, strongly supported by labor, was defeated, and the Trade Act of 1974 has given greater power to the president both to reduce and to impose trade barriers.

The Trade Act has also eased the conditions of providing adjustment assistance to workers and firms who are adversely affected by imports. As a result, adjustment assistance has emerged as an alternative to the imposition of trade barriers. And the adjustment problem assumes increased importance with shifts in international specialization and, in particular, given the increased capabilities of developing countries to export manufactured goods.

The period in question has also seen a quadrupling of oil prices. While concerns expressed regarding the implications for financial markets of the resulting income transfer to the oil-producing countries have proved exaggerated, problems remain with regard to the high cost of oil to developed as well as developing countries, the disposition of the balance-of-payments surpluses of the OPEC countries, and the security of energy supplies. At the same time, the success of the oil-producing countries in exploiting their market position has induced producers of other commodities to attempt or to contemplate similar action.

In the framework of proposals for a new international economic order, recommendations have also been made for stabilizing export prices and earnings for primary producers, while the large Soviet purchases and poor harvests, together with the reduction in United States stockpiles, have led to a call for world-wide action on cereals.

In the field of international investment, concerns about U.S. investments in Western Europe have declined in importance while increased attention has been given to foreign—and especially OPEC—investment in the United States. At the same time, multinational corporations have been attacked on several fronts, with U.S. labor fearing the loss of jobs and the host countries the loss of national sovereignty. In turn, the need for control of multinational corporations by the home countries to safeguard their own interests has been argued.

In the international monetary area, President Richard Nixon's decision to suspend the convertibility of the dollar into gold, the demise of the Bretton-Woods agreement, and the "dirty" floating of the principal currencies have been the major events. While these changes have altered the character of the economic inter-dependence of nations, the Jamaica Agreement of January 1976 essentially granted each country the freedom to determine—and to modify—its exchange rate system and made no advance toward the international control of international liquidity.

PART ONE: TRADE LIBERALIZATION AND THE ADJUSTMENT PROBLEM

The essay by Irving B. Kravis provides an overview of arguments pro and con trade liberalization. Kravis concludes that "the national interests of the U.S. lie in the direction of freer trade. The arguments for a contrary policy . . . are based on incorrect assessments of the facts, draw unwarranted conclusions from true statements of fact, or stress benefits that may be real and important but are either incapable of achievement or can be attained only at large economic and political cost."

One of Kravis's conclusions has been that trade liberalization would not have adverse effects on trade and employment in the United States. Still, the problem of short-term adjustment remains, and hence interest attaches to James E. McCarthy's discussion of the contrasting experiences of two United States industries with trade adjustment assistance in the application of the Trade Expansion Act of 1962.

As noted earlier, the Trade Act of 1974 has liberalized the conditions for obtaining adjustment assistance. It has also eased the conditions for applying escape clauses under which the president may negotiate voluntary restraints and impose quotas or higher tariffs in the event imports cause injury to domestic industry. The act also gives the president sweeping powers to retaliate against unfair trade practices and speeds up the handling of complaints concerning dumping and export subsidization on the part of foreign countries.

While these protectionist features of the Trade Act are balanced by providing the president new authority to negotiate agreements lowering tariff and nontariff barriers and the granting of preferences to developing countries, the future course of American trade policy will only be determined as the act's provisions are implemented. Decisions by President Gerald Ford on several cases taken in early 1976, and reported in an article reproduced here from the *Washington Post,* give evidence of a movement in the direction of freer trade. Apart from international political considerations, possible effects on the consumer and on the rate of inflation have been given weight in taking these decisions.

The future course of international trading arrangements will be greatly influenced by the ongoing trade negotiations at GATT (General Agreement on Tariffs and Trade). Geza Feketekuty examines the objectives of the negotiations and makes recommendations for reforming GATT rules.

PART TWO: OIL, COMMODITIES, AND THE NEW INTERNATIONAL ECONOMIC ORDER

In his essay on "Restructuring the World Economy," Hollis B. Chenery considers possible adjustments following the quadrupling of the price of oil in oil-exporting, developed, and developing countries, and suggests policies for these three groups of countries to ensure continuing growth in the world economy.

Chenery essentially takes increased oil prices as a datum and sees few difficulties in the investment of the export proceeds of the OPEC countries in the developed nations.

Conversely, Thomas O. Enders suggests that the developed countries should take measures to bring about a reduction in oil prices and to reduce reliance on OPEC oil. The proposed measures include conservation as well as stimulus to the development of alternative sources of energy, such as the relaxation of existing policy constraints, the provision of financing, and minimum prices for domestic producers.

The question arises whether the producers of other primary commodities could follow the example of the oil-producing countries in taking joint action. Having considered the case of several nonoil minerals, C. Fred Bergsten concludes they could successfully establish cartels, while Raymond F. Mikesell takes the opposite view. In turn, the tripartite report of fourteen experts from North America, Western Europe, and Japan examines the possibilities of international cooperation in agriculture.

One of the key demands of the developing countries for a new international economic order has been to stabilize the export prices and earnings of primary producers. This would be accomplished through the establishment of commodity agreements that would be part of an integrated commodity scheme under a proposal made by UNCTAD (United Nations Conference on Trade and Development). This proposal is criticized by Mordechai E. Kreinin and J. M. Finger in whose view UNCTAD's emphasis on commodity agreements is mistaken and one should concentrate on stimulating the process of internal transformation in the developing countries instead.

PART THREE: FOREIGN INVESTMENT AND THE MULTINATIONAL CORPORATION

According to Raymond Vernon, multinational enterprises contribute to global welfare, but the equitable distribution of the gains is not assured. The distribution of gains and national sovereignty are key issues regarding the policies followed by the host countries toward the multinational firms that Vernon scrutinizes in the first essay in Part Three. Some of these issues are examined from a U.S. perspective in regard to foreign investments in the United States in the essay by John C. Culver.

The preceding essays consider the effects of multinational firms in the host countries. In turn, Thomas Horst and George H. Hildebrand examine the impact of American multinational firms on the U.S. economy; the former concentrates on trade, taxation, and antitrust issues while the latter focuses on labor's interests. Finally, the essay by John M. Dunning provides a fitting ending to Part Three as it calls for international agreements concerning multinational corporations.

PART FOUR: INTERNATIONAL ECONOMIC INTERDEPENDENCE AND MONETARY REFORM

Multilateral trade liberalization, commodity schemes, and the emergence of the multinational corporation are part and parcel of international economic interdependence. The implications of this interdependence for national economic policy making in the developed countries is the subject of the opening essay in Part Four by Richard N. Cooper. As a result of their increased interdependence, notes Cooper, differences in the national policies of these countries are soon translated into balance-of-payments disequilibria and, at the same time, reduce the effectiveness of national policies in reaching domestic objectives.

The situation is aggravated by inconsistencies in the policy objectives of individual countries, thus leading to international competition in economic policy making that tends to have adverse effects for all participants. To minimize the adverse effects of this competition—Cooper argues—countries can coordinate closely their national economic policies, they may agree on increasing international liquidity, or reverse the process of economic integration by reducing economic links among them.

As H. Robert Heller has shown, uncoordinated increases in international liquidity have contributed to world inflation, with changes in national monetary aggregates serving as a link between the two. This may explain that the control of international liquidity was to be one of the main elements of the proposed reform of the international monetary system. Following the demise of the fixed rate system, however, "we are further away than ever from international control over international liquidity" notes Tom de Vries.

Also, the Jamaica agreement of January 1976 has essentially left exchange-rate management to the discretion of each country, thus creating the possibility of conflicting actions by the individual countries. In order to avoid such conflicts, John Williamson suggests that rules be established for managed floating and that the International Monetary Fund be charged to ensure the practical application of these rules.

Reporting on the deliberation of a group of experts, Balassa expresses the view that, given the differing interests of the individual countries, the chances for an agreement on rules for floating and on their international supervision are slim. He adds that there is a greater chance for reaching an agreement on measures aimed at reducing exchange rate instability within a group of countries, such as the European Common Market, which carry out much of their trade with each other and whose domestic economic activities are intimately linked by their mutual trade.

In the last essay, Robert Triffin looks ahead to the year 2000 when an international credit reserve system will have been established, ultimately leading to the creation of a single international currency. Establishing an international credit reserve system, in turn, would require the harmonization of national economic policies. Only time will tell if Triffin's vision is to be realized by the end of the century.

PROBLEMS OF THE MODERN ECONOMY

Changing Patterns in Foreign Trade and Payments
Third Edition

PART ONE: Trade Liberalization and the Adjustment Problem

The Current Case for Import Limitations

IRVING B. KRAVIS

Irving B. Kravis is professor of economics at the University of Pennsylvania. His is a signal contribution to a volume of essays prepared at the request of the Commission on International Trade and Investment Policy, chaired by Albert Williams, United States International Economic Policy in an Interdependent World.

INTRODUCTION

IF THE BEST interests of the U.S. lie in faster rather than slower growth in output and income and in better rather than poorer relations with other nations, the policy of the U.S. should be to reduce its barriers to imports and to expand its total trade by seeking reductions in the barriers of other countries to its exports.

The basic logic underlying the economic aspects of this statement is simple and incontrovertible. The gain from our trade with the rest of the world consists not of the things we export, but of the things we import. We are not made better off by giving up goods; we are made better off by receiving them. Public policies that limit our ability to obtain goods from abroad freely and cheaply reduce the real income of the nation.

Of course, restriction of imports may help particular groups in the economy, just as any restriction of supply may. Restrictions on the number of doctors raise the income of doctors; restrictions on hours of work of electricians combined with limitations on occupational entry raise the income of electricians; production quotas on petroleum output raise the income of oil producers.

Limitation of imports of cotton textiles or meat raises the incomes of the workers and firms in the industries producing them.

Why not then spread these beneficial effects to everybody? Why not restrict the number and hours of work of each group so as to raise its income? Why not help each group further by protecting it from foreign competition?

The answer is, of course, that every one of these restrictions benefits the individuals concerned at the expense of the rest of the people. Each involves a reduction of production and of the national income and a redistribution of the smaller amount of income in favor of the beneficiaries of the restriction. Practiced on a wide enough scale—i.e., if we all try to better ourselves by restricting the supply of our services—even the "beneficiaries" will be left worse off than if there were no restrictions.

Every current claim for protection, no matter what its guise, is a claim for special preference at the general expense.

Whatever the desired objective that is described, there is no getting around the fact that every successful claim for protection makes a select few better off at the cost of making everybody else worse off. It is not possible to use restrictions of supply to make the nation in general better off. The power of the government to control trade should not be used to favor select groups.

Despite this fundamental truth, there has been in recent years a new wave of sentiment in industry and labor and even in the Congress in favor of import limitations. This is based to a considerable extent upon unfavorable developments in our trade balance which has brought new arguments to the fore and revitalized some old ones. These arguments are assessed in the following section. Each is stated and then analysed.

SOME CURRENT ARGUMENTS FOR IMPORT LIMITATIONS

Trade surpluses have been characteristic of the U.S. balance of payments for nearly a century, and have been large and important during most of the last 25 years. Even after the early postwar shortages in Europe and elsewhere were ended, the surpluses averaged $3.5 billion per annum (1953–67). The trade surpluses helped to provide the foreign exchange necessary to support American foreign investment and U.S. military and economic programs abroad. The decline of the surplus to a little more than a half-billion dollars in 1968 and 1969 has therefore been a cause for much concern.

However, the use of the decline in the trade surplus as an argument for increased import limitation depends upon four propositions:

a. A trade surplus should be an objective of U.S. policy.
b. The decline in the U.S. trade surplus is permanent.
c. Import restrictions can indeed increase the trade surplus.
d. Import restrictions are the optimal way of increasing the trade surplus.

The Need for a Trade Surplus · Whether a trade surplus should be an objective of U.S. economic policy depends in part upon an assessment of the nature of the trade balance that will coincide with a long-run equilibrium position in the U.S. balance of payments and in part upon an assessment of the exigencies of the immediate future when equilibrium may not be attained. The long-run factors seem to suggest that a trade deficit rather than a surplus will be the appropriate position since income from foreign investments is likely, later if not sooner, to grow faster than either new investments abroad or government expenditures abroad (military plus aid).

However, the analytical relationships are very complicated and forecasting the components flows is very uncertain, while the current balance-of-payments pressures are both clear and certain. It is therefore assumed for purposes of this paper that the U.S., as a matter of prudence, should pursue a policy of avoiding trade deficits and achieving trade surpluses. The assumption might not stand up against careful analysis, but if it errs, it errs in favor of the case for import limitations.

Long-run Prospects for the U.S. Trade Balance · No one can really predict with confidence what the long-run prospects with respect to the U.S. trade balance are. A myriad of factors affect both U.S. exports and U.S. imports. The interplay of these factors as they change continually through time will produce a shifting margin between these two aggregates of diverse goods. The record bears out this expectation of great instability in the difference between exports and imports. In the post-war period the export surplus has waxed and waned several times over varying from less than $1 billion to more than $10 billion. Nevertheless, these past ups and downs do not warrant the assumption that there have been no persistent factors adversely affecting the U.S. trade position.

There is also some evidence of structural shifts in the U.S. trade position. In the longer run the U.S. has become a net importer in mineral fuels, motor vehicles, and "other manufactures," comprising such categories as textiles, iron and steel, etc. Chemicals and machinery other than motor vehicles are the only sectors in which there has been an upward trend in the trade balance, but only in the former is this associated with a faster export growth rate. In "other machinery" a very small starting level for imports and a large one for exports has produced larger dollar increases in exports than in imports despite a lower export growth rate; this kind of upward trend contains the seeds of its own destruction. Of course, our perception of these trends is heavily influenced by the sharpening of demand pressures in the U.S., and their relaxation in Europe in the last few years mentioned above.

On the other hand, it is possible to argue that there are basic alterations in the world economic picture that are unfavorable to the U.S. trade balance. The faster diffusion of technology, the spread of U.S. managerial methods and indeed of American management itself, and the greater international mobility of capital all tend to diminish important margins of advantage that the U.S. has had which contributed substantially to the U.S. export position in newer and more sophisticated products.

Of course, it has been true all along that the monopoly that an innovating country enjoys on a new product is apt to be a temporary one. Even before foreign affiliates, licensees, or subsidiaries—let alone multinational corporations—became so common, the knowledge of the new product in almost all cases sooner or later was spread abroad and production was successfully imitated. The innovating country does not necessarily have a long-run comparative advantage in every new product that it develops. Thus, for the United States for nearly 100 years now, the exports of one year have often become the imports of a later year. This has happened to a long list of American products from sewing machines to TV sets.

The transfer of technology, it should be noted, goes in both directions. Some has been from foreign countries to the United States. Thus, the Bessemer and open-hearth processes for making steel were imported from England in the last century and the oxygen process from Austria, Germany, or Sweden and the extrusion process of squeezing cold steel into desired shapes from Italy in more recent years. Also, there is a substantial amount of direct investment by multinational firms other than those of U.S. origin. A recent estimate for 1966 placed the proportion of U.S.-owned international direct investment at 57.4 percent. If the multinational corporation is a transmitter of technology, it seems likely that a lot of foreign technology is also being diffused, and some of it to the U.S. However, it is highly probable that the overwhelming movement has been outward from the United States. The innovating country sometimes still enjoys benefits after the transfer in the forms of licensing royalties or direct profits on foreign production. Also, the position of a continuous innovator is partly protected by the continual development of new products or models that make obsolete or at least less desirable the ones that have spread abroad. The speed with which innovations are being replaced by superior innovations is probably also increasing and this, too, affords some continuing margin of advantage for the innovating country.

In general, however, it seems likely that the net effect of all these changes and particularly of the greatly increased speed with which they have been occurring has been to reduce the margin of technological leadership which the United States formerly enjoyed.

All in all, then, there are grounds for pessimism with respect to the structural influences affecting the U.S. trade balance. However, even if the direction of these influences turns out to be unfavorable, no confident forecast of the future can be made. Many other factors affect the trade balance, and prediction is just about impossible. The most important unknown consists of developments in the relative prices at which U.S. goods are available to foreigners and in the relative prices at which foreign goods are available to Americans. These are proximately determined by changes in domestic price levels and in exchange rates. The movement of each country's domestic price level is heavily influenced by cyclical developments and by public policies that are not related or only partially related to balance-of-payments factors. Even if pessimistic expectations about the structural factors turn out to be correct, we cannot tell whether a future rise in U.S. prices relative to those of foreign countries will accentuate their impact or a future fall offset and obscure them. The possibility of changes in government policies taken to influence the trade balance or the balance of payments in general adds to the uncertainties. No one can say if or when monetary and fiscal policies to affect the price level or commercial policies—tariff and nontariff barriers, export subsidies, etc.—intended to have a direct effect on trade flows will be altered in the U.S. or in one or more of its important trade partners. No one can predict when a key exchange rate will be altered under the pressure of a deficit or of a surplus. All these factors have a powerful influence on the U.S. trade balance, and their net effects can not be known in advance.

In view of these uncertainties, let us again draw the inference that appears to be most favorable to the case for import limitations. Let us assume that a trade surplus will not come about without some deliberate policy action by the U.S. The question then facing the U.S. in the 1970's is whether this should be attempted mainly or even to a major degree by means of trade restrictions.

The Feasibility of Import Restrictions as a Means of Increasing the U.S. Trade Surplus · The hard truth of the matter is that it is not open to the U.S. to improve its trade balance through item-by-item import restrictions. Almost any restrictive move made by the United States can be expected to bring retaliation and to result in an approximately equivalent diminution in U.S. exports. The warnings on this point by responsible foreign authorities should be taken at their face value.

It must be realized that these warnings refer not to new and untried measures but rather to responses that are built into the trading system and for which there is ample precedent and wide acceptance in the community of nations. A basic principle of

GATT (the General Agreement on Tariffs and Trade), which governs the trade relations of the Western countries, is the preservation of the "balance of benefits" which each country derives from the tariffs that have emerged from six rounds of international negotiations in the last quarter of a century. A country that finds its interests adversely affected by an increase in a duty that has been bound or reduced in a GATT negotiation—and this includes virtually every U.S. tariff classification—or by the imposition of a quota is entitled to compensatory concessions. If these are not forthcoming, it is free to restore its balance of benefits through restrictions of its own. Any extensive effort by the United States to use import limitations to improve its trade balance is thus almost certain to set off a self-defeating chain of restrictions on trade that would serve neither the economic nor the political objectives of this country.

Trade Restrictions as the Optimum Way to Improve the Trade Surplus · Even if it were claimed that other countries would permit the United States to improve its trade surplus through limitations of imports, the further proposition would still have to be established that item-by-item import restriction was the best way to achieve the desired increase in surpluses. The item-by-item approach can be defended only if it is argued that the government and not the marketplace should be allowed to determine the changes in the commodity composition of imports by which the trade balance should be improved.

If the objective is to reduce the general level of imports or to limit its increase, then it is logical and efficient to use some general criterion, perhaps a uniform ad valorem tariff surcharge applied to all goods, rather than a series of discriminatory tariff increases favoring the domestic producers of some goods over the domestic producers of others. But if the trade surplus is the true objective, it can be improved through an increase in exports as well as a diminution in imports. Increased exports can be encouraged through export promotion measures such as tax incentives and better credit facilities. However, if a uniform ad valorem tariff were applied to imports, an export subsidy would make the price of foreign currency the same for U.S. exporters and importers and would therefore lead to the most efficient use of U.S. resources as between home and foreign markets in production and between home and foreign goods in consumption.

A uniform tariff and subsidy would be akin to a practical devaluation of the dollar applicable only to trade or perhaps to trade and some service transactions. There are, of course, still other ways of achieving the same effects of making U.S. goods cheaper to foreigners and foreign goods dearer to Americans. One is outright devaluation which would affect capital as well as trade and service transactions. Other less dramatic ways which are much less likely to encounter objections from other countries involve the restriction of future U.S. price movements to rates of increase that are lower than those of the other major industrial countries. This can be accomplished through monetary and fiscal policy or through a wage and price policy, although either means would be politically difficult. All these measures (i.e., partial or total devaluation, restraint of price increases through general or specific policies) would achieve an improvement in the trade balance while leaving it to the market to determine which imports would decrease and which exports would increase.

The United States has, over the years, given many one-sided trade concessions that have opened its markets to foreigners while U.S. exporters find themselves under serious handicaps in foreign markets.

To some degree, this argument is an extension of the previous one. The relative rise in imports is taken as evidence of the opening of the U.S. market and the failure of exports to increase more rapidly as evidence of the discriminatory practices in foreign markets. The trend of exports and imports, however, is not in itself conclusive evidence since many other factors could account for these trends.

Claims that American negotiators over the years have traded away market opportunities in the U.S. without equivalent concessions abroad have never been accompanied by a quantitative assessment of the impact of changes in tariffs and other terms of access. Such evidence as is readily available does not support the view that U.S. commercial policy, either alone or in conjunction with foreign commercial policy, has been responsible for the rapid growth of imports or for the failure of our exports to expand more rapidly.

In the first place, a number of comparative studies of tariff levels have indicated that U.S. tariffs are slightly higher on the average than those of the European Economic Community and slightly lower than those of the U.K. Average post-Kennedy Round tariffs on non-agricultural, dutiable imports are estimated at 9.6 percent for the U.S., 8.1 percent for the Common Market, 10.6 percent for the U.K., and 9.5 percent for Japan; for dutiable manufactures, the rates are 9.9, 8.6, 10.8 and 10.7, respectively, for the same countries.

Of course, even similar average tariffs may have different restrictive effects in different countries, depending on such factors as the structure of the rates, elasticities of demand and supply, the share of imports in domestic consumption, and the composition of imports. When these factors are taken into account, U.S. tariffs, Professor Bela Balassa found in a study of pre-Kennedy Round rates, were more restrictive of imports than those of the EEC and the U.K., though less restrictive than Japan's.[1]

Tariffs for individual commodities and average tariffs for classes of commodities are dispersed around these overall rates in ways that differ from one country to another. In some commodity classes, such as textiles and chemicals, . . . U.S. rates are higher than those of other countries; in others such as transportation equipment and electrical machinery the U.S. rates are lower. Thus, individual U.S. industries sometimes find that the tariffs levied on American goods by the foreign source of supply are higher than the corresponding U.S. rates. For example, U.S. and foreign tariffs on electronic products (tubes, transistors, transformers, loudspeakers, etc.) were cited as an example of inequitable tariff treatment at the House Ways and Means Committee hearings on "Tariff and Trade Proposals." The U.S. rate of 7.6 percent was compared to rates of 14 percent for the EEC and 12.4 percent for Japan.

Where cross-exporting (i.e., two-way trade) of similar products exists or where U.S. firms would be able to export to the foreign

1. Bela Balassa, *Trade Liberalization among Industrial Countries* (New York: McGraw Hill, 1967), p. 59.

source of supply over a lower tariff barrier, an industry might justifiably regard a difference in tariff rates as inequitable. This would, of course, be equally true for a foreign industry facing higher U.S. tariff rates. Very often, however, the difference in rate is of little practical importance because the domestic industry would not be able to compete in the foreign market regardless of the level of the foreign tariff. If in the electronic components industry, for example, Japanese costs are lower than those of the U.S., a lowering of the Japanese tariff to the American level would not have any beneficial effects upon the position of the U.S. industry.

Not only are the present overall tariff levels rather similar among the major industrial exporters, but it is not at all clear that U.S. tariff levels have declined very precipitously in the last 20 years. Tariff Commission figures show that duties collected as a percentage of dutiable imports have varied mainly in the 11 to 12 percent range in the last few years compared to a 12 to 13 percent range in the early 1950's. As the Commission points out, these average ad valorem equivalent duties are not completely reliable guides to changes in the level of protection since, among other reasons, they are affected by changes in the composition of imports. Tariffs reduced to the threshold that made imports possible where there were none before, might still average out to levels above the previous average ad valorem equivalent collected duty. The average might thus fail to decline despite general reductions in duties. On the other hand, there is little doubt that in the various GATT rounds of tariff cutting, particularly before but not altogether excluding the Kennedy Round, there was a systematic search for concessions to offer foreigners that could safely be made without having a great impact on U.S. imports.

The notion that tariff concessions played a major role in the increase in U.S. imports is not strongly supported by the timing of the import changes. If tariff concessions were an important influence, each round of tariff reductions should have been followed by a surge of imports. In fact, neither the reductions made in the 1956 round nor those made in the Dillon Round of 1961–62 appear to have a large gross impact on U.S. imports. The great increase in imports between 1967 and 1968 did come at a time when the first Kennedy Round reductions went into effect, but the 23 percent increase in imports could not have been attributable to any major degree to a cut in tariffs that can hardly have amounted to an average reduction in price to U.S. buyers of as much as 1 percent.[2]

The available evidence thus does not indicate that U.S. firms are generally at a competitive disadvantage owing to differences in tariff barriers or that the U.S. tariff barriers faced by actual exporters to the U.S. have been radically reduced in the last 20 years.

Much of the concern about the relatively unfair treatment of American exports is, however, directed to non-tariff rather than to tariff barriers.

There is no doubt that U.S. exports are limited by non-tariff barriers. Buy domestic policies, safety regulations, and the rebating of excise taxes on exports and compensatory levies on imports are among the many practices that American exporters have found place them at a disadvantage in international competition. However, the United States is not without its own non-tariff barriers, including buy American policies, the imposition upon foreign countries of "voluntary" agreements to limit exports to the U.S. as in cotton, textile, and steel, and direct unilateral restrictions on imports of dairy products, meat, sugar, and oil. Also, the barriers have been increasing rather than diminishing in number and importance. In the last few years "voluntary" quotas on steel and meat, prohibition of imports of firearms other than those used for sporting purposes, and a tariff quota on brooms have been added to the list.

Trends in foreign non-tariff barriers have been more mixed. Between the early 1950's and the early 1960's the trade restrictions maintained by many countries for balance-of-payments reasons were reduced and then eliminated. With the advent of the Common Market, however, some new and important barriers to U.S. trade, particularly the variable import levy, were imposed.

The non-tariff barriers imposed by the United States and

2. The reduction averaged 37 percent, and 20 percent of each reduction went into effect on January 1, 1968. A 7.4 percent cut in an average duty of, say, 12 percent comes out to a saving for U.S. buyers of imports of less than 1 percent.

other countries undoubtedly restrict the volume of foreign commerce but whether they are at present more burdensome to American exporters than to foreign exporters is not obvious. The Japanese restrictions almost surely limit imports more than do the non-tariff barriers of the U.S. and Western European countries. It would take a special study to confirm or deny the widely prevalent notion in the United States that European non-tariff barriers are more restrictive than ours. An important new work by Professor Robert E. Baldwin suggests that relative to the U.K., at least, the U.S. still has a slightly higher rate of effective protection when non-tariff, as well as tariff, barriers are taken into account. (The effective rate of protection measures the degree of protection of value added in manufacturing; it indicates the excess in domestic value added that can be obtained as a result of trade restrictions, as a percentage of what the value added would be under free trade.) Baldwin's estimates for 1972, the year in which the Kennedy Round tariffs came into full force, indicate a 15 percent overall rate of effective protection (tariff and non-tariff) for the U.S. and a 13 percent rate for the U.K.[3]

This is not to deny that non-tariff barriers have been growing in importance, both at home and abroad, relative to tariffs. Furthermore, the common U.S. view that foreign non-tariff barriers are greater than those of the U.S. may well turn out to be more justified in the case of the EEC and still more in the case of Japan. Even so, it seems doubtful that non-tariff barriers can be held responsible for the failure of U.S. exports to grow more rapidly. A relaxation of the barriers would, it is true, give U.S. exporters a fairer chance to enter European and Japanese markets, but U.S. export gains might turn out to be modest. Most of the barriers are aimed at imports in general and are not discriminatory against the U.S. Their relaxation would therefore open each market not just to the U.S. but to other competing countries as well. American exporters would probably enjoy some increase in sales as a consequence, but to gain this and to achieve the still more problematic effect of an increase in the rate of growth in their sales, they would have to meet the competition of other countries.

3. Robert E. Baldwin, *Non-tariff Distortions of International Trade* (Washington, D.C.: Brookings Institution, 1970), pp. 165 and 168.

The dismantlement of non-tariff barriers is an objective that is important to pursue but it is doubtful that it will provide a major key to the resolution of the problems with our trade balance. Even if all—U.S. and foreign—non-tariff barriers were eliminated, it is not sure that our export balance would become larger. Certainly our imports would increase and our exports also, but even if the barriers of foreign countries are more restrictive than ours, the size of the gain in our exports would depend upon the competitiveness of our economy. Non-tariff barriers certainly have a harmful effect on world commerce and income, but they just do not fill the role of chief villain in the story of the disappearing trade balance.

Imports have an unfavorable impact on employment, particularly since they tend to be concentrated in labor-intensive products.

One of the necessary conditions for the improvement of the living standards of a country is the mobility of labor and capital. Some notion of the dynamism of the modern economy is called to mind simply by considering what a small fraction of his consumption expenditure each of us spends on things that are physically identical to those purchased by his father at an equivalent stage in his life.

Some of the changes in production necessary to turn out new products and new product varieties and to use cost reducing methods can be smoothly absorbed by the existing industrial organization without requiring much adjustment either by labor or capital. For example, when the home freezer industry developed, the workers and firms that had previously manufactured refrigerators could move easily into the new good. Other changes, however, require reduction in the number of firms and workers in an old industry as new conditions develop. For the most part, the pressures for change are generated within the internal economy of the United States. This was true, for example, of the losses of employment suffered in the Michigan peninsula when station wagon bodies began to be made of steel rather than of wood. It was true also when the hosiery industry moved out of Philadelphia into the South and more generally when the textile industries of Pennsylvania and other northern states shifted to North Carolina and other southern states. Between 1947 and

1967, for example, Pennsylvania lost 69,700 production jobs in the textile industry while North Carolina gained 32,500. Sometimes, as in the recent contraction of the space effort, a change in governmental needs or priorities is the cause of the disruption of individual lives and of blight for a whole community. In these cases and many more, thousands and thousands of workers and many employers suffered great economic, social, and psychological injuries through no fault of their own as a result of changes in the marketplace. In each of these cases it would have been in the interest of the workers and employers concerned to have government intervention or decision that would prevent the shift to a new product or a new location.

What is the appropriate national policy in these cases? Surely, no one would argue that it would be appropriate to guarantee any industry or firm against a reduction in its level of employment. Any effort along these lines obviously would promote a hothouse economy pockmarked with artificially maintained prices for commodities serving needs that could be more cheaply provided for in a free market. The protection of particular individuals against such disruptions can only be achieved at the expense of the rest of the U.S.

What is worse, such protection tends to freeze patterns of employment that are not in the long-run interests of workers or of the U.S. at large. The jobs that are protected tend to be low-wage jobs relative to those that would be available without protective policies. The Pennsylvania textile workers of yesterday were injured by the shift to the South. Today, their successors are better off than they would be if the government had intervened to keep the textile industry in that stage; they are working in industries that pay higher wages than the textile industry.

The problem is not different when the pressure for the reduction in the employment and number of firms in an industry comes not from another section of the country but from abroad. Today's workers and employers in that industry will be better off if the government intervenes and prevents their loss of jobs and capital. The cost of such a policy in the short run is borne by the rest of the economy which is denied the opportunity to obtain the goods at the lower prices available abroad. In the long run, however, the workers themselves have to be regarded as worse off. By and large, the industries that need protection from foreign competition are low-wage industries and the jobs that are being perpetuated by restrictions on imports are low-wage jobs. At the same time, a policy of import restriction prevents the expansion of export industries which characteristically pay higher wages. This is true because the restriction of our purchases abroad gives foreigners fewer dollars which they can spend in the United States.

In short, protection can at best make a small fraction of today's labor force better off at the expense of the large majority and at the expense also of tomorrow's labor force.

The irrationality of a policy of using trade restrictions to create jobs is shown by data presented to the Congress by a spokesman for industries seeking the restriction of imports. In a statement before the Joint Economic Committee, a representative of the Trade Relations Council reported upon an analysis of the trade position of 313 four-digit manufacturing industries of the United States. In 1967, 128 of these industries had a foreign trade deficit aggregating $9 billion. The excess of imports over exports in these industries was calculated to involve a net loss of 367,552 jobs. The other group, consisting of 185 industries, had trade surpluses which amounted to $10.4 billion. The job-equivalent of this trade surplus was estimated at 201,532 jobs. Although apparently cited as an argument for protection, these data constitute a powerful argument for freer trade. For the labor of a little more than 200,000 men, we received $10.4 billion. This was enough to obtain goods from abroad that it would have taken 400,000 men—twice as many—to produce. To advance these figures as an argument for protection is to embrace a make-work philosophy. It is to argue that we should devise policies that will lead to more, rather than fewer, hours of work to produce a dollar's worth of real income. If this is what we want, protection is a good way to get it. If we want to find ways to increase man-hours per dollar of output, international trade is not for us. International trade increases real product per hour of work rather than raising the hours required to produce a dollar's worth of product.

The magnitude involved in the Trade Relations Council's estimates of the net effect of trade on employment also clearly indicates that the trade balance has only a small net impact on overall employment in the U.S. The size of the trade surplus affects at most a few hundred thousand out of the nearly 80 million civilian jobs. During 1968, for example, when imports soared and the trade balance plummeted, other and much larger influences were at work so that employment expanded by more than 2 million jobs and the unemployed rate dropped from 3.5 to 3.3 percent.

As these events suggest, the level of employment in the U.S. does not depend in any quantitatively significant way upon the level of imports. It is determined to an overwhelming degree by internal influences. The expansion of international trade certainly does not require a higher level of unemployment. International trade is no more inconsistent with full employment than other efficiency-increasing influences such as automation or cost-reducing changes in industrial location. All impose a temporary cost in terms of job displacement.

Advocates of freer trade—like defenders of automation—have sometimes been chided for citing job statistics without sufficient regard to the human beings involved. However, the whole argument turns precisely on human welfare. Is it increased or diminished by changes that are required for greater efficiency? The answer is that there is a restricted and short-run hurt in exchange for a widespread and long-run gain. The extent of the losses to adversely affected individuals will be smaller when the changes occur against the background of a buoyant economy. This is clearly illustrated in the story of the remarkable achievement of the Common Market countries in abolishing tariffs among themselves completely with little disruption of individual firms and workers. Rapid economic expansion was an essential feature of the story. The real gross national product of the Common Market countries increased by 50 percent from 1959 to 1967 while internal tariffs were coming down. It is easy to make room for increased imports when domestic demand is expanding; even where imports enter in very large volume it is not so difficult for businesses to find other lines which they can pursue with greater profit.

The proper means to pursue full employment objectives is not tariff policy but monetary and fiscal policy.

Foreign competition is unfair because it is based on low wages.

International trade raises real income because certain industries, owing to some natural or cultural differences between different areas of the world, are able to produce at a lower cost in one country while others will be able to produce at lower cost in some other part of the world. American producers, when confronted with the natural or acquired advantage enjoyed by a foreign industry, often feel, quite rightly, that they are facing unequal odds. Some years ago, a Pennsylvania oil producer whose wells produced less than a barrel a day felt that it was unfair to have to compete with the wells of the Middle East that produce 5,000 barrels a day. So in a sense it was. However, it was "unfair" in the sense that one would use in a sports contest; the same standard of equity is not appropriate as an economic criterion. No sound policy can be based on the principle of eradicating all the economic advantages possessed by any contestant in order to run a competition that gives an equal chance to all entrants. Such a policy would imply that American firms that have unusual know-how or access to large amounts of capital should be precluded from selling abroad because they have an unfair competitive advantage over less sophisticated and more poorly capitalized European firms. It would be, once again, to reject the view that a main goal of our economy is to maximize per unit of input.

The advantage that most other countries have relative to the U.S. is an abundant labor supply relative to other factors of production. Productivity is low, but wages are sometimes even lower so that labor costs in some industries are below those of the U.S. For example, in 1967 the Japanese GNP per capita was, according the the rather imperfect measures available, about 40 percent of that of the U.S. However, in the iron and steel industry hourly labor cost was only 21 percent of the U.S. level and unit labor cost 40 to 38 percent of the U.S. level. In industries where differences in wage levels are decisive, foreign firms are apt to have the advantage over U.S. firms. Such industries include labor-intensive industries like textiles and shoes and also industries like steel, mass-producing relatively standardized products by well-established, widely known methods of production.

The wages advantage that these foreign industries enjoy is no more "unfair" in the relevant economic sense than is the superiority of the Middle East oil well over the Pennsylvania oil well or of the well-capitalized, technologically advanced U.S. firm over the smaller and less sophisticated European firm. It is easy to understand and indeed difficult not to sympathize with the feeling of workers and firms that the situation is unfair to them. However, the fact remains that no case can be made in the broad public interest for the protection of particular industries on grounds of "unfair" competition even when, owing to low foreign wages, prices and costs abroad are lower than the most efficient producer at home can achieve.

What can be regarded as unfair is to ask the workers and employers in the affected industries to bear the costs of adjustment, particularly if these costs result from a change in national policy designed to benefit the nation as a whole. Relief should, however, be temporary and geared to adjustment rather than to the permanent protection of any share of the domestic market. The experience of the European Economic Community in moving to tariff-free trade suggests that the extent of the dislocation of industry may be surprisingly small. Once the policy of free trade was convincingly laid down in the six Common Market countries, firms had the incentive to adjust rather than the incentive to organize politically for protection.

Someone might wish to argue that the whole level of wage rates abroad is so low relative to wage rates in the United States that all foreign industries or many of them have advantageous labor costs relative to the U.S. industries. If that argument were valid, what would be called for is not protection for particular industries but an across-the-board change in power of foreign currencies to purchase U.S. goods; the objective would be to restore a balance in which some industries had low enough labor costs so that, together with their other advantages, they would be enabled to export enough to achieve a trade balance (or a trade surplus if that were taken as an objective of our policy). Alternative ways of achieving such an adjustment have already been discussed.

The advent of the multinational corporation has so changed the nature of trade relations that the case for freer trade has been made irrelevant.

The rise of multinational corporations has brought forward new problems. In a world organized into nation-states the rise of firms employing a global approach to production and marketing creates new problems with respect to national jurisdiction and national interests with respect to the location and volume of production, exports, and imports, taxation, etc.

However, there is no evidence that the multinational corporation is immune from the economic forces that determine which goods can be most cheaply produced in which countries. On the contrary, it seems likely that the multinational corporation provides decision-makers with better information about the most advantageous location of production than was previously available. Components, such as the Ford engine for the Pinto, are produced abroad when they can be made cheaper.

The effects of multinational corporations on the U.S. trade balance are very difficult to estimate. They have hastened the processes described earlier as probably unfavorable to the U.S.— the diffusion of American managerial methods, production techniques, and capital; but in a shrinking world the pace of this diffusion was bound to increase anyway. Exports from their U.S. plants of the main products produced by their foreign plants have probably been reduced. However, there is at least some validity to the claim made by the corporations themselves that their establishment of production abroad was necessary to protect their holdings of the foreign market against potential foreign competition. To the extent to which this is true, foreign production and even exports from foreign plants may not be at the expense of U.S. exports, and the profits from foreign operations a possible net gain to the U.S. balance of payments, depending upon the use to which they are put. More definite sources of gain to the U.S. balance of payments are exports of machinery and of supplementary product lines, the latter being of potential importance when full-line production is maintained in the U.S. and foreign production limited to models for which there is a large market in the host country.

However the net effects turn out, it seems clear that multinational corporations can hardly be held responsible for import problems in textiles and a number of other areas where the domestic industry has been in difficulty and has sought protection. Multinational companies are important in automobile production, petroleum, tractors, chemicals, pharmaceuticals, office machinery, and farm and construction equipment. In most but not all of these areas the U.S. has a strong export position. In the few cases in which multinational corporations have been conspicuous in industries encountering severe import competition, the products though relatively new, such as electronics, require labor-intensive methods of production.

In any case, the injury to U.S. interests of which multinational corporations are accused by those seeking trade restrictions is not different from others independently claimed as a basis for import limitations and already discussed—viz., a reduced U.S. trade surplus and job displacement. The expansion of the multinational form of corporate enterprise adds many new problems to the relations between government and business and to intergovernmental relationships, but it does not constitute a new argument for protection. Indeed, the retaliatory or at any rate unfavorable responses that can be expected from foreign governments to any U.S. effort to limit imports would make much more difficult the intergovernmental cooperation that is required to cope with many of the problems in this field.

The national security of the United States requires that some industries be protected.

The national security argument is sometimes applied to natural resource products such as petroleum and sometimes to fabricated products such as steel.

It can hardly be denied that petroleum and steel and indeed a vast host of other products are essential to national defense. But direct guarantees do not always achieve their intended results. One is reminded of the old story of the wise town elders who, wishing to accommodate the convenience of all visitors, decreed that one of the town's two taxis always had to be at the railroad station.

In the case of a natural resource product, it has never been satisfactorily explained how a program which encourages the use of domestic reserves rather than the use of the foreign product will assure adequate domestic supplies in case of an emergency. The argument advanced to defend quotas on the import of crude oil and petroleum products is that high domestic prices, which are necessary to maintain a high level of new discovery and exploration, can be kept only by restricting cheap foreign imports. If national security is dependent upon the ready domestic availability of large quantities of petroleum, what is really called for is a program of subsidization for the exploration of petroleum reserves in the United States and a program that would restrict domestic production to the levels necessary to keep a domestic petroleum industry operational and capable of sudden and large expansion in the event of necessity.

What is particularly indefensible is the protection of the domestic petroleum industry through import quotas rather than tariffs. Import quotas have the effect of transferring to private pockets in the form of monopoly profits substantial sums of money from the public purse. If it is felt that tariffs are too uncertain in their effects on import quantities and quotas are desired on this account, the quotas should be auctioned off so that their monopoly value does not accrue to private firms. At a time when important social needs are being denied because of inadequate government revenues, it is particularly inappropriate for the government to confer monopoly power worth over a half billion dollars per annum on private parties.

In the case of a manufacturing industry, such as the steel industry, it is argued that protection is necessary to maintain skills that would be lost were the industries subject to unresricted import competition. The American Iron and Steel Institute, for example, has claimed that the unchecked growth of steel imports presents a direct threat to our national security since a domestic industry will no longer be able to produce the full range of steel products necessary for national security. In addition, it is argued, that under crisis conditions serious shortages might develop.

In fact, the wartime experience of the United States, like that of every other country, including England, Germany, and Japan, demonstrates very clearly that human skills and ingenuity manage very quickly to produce whatever is needed in wartime. The United States during World War II, for example, was able to produce large quantities of airplanes including many kinds which had never been produced before and even to master the production of products like lenses, which formerly had been regarded as the province of highly skilled craftsmen not to be found in the United States.

The national security argument is also weakened by the diminished likelihood of a large-scale conventional war of long duration. A major nuclear war would be brief and horrible and its outcome would not be affected by the size of particular domestic industries such as oil or steel. Non-nuclear wars restricted to particular regions are unlikely to leave the U.S. cut off from all foreign sources of supply.

Protection for national security purposes is also counterproductive politically and diplomatically. Further action to limit steel imports, for example, would strengthen the divisive forces affecting our relations with friendly countries.

THE COST OF INCREASED PROTECTION TO THE UNITED STATES

The benefits of import limitations, it has been shown, accrue to favored groups in the economy at the expense of the population as a whole. Some of the ways in which these costs are incurred have already been described. The disadvantages of a policy of protection are set out more systematically in the following paragraphs.

The insulation of the U.S. economy from foreign competition will reduce consumer choice and the stimulus to innovation.

The maintenance of competition in a market economy under modern technological conditions where the scale of the firm is so large in many industries is one of the difficult problems of economic organization facing the United States. The entry of foreign competitors into the American market makes it more difficult for large firms to pursue a live-and-let-live policy that will produce a quiet life for their managers but which will not be in the interests of consumers or the economy at large. There are on record in recent years a number of cases in which the stimulus to innovation has come from foreign competition—the small car, oxygen steel, and flat glass. The American consumer and the economy in general is better off for each of these cases of increased foreign competition.

Import limitations will lead to higher prices and make the control of inflation more difficult.

Recently, the proposition that import controls or tariffs are likely to lead to higher prices for the protected commodities has been challenged. These challenges usually take the form of citing cases in which products under protection such as cotton textiles have been marked by price increases smaller than the price level in general. These instances have usually been contrasted with other products like coal which although unprotected have risen in price more than average. The juxtaposition of such examples only indicates, however, that there are other price-determining influences that are also at work. It does not mean that the observed price of a protected good whether it has risen more or less than average, would not be lower without the quota or without the tariff. Nobody has yet set out the logic by which it can be claimed that the restriction of a cheap source of supply will not tend to raise the price. Most quotas not only result in higher prices to buyers but, as noted in connection with the discussion of the oil quota above, confer a monopoly profit on those lucky enough to receive the privilege of importing some of the limited quantity of goods permitted to enter the United States.

The upward pressure on prices exerted by import quotas or tariffs also hurts the United States by weakening our export position. Import quotas on petroleum, for example, push up fuel costs for our manufacturing industries and the "voluntary" quotas on steel have enabled increases of steel prices to occur which have raised input costs for our machinery-producing industries. Our machinery industries, which are so important in our export trade, are competing with foreign producers who are able to buy fuel and steel at world market prices.

Protectionist policies will reduce the participation of the United States in world trade and thus lower its rate of growth and income.

Textbook writings on international trade and the current arguments of those favoring increased protection have one thing in common. Both view international trade as leading to a form of specialization in which some industries expand in each country while others contract. To some degree, this is still a correct view. It is likely, for example, that under free trade the textile industry and the steel industry in the United States would grow smaller than they are today while the machinery industries would expand.

However, there is a large and growing form of international trade that does not take this character at all. The trade between the great industrial countries is increasingly taking the relatively new form of intra-industry specialization. It is based on the economies of long production runs for particular variants of products. It owes its origin to the ever-growing variety of specialized materials and machines which is emerging to provide a more and more varied and sophisticated bundle of consumer goods and to meet the needs of industry for labor-saving, cost-reducing methods of production. How can this great growth in variety of output be reconciled with the great economies that can be derived from long production runs? The answer for most producers is to concentrate on a limited range of product variants.

To see the impact that this has on international trade, let us consider, for example, the production of machinery for the use of such industries as printing, baking, and pharmaceuticals. Such machinery is manufactured in the United States, the United Kingdom, Germany, and other Western European countries. However, in each of these countries the equipment is designed to meet local conditions such as the usual scale of output and the prevailing ratio of wages to capital costs. Each country could produce the whole range of equipment but in fact concentrates on the product variants most in demand in its own or in other nearby markets. Thus the European equipment is typically designed for smaller volume, lower speed, and greater variety of purpose than the American equipment for the same industries. Trade arises because in each country there is likely to be some limited need for the kinds of machines produced abroad although the major need will of course be for the type of machine produced at home. Since the direction of technological progress is clearly toward more and more complicated and highly specialized machinery, the volume of intra-industry specialization may be expected to increase.

Intra-industry specialization in the trade among the industrial countries accounts for the apparently contradictory phenomena, that there is on the one hand a great similarity in the commodity composition of the exports of the industrial countries and that on the other hand a substantial fraction of world trade consists of exchanges between the industrial countries themselves.

The expansion of this trade is attractive not only because it lowers costs and raises incomes for the participating countries but also because it brings relatively few of the adjustment problems that are so difficult where specialization by whole industries is involved. From the standpoint of the U.S., it points also to a profitable avenue for the expansion of trade that does not depend upon the maintenance of the technological margin of superiority the U.S. enjoyed in the past.

The experience of the Common Market may again be taken as an illustration. Trade among the six countries tripled in the decade following the establishment of the Common Market in 1957. This expansion of trade was based on neither large technological gaps among the countries nor on the disappearance of entire industries as a result of inter-industry specialization.

Those seeking import limitations are asking the U.S., in effect, to sacrifice the chance to participate fully in this growing trade in an effort to protect the short-run interests of limited groups in the economy.

The political and diplomatic costs of import limitations would be very high.

Any marked movement toward further limitations on imports would, as already remarked, bring retaliations. There is a great danger that a trade war would be set off which would have the economic and political consequences in restricting world trade that would clearly leave all trading countries worse off. What is even more dangerous, however, is the broader impact upon the political leadership of the United States. The United States has in the community of nations stood for the principles of a competitive economy and for the reliance upon markets rather than upon governments for economic decision-making. We have put our great weight behind the reduction of trade barriers. A U.S. policy of protection where competition hurts some American workers and firms, and of free trade where it does not, will hardly strengthen our position of leadership. Rather it will strengthen the position of those cynics who argue that the United States has been using its great power to pursue its own short-run economic interests rather than, as we claim, to create a peaceful, prosperous, and stable world.

A TRADE POLICY IN THE NATIONAL INTEREST

The national interests of the U.S. lie in the direction of freer trade. The arguments for a contrary policy, it has been shown, are based on incorrect assessments of the facts, draw unwarranted conclusions from true statements of fact, or stress benefits that may be real and important but are either incapable of achievement or can be attained only at large economic and political cost.

The strength and pervasiveness of the present trend toward import limitations is evidence of the capacity of men to believe what it is in their economic interests to believe. It reflects also the hospitality the democratic political process gives to the efforts of organized groups to benefit themselves when the gain to them is large and the losses to others are widely distributed. Political leaders may have to yield to such pressures, but if so, the only rational ground is a concern for a special interest or political necessity and not a concern for the national interest. Their need to yield may be less if the special and public interests are clearly distinguished.

Contrasting Experiences with Trade Adjustment Assistance

JAMES E. MCCARTHY

In this essay, originally published in the June 1975 issue of the
Monthly Labor Review, *James E. McCarthy compares the experiences of workers in Massachusetts and in Rhode Island with adjustment assistance under the Trade Expansion Act of 1962.*

THE TRADE EXPANSION ACT of 1962, which authorized U.S. participation in the Kennedy Round of trade negotiations, also authorized this country's first experiment with trade adjustment assistance. The legislation provided that firms or groups of workers which could demonstrate to the Tariff Commission that they had suffered injury from increased imports, as defined in the act, could qualify for assistance. Assistance for workers consisted of (1) trade readjustment allowances, which supplement unemployment compensation; (2) the provision of testing, counseling, placement, and training services by State Divisions of Employment Security; and/or (3) relocation for new employment. Assistance for firms consisted of tax assistance, technical assistance, and loans or loan guarantees. On April 3, 1975, new trade legislation, the Trade Act of 1974, provided for similar but expanded trade adjustment assistance.

Adjustment assistance has been of interest to economists and policymakers for a number of reasons. It promised aid to groups which would otherwise suffer as a result of freer trade. Unlike the escape clause or other broad forms of protection given to an entire industry, adjustment assistance would be given only to those within the industry who genuinely needed help. Instead of forcing consumers to subsidize all firms in an industry by means of tariffs or quotas, government funds would be spent to increase the efficiency of failing firms and to assist the functioning of labor markets.

The shoe industry in Massachusetts has been one of the few

industries which has been able to qualify for adjustment aid. As of December 31, 1972, when this study was begun, a total of 68 cases of worker adjustment assistance involving 30,651 workers from all industries and states had been certified eligible.[1] Both in number of cases (24) and in number of workers (6,505) the nonrubber footwear industry ranked first. About half the footwear certifications (13 cases and 2,989 workers) were from Massachusetts. Thus, it seemed that a case study of worker assistance in the Massachusetts shoe industry would yield some indication as to the program's effectiveness.

To study the worker program, a random sample of 200 workers, stratified by city and by firm, was chosen. Workers from 12 firms were included. Each of these workers was interviewed to obtain information concerning personal characteristics, the job lost due to imports, and the adjustment experience of the individual since layoff. The workers lost their jobs between January 1969 and August 1971. The fieldwork was done between March and July 1973. Information was also collected from the claimant files of the Massachusetts Division of Employment Security.

CHARACTERISTICS OF WORKERS

The personal characteristics of workers receiving adjustment assistance can be summarized in five observations. First, they were old. While workers ranged in age from 17 to 77, their median age was 55, and only 10 percent were under the age of 40. Second, they were overwhelmingly female: 142 (71 percent) of the sample compared to 59 (29 percent) male. Third, they were mostly white and U.S.-born, although 13 percent were immigrants of extractions which varied with the city in which the factory was located. Fourth, they had a generally low level of formal education. On the average, they had completed nine years of school. Only 21 percent had graduated from high school, and only 12 percent had ever had any special job training in addition to their schooling. Fifth, because of their age and sex, only 37.7 percent were the heads of a family unit, while 36.6 percent were

1. Through the end of fiscal 1974, 96 groups with an estimated total of 45,659 workers had been certified. Expenditures totaled $68.3 million.

secondary wage earners, and 25.7 percent were self-supporting. Two-thirds said they had no dependents. While virtually all of the secondary wage earners were women, women also comprised 38.9 percent of the primary wage earners (heads of family units) and 81.6 percent of those who were self-supporting without dependents.

The jobs held prior to layoff included virtually all phases of shoe production. The claimants included unskilled and skilled labor, supervisory, clerical, and even managerial personnel.

Reflecting the age of workers, the average length of service with the affected company prior to layoff was almost 13 years, and 19 percent had worked for the same company for 20 years or more. Mean number of years worked in the shoe industry was slightly above 26, and almost 19 percent of the claimants had 40 years or more experience making shoes.

Wages on prelayoff jobs were generally low: average weekly wages ranged from $30 to $316, but the mean was only $100.40. Roughly two-thirds of the population earned between $61.35 and $139.45. Less than a fourth of the workers earned as much as the average weekly wage in manufacturing.

WORKER ASSISTANCE

Eleven of the 12 firms represented in the survey shut down and permanently laid off all their workers. Most of the workers (71.4 percent) had a month or less notice of layoff. The other company received firm assistance and was still in business at the time interviews were conducted. Sample members from this firm had been temporarily laid off for varying lengths of time, but most had been recalled.

Our study found that the permanently laid-off workers as a group had severe adjustment problems. One-fourth of those laid off never found another job. At the time of interview (an average three years and three months after layoff), half were not employed full time. And real wages for those employed had declined 17.9 percent from prelayoff levels. Yet of the 185 workers who were laid off, only one had participated in a government training program, one had received a relocation allowance, and only five had been placed in jobs by the Massachusetts Division of Employment Security. For most workers, assistance consisted only of trade readjustment allowances (TRA), a supplement to unemployment insurance. Sample members received an average of $1,072 in trade readjustment allowances in addition to a mean $1,635 in regular and extended unemployment benefits.

The scarcity of adjustment services received made it pointless to focus on the effectiveness of the worker assistance program. Instead, the nature of the adjustment experience was examined. Five different measures of adjustment were considered: (1) whether or not the worker found subsequent employment; (2) the number of weeks of unemployment and TRA benefits collected; (3) for those who found work, the number of weeks of unemployment before a subsequent job was found; (4) the difference between the prelayoff wage and the initial wage at the next job; and (5) the difference between the prelayoff wage and the wage at the time of interview. Regression analyses were run for the last four of these, using a variety of independent variables. While 18 independent variables were found to have significant effects on the adjustment process in one equation or another, the important relationships can be described in the following observations.

Men adjusted more easily than women. They found jobs more quickly and, once they found jobs, suffered significantly fewer weeks of unemployment. They also earned wages significantly higher than women both in the short and long run. After controlling for other variables, the difference between currently weekly real wages and prelayoff wages was $41 higher for men than it was for women. Since the mean change in real wages was —$17.81, this would indicate that men had, on the average, increased their real wages and that the burden of adjustment fell on women.

Older workers had a more difficult time adjusting than the young and the middle-aged. This fact shows up most clearly where the dependent variable is weeks of benefits collected. Persons 55 years of age, according to the regression equation, collected 7.7 more weeks of benefits than persons age 45; 65 year olds collected a further 11.1 weeks. This reflects the fact that older people often did not find work: one-third of the 55–64 age group never worked again. To some extent it also reflects the fact that persons 60 or over at the time of layoff were eligible for 13 more weeks of TRA. But even with this extra entitlement, 64 percent of those over 60 exhausted their TRA benefits, while only 39 percent of those under 60 did so. For those who did find work, the age variables showed that the middle-aged were most likely to show wage gains.

Those with more highly paid jobs took bigger absolute cuts in wages at subsequent and current jobs and the loss was more than a short-term one. In fact, it grew as time passed: the negative coefficient for change in wage at the current job was 36 percent larger than that for the first job after layoff.

Workers with the most seniority and experience had a more difficult time adjusting than other workers. Workers with many years in the industry collected significantly more weeks of benefits and suffered significant wage losses which persisted over the entire period. Workers with many years at the company suffered significant initial wage losses in shifting jobs.

Workers who remained in the shoe industry did not suffer negative effects as a result. They had fewer weeks of unemployment and at the time of interview were earning a statistically significant premium of $11.25 a week over their fellows who went to work in other industries. Despite the low wages paid in the shoe industry, it appears that the other jobs open to shoe workers paid even less. The only problem with this conclusion is that the option of remaining in the shoe industry was not open to many workers because in many cases there were simply no shoe jobs available within commuting distance.

High rates and rising trends in unemployment led to longer periods of unemployment before workers found jobs. High unemployment rates also led to more weeks of benefits collected and lower initial wages; but the wage effects were apparently not long-lasting, as no significant effect was found on current wages.

Training, where provided by new employers, had significant positive effects on current wages, averaging $19 per week. That these effects were due to training is supported by the finding that trainees had lower than average wages on their first jobs after layoff.

Apparently workers given more notice of impending layoff were better able to adjust. They suffered significantly fewer weeks of unemployment overall and received higher mean wages (though not significantly so) at subsequent employment.

EFFECTS OF FIRM ASSISTANCE

It is interesting to contrast the experiences of those permanently laid off with those temporarily laid off at the firm-assisted company. Fifteen people in the sample were employed at the firm-assisted company and 185 were permanently laid off. The two groups were similar in personal characteristics (age, sex, years of schooling, percent U.S.-born whites) but their adjustment experiences were markedly different. The firm-assisted group was unemployed fewer weeks, and on the average collected less than half as much in total unemployment benefits as those permanently laid off. In addition, the mean wage of this subgroup rose 27.5 percent between the prelayoff period and time of interview. Adjusted for inflation, the real wages of the subgroup rose 5.1 percent compared to a drop of 17.9 percent for those permanently separated.

The effectiveness of firm assistance in dealing with the firm's problems, however, remains unproven. Only 17 firms had received any trade adjustment assistance by the end of fiscal 1974. Of these, 2 subsequently went out of business and the future of others was still in doubt. Thus, while firm assistance may have positive short-run effects on workers, it may only be postponing the day when workers will be permanently laid off.

LITTLE USE OF ADJUSTMENT SERVICES

Despite the difficult adjustment which most workers faced, there were at least four reasons why the adjustment services authorized by the Trade Expansion Act were not used. First, the time lag between application for and receipt of benefits was so long that most applicants were forced to adjust on their own. Workers in our sample waited an average of 19.4 months from date of layoff to receipt of their first TRA check. Much of the delay was the result of the cumbersome procedures required by the Trade Expansion Act.

Second, knowledge of available benefits was not widespread. In our survey, fewer than 70 percent of TRA recipients knew that they were also eligible to receive retraining or relocation benefits. A more detailed survey of worker knowledge, undertaken by the Bureau of International Labor Affairs, found even less awareness: more than 60 percent of those potentially eligible for benefits were unaware of the training, placement, and relocation aspects of adjustment assistance.[2]

Third, many affected workers were simply not interested in the services. In addition to the few who did retrain or relocate only 17 percent of our sample members expressed any interest in retraining and less than 7 percent an interest in relocation.

Fourth, those workers who were interested in the services often faced insurmountable administrative obstacles in trying to obtain them. Manpower Development and Training Act training classes had long waiting lists, and single referral training was generally available only in Boston, outside the commuting area of most sample members. Relocation allowances were available only to heads of families who obtained employment or received a bona fide offer of employment outside the commuting area, and only if the Secretary of Labor determined that the worker could not reasonably be expected to secure suitable employment within the commuting area. Under these conditions, few even applied.

It should be noted that in most cases the Massachusetts Division of Employment Security did not make much of an effort to provide special services to trade-affected workers. Most claimants only dealt with the unemployment insurance side of the division. The employment service, which would provide counseling, refer individuals to training, or provide other services was a separate branch, sometimes in a different building. Unemployment insurance personnel did refer some individuals for counseling by the employment service, but unless the person was young and unemployed at the time he filed for trade readjustment allowances, he was generally not referred for such counseling.

2. "Survey of Workers Displaced by Import Competition," (U.S. Department of Labor, Bureau of International Affairs, unpublished, 1972), tables XVI and XVII.

A CONTRASTING CASE

The experiences of the workers with regard to receipt of non-cash adjustment services were not atypical compared to the experiences of most groups in other states, but there were a few other groups which had far different experiences. One of these was a group in neighboring Rhode Island, whose experiences were described in *Industrial Gerontology*. Seven hundred fifty-five workers of the Uniroyal Company in Woonsocket, lost their jobs in April 1970 as a result of increased imports of rubber and canvas footwear. In many respects these workers were similar to those in our case study: women made up 68 percent of the group, the average age was 47 years, and average length of employment with Uniroyal was over 20 years. In addition, since they represented 10.1 percent of the community's manufacturing jobs, it was difficult for the labor market to absorb them quickly and they faced severe adjustment problems.

The company had announced its intention to close the plant in August 1969, 8 months before the closing, and had announced a definite closing date January 21, 1970, 2.5 months before production was to cease. Because of this advance notice, the Rubber Workers' union was able to apply for adjustment assistance before the plant closed. The petition was approved by the Tariff Commission on April 20 and certified by the Secretary of Labor on May 13, only a month after the layoffs. The state's Department of Employment Security also became involved relatively early. Officials of the department wrote the plant management offering to provide job placement and training, and later met with union and management officials to draw up a plan of action. The results were in marked contrast to the experiences of our sample.

During the month of July 1970, the Rhode Island State Department of Employment Security transferred three staff members to the Woonsocket office to perform counseling duties and to interview the 755 displaced Uniroyal employees. This staff interviewed 738 individuals in a total of 2,019 counseling interviews to determine specific employment needs and training aspirations. As a result of these interviews, 105 persons were subsequently placed in other positions, and training proposals were prepared and submitted to the Labor Department in conjunction with the State Division of Vocational Education for an additional 313 persons.[3]

Despite delays due to lack of facilities in the area and unwillingness of workers to take training outside the immediate vicinity, 119 people were enrolled in private training during November 1970, and within a year of the plant closing, a total of 305 had been enrolled in some type of training. By use of private as well as government facilities, a wide range of training options was made available. Course titles ranged alphabetically from air-conditioning mechanic to welder; they were concentrated in mechanical, medical, and clerical occupations. Of the 305 who entered training, 253 (83 percent) completed it, and 224 (88.5 percent of those) were placed in jobs, at least 170 of them in training-related jobs.

All of the factors which we listed as limiting the use of adjustment services by our survey subjects were overcome in this instance. There was advance notice of layoff and cooperation among the various groups involved, so that much of the delay in authorizing assistance was overcome. Counseling sessions with 738 of 755 workers eliminated the problem of ignorance about available services. The Rhode Island Department of Employment Security undertook a massive effort to train and place the affected workers. And, as a result, disinterest of individuals in training, such as we found, appears not to have been a factor. All of this combined to produce massive use of adjustment services by the Uniroyal workers.

The effects of adjustment assistance in this case, however, have not been studied. Whether training led to stable employment and higher wages, whether benefits justified costs, and how the experience of workers trained and placed compared with that of others in the group is not known. A more thorough study of this case could help us judge the potential of trade adjustment assistance.

3. Jane Mayerson, "The Trade Expansion Act: An Untapped Resource for the Middle Aged and Older Worker," *Industrial Gerontology*, Spring 1972, p. 41.

CONCLUSION

The experiences of shoe workers in Massachusetts with trade adjustment assistance leads to four conclusions: (1) adjustment assistance, in most cases, consisted entirely of trade readjustment allowances, a supplement to unemployment insurance. While this may have helped to compensate workers for loss of a job, it did nothing to improve their chances of future employment. (2) The slowness of the program effectively precluded the use of adjustment services by most workers. Even a more timely program would have to deal with workers' ignorance of benefits or disinterest in them, and the administrative obstacles which often made benefits unobtainable. Overcoming these factors requires special effort on the part of State Divisions of Employment Security. (3) Workers most in need of adjustment services were women and older workers, especially those with seniority or long experience in the industry. High or increasing unemployment rates in local labor markets and the absence of employment opportunities in the same industry nearby hindered adjustment. (4) Firm assistance appears to have brought significant benefits to workers in the one case where its effects were studied. The effectiveness of this assistance in solving the long-run problems of firms themselves, however, has yet to be proven.

APPENDIX: WORKER ADJUSTMENT ASSISTANCE UNDER THE TRADE ACT OF 1974

A new Trade Act, which became effective April 3, 1975, provides for expanded adjustment assistance to American workers who have lost their jobs because of import competition. The law also provides for improved access to the assistance.

To expedite certification of eligibility and delivery of services, workers who believe they have been or will be injured by increased import competition may simply petition the Secretary of Labor, seeking certification of eligibility to apply for adjustment assistance. No longer do the workers need to establish a link between the injury and an earlier tariff concession. Nor do they have to prove that imports were the major factor causing injury.

If the workers' petitions show that increased imports have contributed importantly to their unemployment and to a decrease in sales or production of the firm(s) from which they have become unemployed, the Secretary of Labor may declare them eligible for adjustment assistance.

The expanded assistance available under the new law includes cash trade allowances amounting to 70 percent (up from 65 percent) of a worker's average weekly wage, not to exceed the national average weekly manufacturing wage (approximately $180 a week in 1974) for up to 52 weeks. An additional 26 weeks of allowances was available to complete approved training. Workers age 60 or older may also receive up to 26 additional weeks of allowances, but no worker may receive more than 78 weeks of allowances. There are also provisions for training, counseling, testing, placement services, and other services through cooperating state agencies.

Workers who cannot expect to find suitable employment within their own commuting area may qualify for job search and relocation allowances. Eighty percent of necessary job search expenses, up to $500, may be reimbursed. Workers who relocate may be reimbursed for 80 percent of moving expenses plus a lump sum (up to $500) equal to three times their average weekly wage.

To be eligible for adjustment assistance under the new law a worker must have been employed for 26 weeks out of the 52 weeks prior to layoff at a firm or plant certified as affected by import competition. He must have earned $30 or more per week.

If the Shoe Fits . . .

*In this article, originally published in the August 18, 1975, issue
of the* Washington Post, *Nancy L. Ross reviews the first decisions
taken by the president of the United States under the Trade Act
of 1976. A postscript entitled "Whose Shoes?" and published
in the* Washington Post *on January 28, 1977, brings the story up
to date.*

THE SHOE DECISION had little to do with shoes.

That, in summary, is the reaction of many shoe industry representatives—as well as others—to the White House announcement last month that the United States would not impose quotas or tariffs on imported shoes and boots.

Instead, President Gerald Ford ordered assistance in the form of increased unemployment benefits and job retraining for the beleaguered American footwear industry.

Overlooked—or overruled—according to manufacturers, were the International Trade Commission's 5–1 recommendation in favor of some kind of tariffs and/or quotas, commitments to the industry made by a succession of presidential special trade representatives, the steady decline of domestic manufacturing and growth of imports, and Mr. Ford's own record of support for the shoe industry when he was in Congress.

"The shoe industry was crucified on the cross of free trade," declared an industry representative, referring to the Good Friday (April 16) announcement. Seymour Fabrick, president of Vogue Shoe, Inc., of Los Angeles, said, "On Wednesday (April 14), we had a deal on 1974 quotas. On Thursday, there was a new deal set up by the Secretaries of Treasury and State and, on Friday, in a sneaky way, they gave us a burial service."

Others in the retail shoe business and in government insist the issue was decided on its merits, and that the shoe industry's recovery from the recession precluded the imposition of quotas or tariffs to curb imports. "The domestic manufacturing industry is enjoying virtually unprecedented prosperity," the Volume Footwear Retailers of America announced on March 15.

In fact, the official announcement made by special trade representative Frederick Dent, plus accounts of the internal debate in the administration that preceded the announcement, tend to support the claim that both domestic and international political considerations helped to shape the final decision.

The official announcement states that import restraints would result in higher shoe prices for consumer, retaliation against U.S. exports which in turn would affect American jobs. It called "expedited adjustment assistance (to domestic footwear industry workers) "the most effective remedy for injury."

The story of the latest effort to help the U.S. footwear industry began in 1974 wih passage of the Trade Act. This contained a liberalized "escape clause" allowing temporary action in the case of U.S. industries that are found to be hurt at least partially by imports. At that time, more than 40 per cent of the domestic non-rubber footwear market was held by imports, a figure that now has increased to 48 per cent.

Accordingly, in the spring of 1975, the American Footwear Industries Association, which represents most U.S. manufacturers, was advised by Dent to file for relief under the escape clause. The association asked for mandatory quotas on a country-by-country, product-by-product basis. The nations primarily affected would be Taiwan, Italy, Spain, and Brazil.

On February 20, the six-member International Trade Commission (ITC) unanimously agreed the shoe industry had suffered "serious injury" from increased imports. Yet, there was no clear majority on the recommended remedy. Three commissioners urged that tariffs on imported footwear be increased 25 to 35 per cent, depending on the price of the shoes, from the present 6 to 15 per cent. Two others voted for a combination of tariffs and quotas. Only one commissioner, Italo Ablondi, favored trade adjustment assistance (TAA).

This program, administered by the Secretary of Labor, includes benefits of weekly allowances of up to 70 per cent of a worker's average weekly wage for 12 months, employment counseling, job retraining, job search allowances, and advances to assist in relocating if necessary for re-employment. The Secretary of Commerce administers adjustments for firms and communities affected. It includes technical assistance, direct loans, or loan guarantees, to aid in modernizing plants or switching to other lines or to attract new industries.

The fact there was no clear majority recommendation was to become a key factor in the ultimate decision. For, under the 1974 Trade Act, Congress has the power to override a chief executive who disapproves or changes a majority decision. White House lawyers quickly made it known they did not consider three out of six a majority.

Meanwhile, the steel case intervened. In January, the ITC had recommended 4–1 that President Ford impose quotas on imports of specialty steels such as stainless. Under pressure from thousands of union steel makers and workers—an industry where unemployment was high and profits very low—and from Congress, Mr. Ford announced on March 16 that he would unilaterally impose quotas June 14 if his negotiators were unable to get voluntary export limits with the major foreign sellers—Japan, the European Economic Community, and Sweden.

It was the first major decision under the 1974 Trade Act, and its protectionist terms alarmed proponents of free trade at home and abroad. Thus far, European negotiations have not proved fruitful.

Shortly after the presidential decision in favor of protection, the specialty steel industry announced selective price increases. This move angered Treasury Secretary William Simon. At a high-level White House meeting during Easter week, he reportedly vowed the shoe industry would never do the same thing if he could help it.

As the ITC recommendation was based on 1974 data, a week or so prior to that meeting Simon's staff conducted an informal telephone poll of about half a dozen U.S. manufacturers to inquire how business was going now. One of these, Sid Schwartz of Vogue Shoe, said he told the caller the factory was busy at the moment with Easter orders. Most of his colleagues gave similar reports.

The footwear industry actually began its recovery from the recession in May 1975, marking the end of a downturn that really began in the spring of 1973. Production for 1976 is up 20 per cent over 1975. Manufacturers counter that they are just now getting back to where they were in 1974, after a disastrous 1975.

Treasury Secretary Simon's thinking is said to have been influenced as well by the Brazilian situation. Brazil is the fourth largest shoe exporter to the United States, having shipped 26.4 million pairs worth $120.6 million last year. Several New York banks argue that Brazil would have difficulty repaying its U.S. loans if its exports to the United States were reduced as a result of quotas or new tariffs. At the same time, Brazil has imposed new duties on entering goods that Simon would like to get reduced, and American restraint in the shoe matter was seen as a strong argument for Brazilian concessions.

The secretary left last week for a visit to Latin America, including Brazil, and was not available for comment.

According to informed sources, the opinions of Simon and Secretary of State Henry Kissinger weighed most heavily in Mr. Ford's decision, especially when his advisors proved evenly divided on the question of tariff/quotas versus adjustment assistance. At the Tuesday meeting of the Economic Policy Board with the president, Simon made a "strong statement," and the meeting broke up with adjustment assistance a slight favorite.

Kissinger, ideologically wed to free trade, joined Simon in writing a letter over the Palm Sunday weekend urging the president not to impose any kind of new import barriers. State Department consumer advisor Joan Braden went on the NBC "Today" show to discuss her concern that tariffs or quotas could trigger international retaliation and could also lead to higher consumer shoe prices domestically.

Rogers Morton, Mr. Ford's campaign chief, is said to have warned that rising shoe prices would be highly visible to voters. The Treasury Department estimated the cost to consumers at between $750 million and $1 billion in the first year, a figure hotly contested by domestic manufacturers.

Also opposed to tariff/quotas were the Secretary of Agriculture, who feared foreign retaliation; the Secretary of Defense, who feared that duties on Spanish shoes might create difficult relations with Spain where the U.S. has important military bases; the Secretary of the Interior; and the director of the Office of Management and Budget.

On the other side stood the president's special assistant for economic affairs, William Seidman, and the Secretaries of Labor and Commerce. On March 5, the Commerce Department had turned out a position paper opposing adjustment assistance on the grounds that "many shoe firms lacked the resources, the expertise and the will to modernize or diversify."

However, Elliot L. Richardson, most recently ambassador to Great Britain before becoming Commerce Secretary, was reported wavering as the result of conversations wih a Spanish minister and U.S. retailers, both opposed to tariff/quotas. (A few days after the decision, he issued a press release saying he would expedite TAA.)

Special trade representative Dent went into the meeting with what amounted to a compromise between the pro- and anti-tariff industry groups and a reluctant acceptance from foreign representatives. But the president did not accept Dent's modified position as he had in the steel case.

After more informal meetings, word of the presidential decision in favor of TAA began to leak out Thursday morning. The official announcement was not made until 2 P.M. Friday afternoon (evening in Europe) on a holiday weekend when Congress was on vacation. The timing offended almost all involved.

The decision was denounced by Senator Thomas J. McIntyre (D-N.H.) and Representative James A. Burke (D-Mass.), both of whom have fought long for footwear workers in their districts. "I consider the president's decision a breach of faith and a violation of the intent of the Trade Act of 1974," McIntyre stated. He added that he had been assured by presidential trade representatives as early as December 1974 that "if the procedures suggest the need for import relief (tariffs or quotas), you can be assured the administration would move expeditiously to provide it."

Calling trade adjustment assistance "ineffective," Burke cited an opinion by Ablondi, the only commissioner to vote in favor of TAA, that there is not enough money available to carry out the intended mission of the (TAA) program. Burke urged the General Accounting Office to conduct a study of the effectiveness of TAA.

Soon afterward, the Commerce Department put out its own study showing the TAA program has had mixed results. Since

1962, seven shoe companies have received $14 million in TAA. Four are still in existence and one has reduced operations. The Labor Department has granted $36.8 million in TAA to 17,800 shoe workers (an average of $2,067 apiece) since 1969.

"I guess we were just naïve to think we could win on the merits of the case," declared an industry attorney. It was not the first time the footwear manufacturers have been disappointed. For the past eight years, since domestic production began its decline, the industry has been seeking relief.

The Tariff Commission, predecessor of the ITC, predicted in 1968 that U.S. production in 1975 would amount to 650 million pairs (it was 433 million), and imports 335 million (they were 320). There are now 350 companies making shoes in the United States compared with 600 in 1969.

In 1969, then-Representative Gerald R. Ford joined Burke and 300 colleagues in requesting President Richard Nixon to ask foreign countries to set voluntary import limitations. Ford voted for the 1970 trade bill, which called for quotas for footwear, among other industries, and increased adjustment assistance. However, because a majority of the Tariff Commission did not find imports the primary cause of the industry's malaise, the White House did nothing.

The latest White House decision was eagerly awaited, not only by shoe retailers and manufacturers, but also by many with no interest in shoes beyond what they put on their feet. Footwear was the second major case since the 1974 Trade Act liberalized the escape clause and many industries decided to test it. Observers were waiting to see if the shoe decision coming after the steel quotas would set a protectionist trend. The answer is no.

Since shoes, Mr. Ford has declined to impose a recommended tariff rate quota on stainless flatwear (knives, forks, and spoons), or continue tariffs on ceramic dishes. He did nothing on asparagus when the commissioners split 3–3 on injury with half recommending quotas. He ordered adjustment assistance for the domestic zipper industry. In the case of mushrooms, on which a decision is due May 17, the recommendation of three out of five commissioners voting is for TAA.

In all of these decisions to date—excepting shoes—Mr. Ford has accepted the philosophy of his Trade Policy Committee, whose chairman is Dent, rather than the generally protectionist stance of the International Trade Commission.

But on blue pigments (dyes), a case that must be judged by June 2, the president faces a 5–1 ITC recommendation in favor of an 18 per cent increase in tariffs. This means that if he decides against tariffs, Congress can override his decision. Unlike steel or shoes, blue pigments are hardly of great importance, with only $2.7 million worth imported annually from the United Kingdom, West Germany, and Japan.

On the whole, U.S. trade policy does not appear at present to be headed in a protectionist direction. Mr. Ford went one way on steel, another on shoes. The political fallout from both decisions remains to be measured.

A POSTSCRIPT: WHOSE SHOES?

The shoe manufacturers are back, wringing their hands, weeping and calling piteously for protection from imports. They are forcing the first real test of President Jimmy Carter's declared intentions to keep American markets open to world trade. If he imposes tariffs and quotas, the prices of many kinds of shoes will rise and the range of choice for consumer will shrink. When the shoe industry pressed this same claim a year ago, President Ford turned them down. Now, with a new administration in power, they are trying again. They've been back to the International Trade Commission—a weak agency, excessively responsive to the Senate Finance Committee—and the ITC recommended an awkward formula of quotas and higher tariffs. That recommendation now goes to the White House.

The issue casts a long shadow. How much responsibility does society have to preserve an individual citizen's job? How much of a cost can properly be put on consumers in general to save a specific factory? Is it right to save one person's job through public action that may also jeopardize the job of someone else? Perhaps you have never fully considered the philosophical implications of the shoe trade.

First, the trade-off in wages and subsidies: The ITC calculates that its tariff-and-quota proposal would create perhaps as many as 10,000 jobs in the U.S. shoe industry as the supply of imports dropped. The cost in higher prices to American consumers would be, also according to the ITC, about $170 million a year. That works out to $17,000 a year per job—which, as it happens, is something over twice the average production worker's wages in the shoe industry. As a formula for protecting the nation's prosperity, that doesn't sound like much of a bargain.

Next, the trade-off in jobs: While the protectionism doubtless creates jobs in the shoe factories, it is equally likely to destroy jobs in the retail stores. Higher prices would mean fewer sales, which in turn would mean the closing of some stores. How many? It's hard to tell. But it's pretty clear that the ITC's tariffs and quotas would subtract jobs as well as add them.

Finally, the trade-off in trade: If the United States discriminates against other countries' sales here, we can expect them to discriminate against our exports. Tit for tat is the rule in world trade strategy. But it's not only that American exports represent American jobs. Economic quarrels pollute foreign policy. It's hard to make another country believe in your pledges of eternal friendship if, meanwhile, you're cutting off its access to the world's richest market. Italy, for example, is a major exporter of shoes to the United States. One of President Ford's reasons for turning down the shoe quotas a year ago was that Italy faced an election in June, and he didn't care to help the Communists win it.

The country owes generous compensation and adjustment assistance to working people whose jobs are hit by imports. It is not fair to load the price of economic growth and general prosperity onto a small number of people in hard-luck industries. But the country can't sensibly commit itself to propping up uncompetitive companies forever, at great cost, to preserve small numbers of badly paid jobs.

In the politics of protectionism, it is always the narrowest interest that is most vigorously represented. It is the threatened companies and unions that push hardest. The interests on the other side of the question are more diffused. In this whole angry process, the national interest is fully represented only at the White House—and that is where the process is now headed.

Toward an Effective International Trading System

GEZA FEKETEKUTY

In this essay, written for the Columbia Journal of World Business *shortly before he joined the president's Office for Trade Negotiations as chief economist, Geza Feketekuty reviews the main issues for the ongoing trade negotiations.*

U.S. NEGOTIATING OBJECTIVES in the trade arena are based on a continuing confidence in the advantages of an open world economy. Although substantial progress has been made in removing trade barriers over the last quarter of a century, some important barriers remain. Significant sectors of the U.S. economy, in particular the farm sector, are now denied the opportunity to export the products the United States as a nation can produce best and at least cost; these are the economic activities from which U.S. residents derive high income. At the same time, U.S. consumers are denied the advantage of buying many foreign goods that are of higher quality or lower price than like goods produced domestically. Estimates place the cost of existing U.S. import restrictions to U.S. consumers at several billion dollars each year.

It will not be easy to remove or reduce many of the trade barriers that remain in effect; their survival after 25 years of negotiations is in itself a sign of their economic importance or, at least, their political durability. The aim, however, will be to remove as many barriers as feasible, including tariffs, quotas, or any other government measures that selectively impede imports or favor goods produced in the home market. Where removal of a barrier is not practical, the objective will be to bring it under international review procedures to assure that every precaution has been taken to minimize the distortion of trade.

TIMELINESS OF TRADE NEGOTIATIONS

A major negotiating effort to reduce trade barriers is timely for a number of reasons:

First, the phased reduction of barriers which was negotiated in the Kennedy Round has been largely implemented. In order to maintain the momentum toward the progressive liberalization of world trade, a new agreement is needed that will in turn provide a framework for future reductions of tariffs and other barriers to trade.

Second, the accelerated effort in Europe to reduce trade barriers on a regional basis has raised the possibility of a reduction in trade opportunities between Europe, on the one hand, and the United States and other industrial countries on the other hand. The removal of trade barriers within a region tends to create new trade within that region, but it also tends to divert trade opportunities from countries outside the region. Suppliers located inside the region gain a competitive edge over suppliers outside the region. The removal of trade barriers within the region also creates internal adjustment problems that can easily lead to political pressures for offsetting reductions in imports from outside the region. And there is always a temptation to speed the process of unification in Europe by creating friction with the United States. The best way of dealing with these protectionist tendencies arising from European economic unification is to negotiate a reduction of the protective trade barriers around Europe. Of course, in order to have any chance for success, such negotiations must be based on overall reciprocity, with the United States making equivalent concessions and commitments.

Third, the international trading system has shown increasing signs of strain in recent years. The existing rules and procedures embodied in the General Agreement on Tariffs and Trade (GATT) have increasingly become inadequate for the resolution of problems that have arisen in international trading relationships, and this has led to an increasing use of governmental measures inconsistent with agreed rules and procedures. While it has been possible to forestall a wholesale return to protectionist policies, the confrontations on trade issues have led to political friction among the major industrial countries, and to an increase in protectionist sentiment in the United States as well as in some other countries.

The initiation of negotiations aimed at a major expansion of overall trade should in itself reduce the economic and political friction over current disputes by putting them into a broader perspective. Trivial issues will appear as trivial when the focus is on a broad increase in trade. In a context where everyone stands to make substantial gains from the successful completion of comprehensive negotiations, it will not matter as much whether the outcome of a particular issue on balance seems a little more favorable to one party or another.

Over the longer run, the avoidance of escalating economic and political friction over trade issues has to be based on an improvement in the international trading system, i.e., the rules and procedures embodied in the General Agreement on Tariffs and Trade. The existing system was negotiated and functioned relatively well when trade was severely hampered by trade barriers, but it is not capable of dealing with problems that arise in a substantially integrated world economy. The economic integration that has resulted from the removal of trade barriers has increased the sensitivity of economic activity in one country to developments in another and, perhaps more importantly, to policies pursued by other governments. This higher degree of economic interdependence calls for more sophisticated political arrangements among governments to coordinate their policies and to resolve conflicts.

The difficulty of managing international trade relations should not be underestimated. The world trading system as constituted under the GATT is based on the notion that market forces result in an optimal allocation of the world's resources. Moreover, the rules of the GATT establish this principle as an ethical norm. It is a fact, however, that most governments adhering to the GATT intervene in the market on a broad scale in pursuit of a wide spectrum of political, social, and economic objectives. There is thus a natural tension between the free-market principle on which the GATT is based and the practical reality of extensive government intervention in the economy. What is needed to relieve these tensions is a political process that will keep the disruptive effects of government intervention within tolerable bounds.

In each national economy, political procedures exist for determining whether the goals that are to be achieved through government intervention in the economy are worth any losses in economic efficiency that might result. A similar decision has to be made on the international level, though one would expect the criteria for legitimacy to be rigorous. Generally, the test that one would apply would not be whether the intervention is worthwhile, but whether it does not excessively impair the interests of foreign consumers and producers. Ideally, therefore, the international trading rules and procedures should allow each country considerable leeway in pursuing its own policy objectives, but should also require each country to minimize the disruptive impact of its policies on international trade and the policies of other countries.

TRADE LIBERALIZATION GOALS

As in the past, a major focus of the negotiations will be on a reduction of tariffs. While past trade negotiations have reduced the relative importance of tariffs, they remain the most visible obstacle to trade to the average citizen. Approximately 60 percent of all trade in industrial products remains subject to tariffs in the major industrial countries, and the average value of such tariffs is about 10 percent. Moreover, while in the aggregate tariffs have been substantially reduced, some relatively high tariffs remain on a few important consumer goods. Four percent of all trade is still subject to tariffs of 20 percent or more. It is hoped that the negotiations will result in a substantial expansion of the duty-free category as well as a substantial reduction in the average tariff on the remaining dutiable items.

In terms of the relative impact on trade, however, the most important negotiations will not be over tariffs, but over a wide variety of nontariff barriers (NTBs). These barriers, ranging from the very obvious to the subtle, include import quotas, preferential government procurement policies, product standards which have the effect of discriminating against foreign goods, and various administrative provisions which can be applied in a discriminatory fashion to handicap imports. Also included under this category are special advantages to domestic producers or sellers of domestic products, such as export subsidies, investment subsidies, and preferential access to financing.

Most of these NTBs, like tariffs, are designed to protect particular industries. The objective of the negotiations will be to remove as many of these as is politically feasible. Where it is not possible to remove them, they should be subjected to periodic review to assure that the level of protection offered is the minimum necessary to achieve legitimate domestic objectives.

Some NTBs are not protectionist by intent, even though they have the effect of impeding imports. The protectionist effect may be only the unintentional by-product of domestic policies in such areas as health, safety, the environment, and so on. This effect can frequently be avoided, however, by a change in administrative practices, by a modification of the policy tools used to achieve the desired objective, or by a harmonization of policies among the major countries. The objective of trade negotiations in such cases is to bring about whatever modifications in the implementation or design of domestic policies will minimize the trade distortions. Of course, disentangling what is an avoidable and what is an unavoidable impediment to trade in the pursuit of legitimate domestic objectives is not always an easy task, and elimination of all such NTBs should not be expected. Some differences in competitive conditions among countries due to government policies are unavoidable, and need not undermine the basis for market-directed trade. After all, trade is largely based on differences that give each country its particular character, such as climate, the temperament of the people, the quality of public education, and so forth.

The negotiations on NTBs must be approached with a great deal of realism and pragmatism. For only a limited number of nontariff barriers will it be possible to agree on a specific plan for phasing them down or out. In most cases, the negotiations will have to proceed on three levels.

1. Agreements on general principles that can guide national governments in designing their domestic programs so as to minimize the foreign trade impact. While such principles are frequently honored more in the breach than in practice, they pro-

vide a useful measuring stick against which government actions can be evaluated.

2. Fairly detailed understandings on how specific laws, regulations or administrative practices might be changed to reduce their discriminatory impact on foreign trade. Such agreements give all governments the assurance that politically difficult actions or commitments in the interest of the world as a whole are reciprocated by equivalent actions or commitments by other governments.

3. Agreements on procedures involving exchanges of information on governmental actions, joint reviews of such actions in the light of agreed principles and national commitments, and procedures for the settlement of any disputes that may arise.

Many nontariff barriers such as export subsidies and customs valuation procedures, are already covered by existing codes or agreements. Moreover, discussions have been in progress in such areas as government procurement; health, safety, and environmental standards; and domestic investment subsidies. In the context of the negotiations it should be possible to accelerate whatever work has been in progress, and to conclude agreements where sufficient progress has been made at the technical level. Given the complexity of the issues arising from most nontariff barriers, no single agreement will ever solve all problems that can be identified. Thus it should be possible to pull together what can be agreed upon at a politically convenient time, and to supplement such agreements when the need arises and the state of international understanding permits.

Where shortcomings have already become obvious with respect to existing agreements, it may be desirable to conclude supplemental agreements. In only a limited number of cases will it be necessary, however, to change a past agreement.

Perhaps the most difficult negotiations will be in the area of agriculture. International trade in agricultural products is surrounded by virtually every available form of tariff and nontariff barrier. Twenty-five years of trade negotiations have not resulted in a substantial liberalization of agricultural trade. Both income to farmers and availability of food are potent political issues in almost all countries, and most countries have found that the easiest way of dealing with these issues is by raising the prices of domestic farm products and limiting imports of foreign farm products. Where these policies have led to overproduction, subsidies have been used in competition for export markets.

The distortions created by this combination of internal and external measures have become increasingly apparent, and for purely domestic reasons political pressures have developed in most countries in favor of an overall reform of these policies. The trade negotiations thus provide a timely opportunity to put agricultural trade barriers as well as domestic agricultural programs in a more rational framework, one that will protect farm incomes while at the same time making food available to everyone at lower prices.

At this stage it is still too early to tell what form arrangements in agricultural trade might take. They will need to meet four criteria.

1. Expanded possibilities for trade in agricultural goods, so that efficiency in world production of food can be increased and prices can be reduced. Reductions in the prices of meat and other income and price-elastic foods could lead to a significant increase in their consumption, increasing both the welfare of consumers and income opportunities for farmers.

2. Increased responsiveness of agricultural production to market forces. While a strong case can be made for evening out short-term fluctuations in agricultural prices by appropriate agricultural stock management policies, such policies must remain sensitive to underlying shifts in demand and supply both at home and abroad.

3. Continued protection of farm incomes. Most countries have programs designed to protect the income of farmers.

4. Guarantees on the availability of foodstuffs. Food is the basic necessity of life, and every government must be able to assure its people an adequate supply of food.

REFORMING THE INTERNATIONAL TRADE SYSTEM

Another major objective for negotiations is to reform the international trade system. The negotiations to lower nontariff barriers will in themselves result in new rules and procedures that should reduce possible areas of conflict among national policies, and improve the means for settling any conflicts that do arise. In addition, the negotiations will provide a convenient time and place for reforming many of the rules which deal with the exceptional circumstances under which governments may break commitments they have made on liberalizing trade. In the case of three major types of actions that governments might take— safeguards, balance-of-payments measures, and countervailing duties—the need for reform has become quite apparent.

Safeguards include all those actions which governments might take to prevent a disruption of domestic production in a particular industry as a result of a rapid rise in imports. Safeguards, or escape clause actions as they were previously called, are covered in Article XIX of the GATT. These rules have not worked very well. Briefly, the GATT articles require that countries affected by foreign safeguard actions either be compensated by a reduction of trade barriers in other commodities or be allowed to retaliate by increasing some of their trade barriers. In practice, however, the country imposing safeguards has succeeded in negotiating agreements with the major supplier countries, with the stipulation that no compensation would be required and no retaliatory actions would be taken. There has thus been a de facto change in the accepted international standard of conduct, even though the rules themselves have not been changed. It would be desirable that this new standard be incorporated in the rules in the form of an agreement supplementing Article XIX. This would be desirable for two reasons. First, to the extent that safeguard actions have been negotiated on a bilateral basis between the consumer country and the major supplier countries, the interests of third countries have not been directly taken into account. Making such actions legal under the GATT would bring the consideration of such actions back into the multilateral context. Second, tacit acceptance of consistent violations of the GATT articles will tend to undermine respect for the GATT as a whole.

Balance-of-payments measures are likewise covered by the GATT in Article XII. As in the case of safeguards, practices have generally not been in conformity with the rules. The GATT provisions permit countries to impose quotas, but not tariffs, when they are faced by major balance-of-payments deficits. In practice, however, countries have found it preferable to use surcharges on tariffs, and this practice has met with the tacit consent of the international community in most cases. As in the case of safeguards, it would be desirable to bring generally accepted governmental practices into conformity with international rules. This could be done either by a formal amendment of GATT Article XII, or by a supplementary agreement which would in effect suppress the prohibitions of Article XII, under specified circumstances.

Countervailing duties are covered in GATT Article VI. The provisions of this article have not been broad enough, however, to deal in a comprehensive way with the issues that arise with respect to the use of subsidies and the imposition of countervailing duties. It would be desirable, though difficult, to reach agreement on a two-part code dealing with subsidies on one hand and the use of countervailing duties on the other hand. It will not be easy to negotiate such a code because most governments consider the use of subsidies an essential method of achieving a variety of social and economic objectives. On the other hand, countries whose trade might be affected by such subsidies will continue to use countervailing duties, and in the absence of a code will use their own judgment as to what constitutes an illegitimate subsidy. Needless to say, this could easily lead to disagreements among countries, with the possibility of further retaliations and counterretaliations. In order to reduce the risk that such disputes might pose for harmonious economic relations, it is in the interest both of countries extensively using subsidies and countries affected by such subsidies to reach agreement on a subsidy cum countervailing duty code.

PART TWO: Oil, Commodities, and the New International Economic Order

Restructuring the World Economy

HOLLIS B. CHENERY

In an article published in the January 1975 issue of Foreign Affairs, *Hollis B. Chenery, vice-president for development policy at the World Bank, suggests a cooperative approach with the participation of the oil-producing, developed, and developing countries to ensure the continuing growth of the world economy.*

THE WORLD ECONOMY is currently in a state of disequilibrium of a magnitude not seen since the aftermath of World War II. The symptoms of underlying stress have been manifested over the past two years in the form of raw-material shortages, a food and fertilizer crisis, a dramatic rise in petroleum prices, and finally, worldwide inflation and threats of impending financial disaster.

The immediate cause of most of these problems was the rapid growth of almost all parts of the world economy in the previous decade, culminating in a strong cyclical upswing in the industrial countries. In 1972–73 the economies of the advanced countries as a group were growing at an unsustainable rate of over 6 percent, pushing against existing productive capacity and outstripping the potential rate of expansion of world supplies of many raw materials. This spurt in demand provided the opportunity for primary producers in both developed and developing countries to raise their prices, with or without collusive action among producers.

Some of the symptoms of commodity shortages and high prices are purely cyclical and are already disappearing as a result of the current stagnation in world incomes. Others, however, reflect long-term shifts in demand and supply that were merely accelerated by the recent period of rapid growth. This is notably true of the supply of energy and foodstuffs, where the evidence of shifts in the balance of supply and demand was apparent before these markets were disrupted by booming demand, crop failures, and the behavior of the Organization of Petroleum Exporting Countries (OPEC). Before the world economy can return to a condition of orderly development, substantial redirection of investment and production in these and related sectors is imperative.

While the present dimensions of the oil, food, raw materials and balance-of-payments problems are by now well-known,[1] international attention has centered on their immediate impacts on different groups of countries and on the interim measures needed to offset them. There has been little analysis of the adjustment mechanisms that are available to restore the world economy to a condition of orderly development. Yet, since all of these problems are connected through the international system of trade and capital movements, to prescribe separate cures for each of them is hardly desirable. And for poor countries that are importers of both oil and food, the problems must be considered together because their combined impact threatens to be disastrous.

In trying to provide a longer term perspective on the present disequilibrium in the world economy and to outline adjustment processes through which equilibrium can be restored, my analysis is couched in terms of the economic and political relations among three groups of countries: the older industrialized countries, which are members of the Organization for Economic Cooperation and Development (OECD), the newly rich but still developing oil producers (OPEC), and the other developing countries (LDCs). Only passing attention is given to the fourth major group—the socialist countries—which has a limited impact on the problems considered here.

1. See, for example, in *Foreign Affairs*, Gerald A. Pollack, "The Economic Consequences of the Energy Crisis," Lyle P. Schertz, "World Food: Prices and the Poor," Bension Varon and Kenji Takeuchi, "Developing Countries and Non-Fuel Minerals," April 1974; Walter J. Levy, "World Cooperation or International Chaos," July 1974.

II

To define the dimensions of the structural changes that are needed in the world economy, we must first separate out the cyclical effects of the recent boom that are likely to be corrected by market forces over the next several years. The coincidence of shortages and price rises for most commodities during 1972–73 has left the impression of a general "commodity problem" and led to a number of false analogies between petroleum and other commodities. Price reductions since the ending of the boom nearly a year ago confirm the diagnosis that most of these were cyclical phenomena: hence, we can now identify more clearly areas in which longer term adjustments are needed.

The interpretation of movements in international prices is also complicated by the persistence of inflation on a worldwide basis. While the sharp rise in commodity prices in 1972–73 was a significant factor in causing inflation to accelerate, this is no longer the case; the overall effect of trends in commodity prices—including oil—is now deflationary.

The fact is that the commodity boom itself varied greatly among different types of commodities. A good way to measure its scale is in terms of the ratio of prices of primary commodities to those of manufactured goods for a recent period of stable prices, e.g., 1968 to 1970. Compared with this benchmark level, at the peak of the boom in early 1974 basic foodstuffs were up by 100 percent, fertilizer by 170 percent, and petroleum by more than 350 percent; however, other primary commodities averaged only 25 percent higher. With several important exceptions, relative prices of most commodities have already started to fall, and supply and demand conditions are such that a return to the earlier levels of relative prices is likely to take place within the next year or two.

Now that the normal cyclical adjustment is under way, there are only a few commodities whose high prices (or short supplies) are likely to have an important continuing effect on the economic welfare of large numbers of people. These are primarily petroleum, some of the major foodstuffs (grains, oilseeds, beef, sugar), and fertilizer. While there is some dispute as to the ability of producers of other minerals to follow the OPEC example and keep prices higher by restricting production,[2] the value of exports of the leading candidates (bauxite, tin, copper) is relatively small, and the range of possible prices is so limited that successful action would not disrupt world trade and development. In short, the world commodity problem focuses on petroleum and foodstuffs—primarily grains—and the fertilizer needed to produce the latter.

Although recent events have shown that relatively small changes in the supplies of petroleum and foodstuffs can have a very disruptive effect on world trade and development, in most other respects these two commodities are very different. Petroleum has a dominant impact on world trade because it supplies nearly half of world energy consumption, and resources are concentrated in a small number of countries. Consequently, two-thirds of all petroleum produced moves in international trade. The present and prospective value of petroleum exports (even if present prices were somewhat reduced) roughly equals the value of all other mineral and agricultural exports combined. For this reason the position of the petroleum exporters is unique; it is hard to conceive of any combination of producer cartels that would have as much effect on world trade in the next few years as an increase of even $1.00 in the price of oil.

As is now well known, the actions of the OPEC countries in late 1973 raised the average price of oil in the Persian Gulf from about $2.40 per barrel in the early part of 1973 to about $9.60 per barrel in 1974. (This and all subsequent figures in this article are in 1974 dollars except as specifically noted.) The short-run effect has been to increase the value of OPEC exports in 1974 by over $80 billion, about 10 percent of the value of world exports in that year. Only a fraction of this increase has so far been absorbed by increased OPEC imports, and the resulting surplus of some $60 billion is a measure of the present disequilibrium in world trade.

At first glance the effects of rising food and fertilizer prices on the world economy appear to be of quite a different order of magnitude from the oil impact. Even though the total value of

2. See Varon and Takeuchi, "Developing Countries."

grain produced in the world is considerably greater than that of petroleum, most countries are relatively self-sufficient in grain, and only marginal quantities are traded. While the position of the United States and Canada as grain exporters is as dominant as that of the Persian Gulf countries in oil, the total value of world grain exports is only one-fourth that of petroleum.

Yet the disruptive effect of the rise in food and fertilizer prices on world development is much greater than this comparison would suggest. As in the case of petroleum, the developing countries had come to depend on cheap grain imports to supplement their own production, and implicitly on grain stocks in the exporting countries. With hindsight it is now clear that they overestimated the increased productivity stemming from the "green revolution," relied too heavily on continued availability of cheap imports, and devoted insufficient resources to agricultural development. Although the shortfall in LDC production of foodstuffs in the past several years has been relatively small, the rise in import requirements combined with large price rises have had as damaging an effect on the growth prospects of many developing countries as have rising oil prices. The current shortage of fertilizer, while primarily a cyclical phenomenon of lagging capacity, seriously limits the speed with which developing countries can increase agricultural output unless they are given some priority in competing for available supplies.

Although the longer term solutions to the oil and food problems will be very different, in the short run they have a similar effect on the prospects for the developing countries. Increased petroleum prices have added $10 billion to the import bill of the LDCs while the increases in prices of food and fertilizer have added another $6 billion. For the poorest people in these countries the impact of high food prices and shortages is much more serious, since most of their income is spent on food. Even allowing for gains from other commodity exports, such increases in import costs have reduced the external purchasing power of the developing countries by approximately the amount of the total foreign assistance that they receive. The number of countries seriously affected is also likely to increase over the next several years, since the prices of other primary exports are likely to fall more than those of petroleum and foodstuffs. This impact affects disproportionately the poorest countries of South Asia and Africa, which contain about half the population of the Third World.

III

The nature of the present world economic crisis has been aptly characterized by Helmut Schmidt as "The Struggle for the World Product."[3] When viewed in these terms, the rise in oil prices is only the most dramatic of a series of events—some deliberate and some resulting from market forces—that have been operating to change the distribution of world income through the system of international trade and capital flows.

Although the changes in relative prices described above will have a substantial effect on the distribution of the world's income and wealth, their direct impact can easily be exaggerated. To measure this, assume that the OECD countries and the non-OPEC members of the Third World had been able to pay for the increase in the cost of imported oil by shifting $80 billion worth of commodities per year from domestic use to increased exports to OPEC. The result of this one-time cost increase would have been to reduce total national income in the OECD countries by 2 percent and in the non-OPEC Third World by 3 percent, while nearly doubling the total income of the OPEC countries. Although these are large amounts, the direct losses would amount to giving up six months' worth of growth—with the lively hope of then resuming the pattern of 4 to 6 percent average growth thereafter.

In reality the threat to the world economy from the rise in oil prices comes not so much from the need to transfer 2 percent of world income to the oil-exporting countries as from the uncertainties that are inherent in the policies adopted to effect this transfer. If there were in fact a market for their exports, the oil importers—both developed and underdeveloped—could achieve the required 11 percent increase in export quantities over a period of 3 or 4 years without much strain on their economies, which are already developing excess capacity as a result of the

3. See *Foreign Affairs*, April 1974.

current recession. However, it will take the several OPEC countries from 5 to 20 years to develop their economies sufficiently to absorb their increased foreign-exchange earnings in the form of imports. In the meantime, if they export oil at the levels and prices now predicted, they will have to accumulate large surpluses in the form of loans or direct investments in the importing countries. For their part, the principal customers, the OECD countries, will have to accept the corresponding deficits in their balance of payments and arrange to reallocate (or compensate for) the flow of OPEC funds through the process now known as "recycling."

To put the point differently, the major consequences of the change in OPEC price policy stem more from its suddenness than from its magnitude. If the price of oil had reached its present level by 3 percent annual increase in its relative price over the past 25 years, the adjustments needed to accommodate this increase would have had little effect on world growth and indeed some benefit in directing behavior patterns and technological efforts toward more efficient use of energy. Instead, the progressive cheapening of oil for 20 years led to its wasteful use—particularly in the United States—and postponed the development of other energy sources. We are now faced with accelerated changes in consumption patterns and large investments for the development of non-OPEC sources of supply, in addition to financing the cost of the imports that will still be required. And the danger is that in adjusting to these changes the OECD countries may adopt policies that will operate to freeze or reduce their growth so that it does not move back soon to the past pattern of 4 to 6 percent growth.

While the food aspect of the world restructuring problem does not loom so large as the oil aspect in global terms, it raises issues that are just as acute for the LDC countries involved. On optimistic assumptions, it will take at least five years to make up for the lags in fertilizer capacity and in agricultural investment in the developing countries so as to balance supply and demand, restore stocks, and bring food prices down to more normal levels. In the meantime, some restraint will be needed in the high-income countries of the OECD to avoid bidding away the limited supplies of foodstuffs and fertilizer from the poorest countries, whose consumption cannot be compressed further.[4]

For the past year we have watched these adjustment processes begin to unfold with relatively little assistance from governments. Under the circumstances the international banking system has functioned with considerable efficiency to initiate the recycling process. However, existing financial arrangements will soon prove quite inadequate to the magnitude of the problem, particularly for the weaker economies. The laissez-faire approach has already had very harsh consequences for the distribution of food and fertilizer, where the lack of foreign exchange to pay prices that have been bid up by the richer countries has brought several of the weakest economies to the brink of disaster.

There are two great dangers in the present situation, the first involving the relations between the OECD and OPEC countries, and the second involving their common relationship to the LDCs. At present, individual OECD nations are acting on their own to protect their balance of payments in ways that are inimical to their collective interest in increasing their trade and their GNPs. Moreover, given their uncertainty as to future OPEC oil price policies, OECD governments are also taking steps both to limit oil imports and to invest in high-cost substitute energy sources to an excessive extent that affects their future growth. Thus, the continuation of uncoordinated responses to the oil problem will almost certainly result in a lower rate of OECD growth and make the transition much more costly in the end.

Such an outcome is clearly not in the interests of the OPEC countries, whose oil markets and investment returns would suffer in the process. However, it can only be avoided if both the OPEC and OECD countries achieve a better understanding and acceptance of less disruptive adjustment processes.

Secondly, the future of the LDCs—and particularly the poorest among them—depends on the ability of the OPEC and OECD countries to work out some agreed basis for financing the 100

4. More complete statements of the nature of these transitional problems and the changes in agricultural production that are needed are given in the United Nations World Food Conference, *Assessment of the World Food Situation.* See also, Lyle P. Schertz, "World Food: Prices and the Poor"; and Lester Brown, *By Bread Alone* (New York: Praeger, 1974).

percent increase in LDC balance-of-payments deficits that has resulted from the higher prices of oil and food. Although the problem of the most seriously affected is only 5 percent of a $60 billion global disequilibrium, existing mechanisms for balance-of-payments adjustment and capital transfers are clearly unable to cope with it.

Moreover, there is a direct connection between these two dangers. It seems most unlikely that the more fortunate countries of the OECD and OPEC groups will do a great deal about the poorest nations until they reach some understanding on the evolving patterns of trade and capital movements among themselves. So long as the present atmosphere of mutual recrimination continues among the more affluent, the poorest countries will remain their unwilling hostages.

IV

To analyze the possible adjustments to the oil problem more concretely, let us first examine the varying positions of the principal oil exporters. The members of OPEC are all developing countries for whom petroleum is the principal source of foreign exchange and the key to their further development. They differ greatly, however, in their current needs for imports and in the volume of their oil reserves in relation to present levels of production. Assuming that OPEC will continue to set prices cooperatively, countries in different resource positions will have different views as to the best price and output policy for the group.

To indicate the effects of differences in resource positions on the production and price policies that might be followed, the 11 principal oil exporters are grouped in Table 1 below into three categories having the following characteristics:

Group 1 (Saudi Arabia, Kuwait, Libya, Abu Dhabi, Qatar) has 65 percent of proven reserves and 48 percent of current output, but only 12 million population and limited levels of absorption for economic development. The five countries in this group must take a long-term view of petroleum policy; their reserves have a potential life of 50 years or more, and they have few other natural resources.

Group 2 contains four countries (Venezuela, Iran, Algeria,

Iraq) that have already achieved considerable economic development and are depleting their petroleum reserves at higher rates than Group 1. They contain 70 million inhabitants and are in a position to make effective use of most of their increased oil revenues for internal development within the next decade, although they will accumulate substantial surpluses for the next several years. This group is more likely to try to secure maximum revenues in the short run because of the greater opportunities for productive investments within their own economies.

Group III consists of two large countries (Indonesia and Nigeria) that have only a limited share of OPEC resources and little problem absorbing all their oil revenues in the near future. They will not accumulate significant financial surpluses.

Table 1. OPEC Countries: 1973 Oil Production and Reserves

	Population (millions)	Proven Reserves (billion tons)	Output (million barrels per day)	Reserves Years of (at 1973 output rate)
Group I				
Saudi Arabia	8.1	19.3	7.5	51
Libya	2.1	3.4	2.1	32
Kuwait	.9	10.1	3.0	66
Qatar	.2	.9	.5	31
Abu Dhabi	.1	2.9	1.2	45
Subtotal	11.5	36.4	14.3	50
Share of OPEC		65%	48%	
Group II				
Iran	31.9	8.2	5.9	28
Venezuela	11.3	2.0	3.5	11
Iraq	10.4	4.3	2.0	44
Algeria	14.7	1.0	1.0	20
Subtotal	68.3	15.5	12.4	25
Share of OPEC		28%	41%	
Group III				
Nigeria	73.4	2.7	2.0	27
Indonesia	125.0	1.4	1.3	22
Subtotal	198.4	4.2	3.3	25
Share of OPEC		7%	11%	
TOTAL	278.2	56.1	30.2	

SOURCES: *Oil and Gas Journal* (Reserves), World Bank.

While maintaining or even increasing the 1974 Persian Gulf price level of approximately $9.60 per barrel (in 1974 prices) might seem to be in the interest of countries in the second and third groups, this price is well above the long-term costs of major alternative energy sources. Accordingly, such a policy could be expected to induce a maximum effort by the OECD countries to cut back on consumption and to develop alternative energy sources (such as North Sea and Alaskan oil, coal, oil shale, tar sands, and of course nuclear energy). Studies by the OECD, the Federal Energy Administration, and the World Bank suggest that such a maximum effort, although involving a considerable amount of investment that would be uneconomical at somewhat lower prices, could have the effect of leveling off the demand of the OECD countries for OPEC oil.[5] By 1980 OECD imports from OPEC would be no greater than at present and would be likely to decline thereafter.

However, if the Persian Gulf price were reduced to $7 or $8 per barrel (in 1974 prices), with some assurance that supplies would be forthcoming at this level, the OECD countries would probably forgo the uneconomical forms of investment in higher cost energy sources and would be less likely to limit growth of consumption. Thus, OPEC exports of oil to the OECD countries would continue to rise in 1980 and beyond. The total revenues available to OPEC for the next decade would probably be as great as through maintaining higher prices, and total OPEC production in 1980 and 1985 would correspond roughly to the productive capacity now planned by the OPEC countries.

In this situation the OPEC countries are faced with the classical monopolist's dilemma of trying to estimate the speed with which alternative supplies will be developed and whether the gains of maximizing short-run profits will exceed the losses from lower volumes (and perhaps lower prices) in the future. Unless a high discount is applied to the future, the OPEC countries—and particularly the Group I countries with large reserves—would benefit in the long run from reducing the price of oil to the cost of major alternative sources in order to maintain their

5. OECD, *World Energy Outlook: A Reassessment of Long-Term Energy Developments and Related Policies* (Paris, 1977); Federal Energy Administration, *Project Independence Report,* November 1974.

share of future market growth.

This conclusion is illustrated in more concrete terms in Table 2. Case I assumes that the price is maintained at $9.60 (in 1974 dollars) by upward adjustments to offset inflation. Case II assumes that the price declines gradually by some 30 percent to $7.00 (again in 1974 dollars). In both cases, it is assumed that total energy demand in OECD countries would continue to grow, but at a rate of only 3.8 percent in Case I as compared to 4.3 percent in Case II (both, of course, reduced from the recent 5 percent rate for OECD as a whole). As to investment in alternative sources, the underlying assumptions are conservative, not assuming development of domestic or other energy sources that will cost more than imports.

Even so, the table indicates that after 1985 total OPEC revenues would be considerably greater under Case II. Moreover, if the higher prices assumed in Case I should lead to even stronger OECD efforts to reduce imports—as seems quite likely —the lower price policy might well be more profitable to OPEC beginning as early as 1980.

Although the elements underlying this calculation are subject to considerable technological and political uncertainties, the main conclusion that in the longer term OPEC would benefit

Table 2. Projections of OPEC Revenues and Capacity[a]
(in billions of 1974 dollars and millions of barrels per day)

	Group I	Group II	Group III	Total Revenue	Production Total
Case I					
Price Remains at $9.60					
1980	$49	$47	$13	$109	33
1985	51	54	16	121	36
1900				88	26
Case II					
Price Declines to $7.00 by 1980					
1980	$52	$41	$11	$103	42
1985	58	52	12	122	49
1990				135	55
Planned Productive Capacity					
1980	27.8	16.3	4.5		49

a. Based on estimates of the OECD and the World Bank.

from somewhat lower prices remains valid under a considerable range of assumptions. From the standpoint of both the OECD and OPEC countries, the difference between Case I and Case II is particularly great in terms of the decisions on investment in alternative energy sources. In round numbers, if the OECD countries felt compelled to reduce their demand for OPEC oil by 1985 by the 13 million barrels a day difference between Case I and Case II, they would need to make additional investments on the order of $100 billion in this period. The expansion of OPEC capacity, on the other hand, would involve much less cost. In short, since decisions on tens of billions of dollars of investment in both OECD and OPEC over the next several years will hinge on the assessment that is made of future OPEC price and production policy, this becomes one of the most critical determinants of the future pattern of world trade and capital flows.

In order to maintain any given price, the oil exporters need to have some form of agreement as to how any needed reduction below capacity production will be allocated. Then, in deciding on its preferred production level, each country must estimate two elements: its current need for foreign exchange for internal development, and the prospective return on its investment of any surplus revenues in comparison to the prospective appreciation in value of oil reserves. At current prices there is only a limited prospect for a further increase in value of oil relative to other commodities over the next ten years and a greater probability of decline. Even if the real return on their investment of surplus funds is negligible and only offsets the effects of inflation, exporting countries are better off producing than keeping their oil in the ground. Countries with growing needs for foreign exchange for internal development will have a stronger incentive to increase output than those producing in excess of current needs.

Weighing the several factors that affect these decisions, it seems to me likely that oil prices will come down by 1980 to a level approximating the long-term cost of non-OPEC sources of energy, which is currently estimated to be the equivalent of $7.00 to $8.00 per barrel (in 1974 prices) in the Persian Gulf. This reduction would make possible relatively full use of the presently planned expansion of OPEC capacity to 49 million barrels per day by 1980. On this assumption, oil prices would still be three times as high as their relative level in 1970 and twice as high as the peak period of the early 1950s.

V

The main threat the oil crisis poses to the OECD countries, as mentioned above, lies in the possibility of a serious reduction in their growth rates rather than in the need to transfer 2 percent of their national incomes to the OPEC countries. The question of growth rates hinges on the policies followed by the OECD group, and particularly the degree of their willingness to accept the accumulation of major claims on assets (borrowing in the broad sense) from the OPEC countries.

The preceding discussion has already considered three of the actions the OECD countries are taking in the face of the oil crisis, namely, the reduction of nonessential energy needs, the development of their own energy sources and those of other non-OPEC countries, and trying to persuade the OPEC producers to lower the price of oil. Even with some success in each of these efforts, the OECD countries confront a substantial financial problem of, in effect, borrowing from OPEC to finance continuing balance-of-payments deficits with those same countries. Because of the limited absorptive capacity of the OPEC countries, the OECD countries—even under the Case II assumption of gradually lowered prices—would have to finance aggregate annual deficits of $30 to $40 billion (in 1974 prices) until the early 1980s. (Imports would be lower and the deficits slightly higher under Case I.) Unless the OECD countries further reduce their oil demand through rationing and economic stagnation, they will cumulate to a total of up to $300 billion by 1980 (in constant 1974 dollars).

There is an inclination in many quarters to regard the task of financing any such amount as both unmanageable and unsound in the light of traditional principles of financial management. But it is hard to sustain either of these conclusions on economic grounds. Both the postwar experience of the European Recovery Program and the current management of capital flows to developing countries demonstrate the adjustment mechanisms that are needed. The economic desirability of borrowing from the OPEC countries should be judged on the basis of the cost—in terms of lower incomes and higher unemployment—of not borrowing. The feasibility of borrowing in the amounts indicated depends on the burden of debt service and future repayment over the next several decades. Because of the large sums involved, there is a tendency to exaggerate these prospective burdens and to ignore the cost of lower rates of growth.

In many respects the economic adjustment now required of the OECD in relation to OPEC is similar to the typical problem of developing countries that have increased their capital inflow in order to accelerate their rates of growth. It is quite normal for them to finance 20 to 30 percent of import requirements through external borrowing for periods of 10 or 20 years while new exports are being developed. The service on this external debt often rises to as much as 20 or 25 percent of export earnings (or 3 to 4 percent of GNP) without jeopardizing the country's economic prospects or its future ability to repay. The desirability of incurring external debt depends on the additional growth that can be secured from greater imports and investment in relation to the real cost of borrowing.

The OECD oil deficit differs from the normal trade gap of less developed countries in one significant respect: its current magnitude is determined primarily by the ability of the lending countries to utilize imports from the borrower rather than by the latter's ability to supply them. This fact does not create any added problems for the OECD as a whole unless the OPEC countries decide not to continue to supply oil in the quantities indicated in Table 2. On the contrary, having to borrow to pay for oil instead of suddenly increasing exports cushions the immediate impact of the rise in prices and supplies additional resources to offset the large investments needed for alternative energy sources.

Another way to judge whether this process of adjustment is feasible is, however, to compare it to the last major adjustment involving the European members of what is now OECD. In the wake of World War II, these countries engaged in a program of reconstruction that lasted through the period of the Marshall Plan and extended to about 1955. During this period there was, in effect, a massive transfer of resources from the United States to Europe, while Europe developed the productive capacity to meet what was then called the "dollar gap"—that is, to export sufficient goods and services to pay for their import requirements from the United States. In a very real sense, the position of the United States at that time corresponded to the position of the OPEC oil countries today.

The main interest in this comparison is in the relative magnitudes of the "structural" deficits in the balance of payments in the two periods, the time needed to eliminate this deficit, and the capital inflow required during the period of adjustment. The main difference of course was that during the earlier period the United States itself financed a large share of the transfers through grant aid. This difference must be allowed for in making the evaluation. Similarly, while the United States and Canada should be omitted from the "debtor" group in both periods (since they can finance their future oil needs without great difficulty), Japan and the Oceania members of OECD must be included in the second, or OPEC, period.

To make the comparison real, let us assume that in both periods the "debtor" group of nations was required to repay the principal of the total "debt" over a period of six years, beginning in 1952 and 1974 respectively, and that the "interest" (actual interest on debts, plus dividends on investment) was at identical rates of 5 percent. On this basis, Table 3 below shows (in 1974 dollars for both cases) the growth of GNP, international trade levels, capital inflows, and debt service requirements for 1947 to 1955, and projections of the same magnitudes for 1974 to 1985.

When put in these terms, the adjustment to higher oil prices that is now required is shown to be of somewhat lesser magnitude than the postwar adjustment process. The proportion of imports to be financed by external capital in the first five years is only half as great, and it will not be necessary to limit the growth of non-oil imports in order to close the trade gap with OPEC. Although there was little repayment of the actual postwar debt, the growth of exports and GNP after 1950 was rapid enough to have permitted such repayment with little effect on continued growth. The important lesson of the postwar period is that such a large restructuring was accomplished with relative ease because economic growth was sustained at a high rate.

Even without much fall in OPEC oil prices between now and 1980 the OECD countries of Europe and Japan will reach a maximum indebtedness to OPEC in the early 1980s. At its peak, the service on this debt will be less than 2 percent of their GNP. Table 3 shows that borrowing to pay for part of the increased oil costs has the advantage of spreading out the diversion of exports needed to offset the worsening of the OECD terms of trade; even if interest on the debt reaches 5 percent in real terms (much more than is now being paid), the total burden of debt service will be less than 10 percent of projected exports.

By 1990 almost all of the OPEC countries are likely to have reduced their outstanding investments in the OECD very substantially as their internal absorptive capacity continues to grow. While capital may then flow in the opposite direction to support the continued growth of the oil producers as their oil revenues

Table 3. Comparison of Adjustment Processes:
1947–55 and 1974–85 (billions of dollars in 1974 prices)

A. 1947 Adjustment (OECD Europe)

	1947	1950	1955
1. Gross national product	350	435	578
2. Exports	51	94	134
3. Imports	75	90	116[a]
4. Net capital inflow	31	11	2
5. Total debt	31	74	92
6. Hypothetical debt service[b]	1.4	3.6	17.9
7. Debt service/GNP	0.4%	0.8%	3.1%
8. Debt service/exports	2.8%	4.0%	13.0%

B. 1974 Adjustment (OECD Europe and Japan-Oceania)

	1974	1980	1985
1. Gross national product	1,921	2,695	3,082
2. Exports	361	524	776
3. Imports	329	460	710
4. Net capital inflow	40	45	34
5. Total debt	40	285	500
6. Hypothetical debt service[b]	8	48	51
7. Debt service/GNP	0.4%	1.8%	1.6%
8. Debt service/exports	2.2%	9.2%	6.6%

a. Actual imports were reduced to take account of the need to service hypothetical debts.

b. Hypothetical debt service calculated at 5 percent interest, repayment of each year's borrowing over six years beginning in 1952 or 1974.

stagnate or decline, the magnitudes will not be so large as to interfere with the growth of the OECD countries. Therefore, it is difficult to argue on economic grounds that the world economy cannot sustain capital flows of the required magnitude, or that the OECD countries need to suffer heavily in the process.

The other major obstacle to acceptance of borrowing from OPEC countries as a desirable solution to the oil problem is the fear that they will acquire excessive ownership and control of OECD assets. The magnitudes involved—up to $300 billion (in 1974 prices) by 1980—must be judged in relation to the total assets of the OECD countries including the United States. The figure of $300 billion would be perhaps 5 percent of the value of all stocks and bonds in the major OECD countries in 1980 or 2 percent of their fixed assets. These are considerably smaller proportions of foreign ownership than those experienced by many countries in the past. Moreover, it is clearly within the power of the recipient countries to limit the forms of assets that are held so as to avoid any undesirable forms of external control.

Thus, instead of worrying about foreign control of existing assets, we should be more concerned with the loss of income and wealth that is likely to occur through misguided efforts to limit the oil deficits. A reduction of OECD growth from its normal 5 percent to 3.5 percent would wipe out some $300 billion in potential asset formation by 1980 and cause considerable unemployment, which is a much greater cause for concern than the risks of OPEC control.

In sum, there do appear to be reasonable ways by which the adjustment process between the OECD and OPEC countries can be eased and made bearable. If the analysis in Table 2 were accepted, some reduction in the oil price would be a part of the overall answer. But even if this were not done, a better coordinated international system should be capable of handling the required transfers through the transition period. In economic terms, the problems between the OECD and OPEC countries are soluble.

VI

Let us return now to the problem of the LDCs.

The events of the past several years have had very diverse

effects on the two billion people who constitute the Third World. Although the commodity boom of 1972–74 improved the terms of trade of most primary exporters, this trend has now been reversed, with the exceptions noted above of petroleum and some minerals and foodstuffs. The impact of oil and food prices on the non-OPEC members of the Third World has been to double their balance-of-payments deficits—from $10 billion in 1973 to $20 billion in 1974—offsetting the effects of the present flows of concessionary loans and grants.

These developments have initiated a process of fragmentation of the Third World that is likely to continue. The beneficiaries of these changes comprise some 400 million people living in countries exporting oil and minerals, whose development prospects have greatly improved. A second group consists of some 600 million people in the upper income tier of the developing countries—Brazil, Turkey, Korea, Thailand, etc.—many of which have suffered losses similar to those of the OECD. Although they will have to borrow large amounts to offset their oil deficits, most of them have sufficiently flexible and diversified economies to adjust to the increased exports and changed internal allocation of resources. This group will experience a temporary slowdown in growth, but their long-term prospects need not be seriously affected, providing they continue to have access to capital markets and other recycling facilities.

For the billion people in the lower tier of less developed countries the situation is quite different. For most of the poorest countries—mainly in South Asia and East and Central Africa—export prices have lagged behind the general inflation while import costs have risen sharply. As a result, their terms of trade have worsened by 20 percent in the past two years, twice as much as the fall for the OECD countries. For many of these countries—and notably India and Bangladesh, which comprise two-thirds of the population—development prospects have been set back ten years or more. In many cases, food shortages and high prices are as important as the rise in oil costs in pre-empting the available foreign exchange and stopping the import of other goods needed for development. It is in this "Fourth World" that the oil and food crises come together and require a joint solution.

In general, the ability to adjust to changes in external economic conditions diminishes at lower levels of development. The margins for reduction in consumption of oil or food become narrower, and there is a more limited range of potential exports that can be increased in the near future. For many of the poorest countries, the possibilities of internal adjustment are rapidly being exhausted. While some of them accumulated foreign-exchange reserves during the commodity boom, these reserves will not long offset the increased cost of imports. Since it will take several years to develop new exports, growth can only be sustained even at reduced levels by an increase in concessional lending of $3 to $4 billion per year (in constant prices) over the next few years.[5]

Since India makes up more than half the population of the lower tier of developing countries and has somewhat greater opportunities to adjust, it deserves separate comment. Although India has had considerable success in developing an industrial base and a supply of human skills over the past two decades, it has been one of the last countries to maintain the inward orientation of its development effort instead of following Korea, Brazil, Mexico, and most other industrializing countries in shifting into manufactured exports. It was thus in a very poor position to meet the impact of higher oil, food, and fertilizer prices, which added $2 billion to its existing import bill of $3 billion between 1972 and 1974. Unlike the other very poor countries, however, India has an industrial structure that could provide a basis for rapid export growth if it were to give the priority to this effort that has proved necessary for other successful exporters.

In summary, it is worth stressing the basic differences between the more limited adjustment mechanisms available to the less developed countries and those that can be employed by the advanced countries.

1. OPEC surpluses will be automatically invested in the capital markets of the advanced countries; special efforts (such as guarantees or subsidies) will be needed to redirect some of these funds to the developing countries or to have the OECD countries relend them.

5. Robert McNamara, Address to the Board of Governors of the World Bank Group, September 1974.

2. Energy conservation provides a large element of the adjustment for the rich countries, but there is much less scope for it in the less developed ones.

3. Since three-quarters of the OPEC surplus is with the OECD, the latter countries cannot reduce it by expanding exports to one another. However, the OECD countries should accept a continued expansion of exports from the developing countries, since this latter group can only depend on recycling to a limited extent.

VII

Despite widespread predictions of impending economic disasters, these events are no more inevitable now than were similar predictions in 1946 and 1947. The basic problem we face is to adjust to the claims for a relatively small redistribution of world income among countries without incurring any greater loss of welfare than is necessary. While one solution to the problem would be for the producers of petroleum and foodstuffs to moderate their claims, a return to previous price relations can be virtually ruled out, and some degree of structural readjustment must be pursued.

The policy conclusions to this analysis can be summed up in three propositions: (a) once the dimensions of the basic problem are accepted, it should be quite feasible to devise a set of policies to enable the several parts of the world economy to resume satisfactory rates of development; (b) the various elements of the solution are highly interdependent and require a quality and sincerity of international cooperation that has been lacking since the early 1950s; (c) the effects of a failure to make the adjustments in the international system would be considerably more costly to most of the participants than the gains that each country can hope to achieve by acting independently, and the burden of such a failure would fall disproportionately on the poorest countries.

Although it is not my purpose to analyze the various institutional changes that are needed to bring about these results, the principal elements in a cooperative approach to a solution can be sketched out:

1. Reduction of uncertainty in oil marketing. Uncertainty as to

OPEC oil policies and the desirable responses to them is the main obstacle to the acceptance of the problem of higher prices by the importing countries. Reduction of this source of uncertainty would greatly aid the adoption of other measures to restore equilibrium in the world economy.

2. Financing oil deficits. It is generally agreed that the existing recycling mechanisms—OPEC loans to preferred governments, limited use of the international institutions, direct OPEC investments, and the private banking system—will become increasingly inadequate to the magnitude of the OPEC surplus. Although a more satisfactory system would expand use of all of these routes, it should also guarantee a volume of lending adequate to finance the oil deficits of the OECD countries and the upper tier of those developing countries which are able to assume additional debt. Such guarantees are needed to avoid "beggar thy neighbor" policies through which importing countries attempt to reduce their individual oil deficits at each other's expense. However, the poorest countries are not able to assume much additional debt other than on concessional terms.

3. Support for OPEC development. Since the main object of the OPEC governments is the rapid and secure development of their economies, their willingness to cooperate in solving the problems of the rest of the world is likely to be increased by measures that would enable them to reach that goal. Such measures should include a secure return on external investment and assistance in their internal development. In return they might be willing to forgo high short-run profits in favor of a larger and more secure future market for their oil.

4. OECD growth. Even with adequate recycling mechanisms, some short-term reduction in the growth of the industrial countries is virtually inevitable as part of the worldwide effort to control inflation. However, a restoration of the trend rate of 5 percent growth of GNP for the OECD countries by 1976 is quite feasible and would make an important contribution to the solution of the problems of the developing countries.

5. Restoration of LDC growth. In the present atmosphere of inflation, payments deficits, and economic recession, it seems politically impossible for the industrial countries to give adequate attention and support to the developing countries. This condition

is unlikely to be reversed until the OECD countries are on the way to solving their own problems. Until that is achieved, the erosion of aid by inflation is not likely to be offset, and the tendency to restrict LDC imports will be hard to resist.

In quantitative terms, the needs per year of the developing countries for additional support to restore reasonable rates of growth are modest: $3 to $4 billion (in 1974 prices) for the rest of this decade. Depending on the rates of growth of the OECD countries, this would bring total concessional lending back to between 0.3 and 0.4 percent of the gross national products of the OECD and OPEC countries. These were the levels that were reduced by the effects of the inflation. But to achieve them will require substantial increases in current appropriations, in order to offset higher prices.

Without some expansion of aid, restoration of growth in the rest of the world will do relatively little for the most seriously affected countries because they cannot readily shift their exports to take advantage of it. Nor can they make extensive use of recycling facilities on conventional terms. Thus there is no short-run adjustment mechanism available to them except to reduce their growth. Some special assistance—either in the form of reduced prices for oil and food or increases in concessional lending—is needed to avoid inflicting on them the main burden of both the oil and the food adjustments.

VIII

Since the series of negotiations and institutional changes required to bring about this rather optimistic scenario will require an appreciable period of time, we will have to improvize temporary solutions. In the short run, there is no alternative to the use of existing institutions for recycling, the reallocation of aid budgets and food stocks to the most affected countries, and an ad hoc sharing among the stronger OECD and OPEC countries of the burdens of adjustment and risks of lending.

In the longer run, the world does have a choice. It lies between mounting a cooperative effort on the model of the postwar period or accepting the much higher costs of an uncoordinated readjustment in which all parties are likely to suffer.

OPEC and the Industrial Countries

THOMAS O. ENDERS

A former assistant secretary of state for economic affairs, Thomas O. Enders suggests that, in order to improve their power position vis-à-vis the OPEC countries, the industrial countries should reduce their reliance on OPEC oil. His essay was published in the July 1975 issue of Foreign Affairs.

FROM 1947 to 1973 the shift of power is exponential. In 1947 the United States ceased to be a net exporter of oil; the basing point for oil prices moved from the Gulf of Mexico to the Persian Gulf, and with it the underlying leverage. Although the Organization of Petroleum Exporting Countries (OPEC) was formed in 1960, its membership was so disparate that at first it did little to exploit the shift. With prices low, U.S. dependence on imported energy grew to 14 percent of energy consumption in 1972. Europe's dependence on energy imports grew from 33 percent in 1960 to 65 percent in 1972; Japan's from 43 to 90 percent in the same period. By the late 1960s OPEC members were acting more masterfully to turn the increased dependence to advantage; prices began to move up. The 1973 October War revealed OPEC's full power.

It is important to be precise about the implications of this shift for the industrial countries. First, the cartel action continues to pose a short-term problem of economic management. The sharp jump in oil prices accounted for about a quarter of the average 14 percent inflation experienced in 1974 among the member countries in the Organization for Economic Cooperation and Development (OECD). Industrial dislocation and unemployment caused by the 1973–74 embargo, and conservative demand-management policies in Europe and Japan designed to overcome oil-caused balance-of-payments deficits helped trigger the present recession. No doubt the effects of the continued high price of oil on internal demand will make it more difficult to design policies to return the industrial economies to a high rate of growth. All of these difficulties are important and costly, but they are—or can be made—transitional.[1]

Second, there is a medium-term problem of financial management. Most recent studies suggest that the accumulation of financial assets by OPEC will peak in the late 1970s or early 1980s at levels perhaps in the range of $200 to $250 billion in 1974 dollars. This is an enormous total by present comparision—official holdings of financial assets by all the OECD countries totaled $118 billion at the end of 1974—but it is less than was estimated a year ago. Although the political and financial implications of the expected accumulations cannot yet fully be judged, recycling of oil dollars has proceeded more smoothly than feared, and this problem appears manageable.[2]

Third, however, there is a major long-term transfer of real income, which has only begun. The exact time-path of the transfer is difficult to determine, since it depends in part on how rapidly the financial assets OPEC is accumulating are converted into imports of goods and services and how long the high price is sustained. In 1974 OPEC increased its imports of goods and services from OECD countries by about $8 billion in real terms (equivalent to somewhat more than 0.2 percent of OECD's 1974 gross national product). Into the future, OPEC imports from OECD countries, financed by its accumulated financial assets, will continue to grow for some time after its export revenues peak. It is possible that they will reach $110 billion by 1980 (in 1974 dollars), as opposed to about $30 billion in 1973 (in 1974 dollars). The $80 billion gain, equivalent to more than 1.7 percent of the expected GNP of the OECD group in 1980, can be taken as an estimate of the peak value of the real annual cost of the cartel action to the industrial world.

These costs, imposed at a time when most of the industrial countries are having increasing difficulty in meeting the social, economic, and security requirements of their people, are of major significance. It is important to realize that these are not one-time

1. See Hollis B. Chenery, "Restructuring the World Economy," *Foreign Affairs*, January 1975 (reprinted in this volume).
2. Compare Khodadad Farmanfarmaian et al., "How Can the World Afford OPEC Oil?" *Foreign Affairs*, January 1975.

costs; they accrue each year.

Fourth, and perhaps most important of all, there are the political and strategic implications of vulnerability to a new interruption in supply. Existence of the cartel, and the high price for oil that it has imposed, are coordinate with that vulnerability; one presupposes the other. As long as the cartel is effective, the central element of energy in the industrial economies will be subject to manipulation, both as to prices and availability, by supplying countries which do not have, and may well not develop, an inherent interest in their prosperity. We must be ready for the exercise of this power in a new Middle East conflict; whether and how it would be used in other circumstances we do not know. But clearly the threat to the maintenance of stable economic conditions is significant.

As long as the cartel is effective, it will also impose a permanent tension among the consuming countries because of the wide disparity in their dependence on imported oil. Canada, the United States, and soon Britain have options that Japan, Spain, and Italy do not have. Competitive offers of special economic and political terms to secure petroleum supplies are widely recognized as likely to degrade the bargaining position of the consumers as a group. Such protective mechanisms as oil sharing in an emergency and financial solidarity can provide a counterweight, and these have now been effectively agreed upon, largely through the International Energy Agency (IEA).[3] But over the long term the impulse will be strong to substitute producer/consumer lines of force for those now existing among the industrial countries of Europe, America and Japan. If that occurs, the internal contradictions between the security and the economic interests of the industrial countries will grow and their political coherence will dissipate.

So far, the short-term problems of economic and financial management have received the greatest public attention in the industrial countries. Exaggerated fear of their difficulty has given way to relief that they are not intractable. But the real costs of the cartel—the longer-term transfer annually of goods and services, and the potential deterioration of the security and political

3. See Henri Simonet, "Energy and the Future of Europe," *Foreign Affairs*, April 1975.

position of the industrial countries—have yet to be fully faced.

The real-income losses of the consumers are the gains of the producers, but in other respects the effects of the cartel action are not reciprocal. Producers share with consumers an interest in effective management of the short-term economic and financial problems. Return of the industrial economy to a high rate of growth strengthens demand for oil and thereby strengthens the cartel, and the protection of financial assets now is essential to future real transfers and growth. It is only by de facto integration into the industrial economy, through massive increases in trade, industrial investment, and technological transfer, that the producers can realize their real-wealth gains. Four-fifths of OPEC's imports now come from the OECD group; as they rise, the interpenetration of consumer and producer economies will become a central datum of the international structure.

In politics, the lines of potential development lead in different directions. When the October War revealed its power, OPEC was the loosest of coalitions, harboring at least four contenders for leadership (Iran, Saudi Arabia, Algeria, and Venezuela) and a spectrum of traditional state rivalries. But to consolidate its gains and survive the 1975 slump in oil demand, OPEC had to develop more coherence. Saudi Arabia, which some believed might play the maverick and use its vast producing capacity to bid the oil price down, swung into a supportive role. The Saudis engineered the overall price increase at Abu Dhabi, in November 1975, then created conditions for, or acquiesced in, production cuts deep enough to balance OPEC supply with demand. (Saudi production in April 1975 was less than 6 million barrels a day [mmbd], down from 9 mmbd at the peak the previous summer; meanwhile Saudi capacity reached more than 11 mmbd.) Leadership competition among the major states was muted. An informal system emerged in which states wishing to increase exports could do so by shaving quality differentials and lengthening credit terms, while the basic government take of $10.12 per barrel remained intact.

This growing cohesiveness of OPEC gave it an opportunity to bid for the leadership of the whole developing world. The raw materials doctrine developed by Algeria—that the market power of consumers has long kept down raw material prices and thus the economic development of producers, and the cartel action is needed to "revalorize" earnings, along with "indexation" to protect the new wealth by increasing oil prices in proportion to increases in the prices of OPEC imports—served first as a defense against the resentment of other less developed countries whose growth prospects have been damaged or halted by high oil prices. Increasingly, the doctrine is becoming a means by which the oil producers cement their own unity and that of the LDC bloc as a whole.

At the same moment that their economic integration into the industrial world is accelerating, OPEC members are asserting their political identity with a coalition of developing states intent upon challenging the industrial world. In doing so OPEC is making negotiation of stable new institutional ties with the industrial countries far more difficult, as the failure of the producer/consumer preparatory meeting in April 1975 showed. In time, the oil producers will expose themselves to escalating demands from the LDCs. And the tension between OPEC's economic and political interests will eventually increase.

II

It is in the interest of the industrial countries—indeed, of all consuming countries—that conditions be created in which OPEC loses and cannot subsequently regain the power to set oil prices at artificially high levels. What are these conditions? Essentially, that the market for OPEC oil be compressed to, and held at, a volume at which the mechanism for allocating production cuts within OPEC can no longer function.

It is possible to imagine a number of scenarios in which individual producers break ranks and slash prices. But none of these has much plausibility in view of the great economic and political interest all OPEC members have in high prices, and because of the political pressure from their colleagues to which many are vulnerable. In order to predict with some confidence that several members will cut prices in attempting to increase their market share, the following conditions must be present:

1. Such a group of countries must have significant unused

capacity, and practical possibilities for shifting production cuts onto the "low absorbers" such as Saudi Arabia must have been exhausted.

2. They must be unwilling to accept a stretch-out of their development and military-spending programs.

3. They must be in payments deficit on current account.

4. They must have reached the limits of drawing down accumulated financial reserves and of borrowing within or outside OPEC.

5. Relief through increases in the real price of OPEC oil must have been exhausted.

III

How can the consuming countries increase the possibility of an outcome in their favor? And at what cost?

First, by conservation. If President Gerald Ford's conservation proposals of January 1975 were fully adopted, and if they were matched by similar European and Japanese programs, they could be decisive. These measures were originally designed to reduce U.S. imports by 1 mmbd by the end of 1975, 2 mmbd by the end of 1977, and over 4 mmbd in 1985 (below what they would otherwise be).

Through the actions announced by the president on May 27—increased import fees and the proposed decontrol of "old" domestic oil prices—the United States can still make progress toward his goals. However, what Congress will finally do, as well as the actual impact on consumption, may not be clear for some time. Meanwhile Europe and Japan have moved faster than the United States to take effective conservation measures, but the combined bulk of their savings is not yet large.

Second, by stimulus to the development of alternative sources. Here three sorts of action are required:

1. Relaxation or removal of existing policy constraints. Almost every form of energy enterprise in the industrial world is encumbered: U.S. and Canadian gas and oil by price controls; nuclear power everywhere by inadequate or outmoded utility rate structures and by siting restrictions; coal by environmental limits; new hydrocarbon exploration by legal restrictions. The relaxation

of these constraints is above all a domestic political question, although it can be spurred by international review and analysis.

2. Provision of financing. Estimates of financing required over the next decade for energy development in the industrial countries center in the trillion dollar range (in 1974 dollars), equivalent to a fifth or a fourth of expected total capital formation. The question posed is whether energy investment should receive some form of priority access to capital markets, through the use of government guarantees or government-sponsored intermediaries. For such costly developments as oil from shale, tar sands, or coal liquefaction (which may come in the range of $15 a barrel), substantial government financing, including such devices as the sharing of initial "front-end" costs, must be employed. Such projects lend themselves to international cooperation, with possible deals combining funding with access to technology and, in an emergency, access to product. On the other hand, many governments have so far hesitated to provide assistance to conventional energy enterprises, believing it disadvantageous to substitute political priorities for economic calculation. But some support is inevitable even in this area.

3. Protection against "downside risk" for private capital investment. To the extent that the financing of new energy sources is provided through government channels, such capital investment need not be seriously affected by changes in the overall price of oil, or of energy in general. As suggested above, government financing is likely to be the preponderant mechanism for most of the "non-conventional" energy sources such as solar and geothermal power, oil shale, or the Canadian tar sands.

The real problem concerns the major expansion of "conventional" sources, for which private investment must be the principal mechanism, but for which the anticipated costs are significantly higher than the price level to which OPEC oil might conceivably fall over the next ten years. New North Sea oil (less the share taken directly by governments) comes in many cases at $5 or even $6 a barrel. Conventional nuclear facilities, coal, and the vital OCS and NPR-4 may all be in the $6 to $8 range for their energy-equivalent output. All of these investments are price sensitive both at the outset and as they go along: they may not be undertaken, or may be delayed, if there is an actual or perceived risk that international prices will fall to or below that range in the course of development.

Such downside risk is closely linked to the future viability of the cartel. If, for example, the cartel were to lose its ability to maintain a high price in the stress period of 1978–80, the development of OCS, NPR-4, and North Sea oil could all be retarded or stopped. That in turn would result in a substantially higher OPEC export market than would otherwise occur, and conditions for renewed cartel action could be created. Put the other way around, by protecting against downside risk it is possible to be fairly certain that expected major energy investments will occur, and thus increase the odds that in the early 1980s the cartel will lose its power to set the oil price and not regain it thereafter.

IV

The problem of downside risk for investment in conventional energy sources is widely recognized. But there is much controversy over its solution. Broadly speaking, two main concepts have been put forward.

The first of these may be labeled that of "deficiency payments." Under this approach, private firms engaged in the development of energy sources would receive a subsidy from their national governments if the overall oil price falls, possibly set to cover the difference between some base price and the market price.

The advantage of this approach is that any drop in price is passed on to the consumer. The major disadvantage, however, is that under this approach it would almost surely be impossible to meet national self-sufficiency targets. In the event that overall oil prices fall, consumption is bound to be restimulated, and by substantial amounts. Thus, in contrast with the forecast that demand for OPEC oil by 1980 might be in the range of 25 mmbd at present oil prices, the demand for OPEC oil can be estimated to rise to 35 mmbd if the overall oil price were to drop to, say, $4 per barrel (in 1974 dollars). Even a remotely comparable rise in consumption would leave the industrial world still highly vulnerable to embargo and would in turn lead to new cartel action, as surely as the low prices and high dependency of the 1960s and early 1970s stimulated it in the first place.

Other drawbacks of the deficiency payment approach are the high costs to the taxpayer and the uncertain credibility of a system dependent on annual subsidy appropriations for energy companies by the American Congress or by the parliaments of OECD countries.

The second approach to the problem can be described as "border protection." The object of this approach is to prevent imported oil from being sold to the consumer within the industrial economies at disruptive price levels, i.e., at levels below the amounts required to offer the prospect of a fair return to the investors in expanded energy sources. The means required to implement this approach could be varied according to the national choice of the individual consuming countries; tariffs, import quotas, or variable levies might be used separately or in combination to produce the intended result. But the price levels maintained to assure adequate domestic investment, it may be emphasized, would be fixed only in terms of price levels to the consumer. The price actually paid to the OPEC producer would continue to be determined by the international market situation —in effect, by the relative bargaining power of consumers and producers. This is not, in short, a system for guaranteeing the return to the OPEC countries; indeed, its basic objective is to permit market forces to operate, eventually in favor of the consuming countries.

The major advantage of this approach is that national self-sufficiency goals can be protected. Through the stimulation of the necessary investment in expanded conventional sources, this approach provides high odds that OPEC's market will in fact be compressed to a volume inconsistent with continued cartel action.

The principle disadvantage of the approach is that the citizen as consumer does not receive the full benefit of whatever price drops may result over a period of time; on the other hand, the citizen as taxpayer in the consuming countries should have a very much lower burden under most of the possible techniques for achieving the basic goal. As for the question of continuing credibility, the "border protection" approach cannot be described as 100 percent credible, since Congress or parliaments would be under substantial pressure to remove protection and to favor the consumer when and if prices fall. However, the credibility of this approach should be greater than that of the deficiency payments approach because border protection can be legislated or decreed in advance. Once in place, and once investments have been made with reference to it, the system would develop a political constituency that would tend strongly to validate it.

Any policy of downside protection, however, will be of limited help and may disadvantage the countries that adopt it if only a few do so. Here, as in every other aspect of the energy problem, it is important to develop a new calculus of interest:

1. Energy-poor countries are interested in low prices to their citizens, but also in seeing energy-rich industrial countries develop their resources. For only if they do will demand on the international market fall and oil prices come down.

2. Energy-rich countries like Britain, Canada, and the United States are interested in seeing energy-poor countries like Italy and Japan adopt the same level of protection. For the main burden of investment must fall on the energy-rich, while the primary advantages of lower prices caused by the resulting compression of OPEC's market will accrue to energy-poor countries that import much of the energy they need. Without a common level of protection, this would leave the former locked into a high-cost energy economy, and at a competitive disadvantage.

3. All industrial countries have an interest in putting OPEC in the position of residual supplier of oil, with a market kept small enough to prevent renewed cartel action.

Recognizing the basic common interest that underlies this calculus, the industrialized consuming countries, meeting in the International Energy Agency, have already reached a preliminary agreement in principle. They have agreed on a minimum safeguard price system, under which each country would use means of its own choosing to prevent oil from being sold in its domestic economy below an agreed common price.

The question that remains is, of course, the level to be adopted for the agreed common price. Here the divergent interests of the energy-rich and energy-poor members of IEA must be reconciled. Broadly speaking, a high level for the agreed common price would benefit energy enterprise and thus countries with important energy resources. A low level would favor consumers, and thus countries that must import most of their oil.

The costs and benefits of a given system and price level can be analyzed as follows. If the level of protection is set unnecessarily high, the result will be that more investment would be undertaken than turned out to be required. With an annual investment bill estimated at roughly $100 billion per year, the real cost of any excess investment would be some relatively small part of this amount.

The opposite risk is less easy to measure precisely. If the level of protection is set too low, the result would be not enough investment to deprive OPEC of its ability to set prices. Broadly speaking, what would then be lost to the consumer countries would be the difference between the level of their real-income transfers to the producer countries at cartel-set prices and the level of the same transfers if the cartel fails; in addition, the growth-retarding effect of higher prices must be weighed. As analyzed above, it does not seem excessive to estimate this potential difference at as much as $60 billion or more a year (in 1974 dollars). More important, the cartel would retain its power to disrupt the industrial economies by embargo, and the risk that its economic power over the consumers will be transmuted into political power would grow.

In short, the level of protection chosen must be evaluated, in effect, like the premium on an insurance policy. The penalty for guessing wrong and doing too little is incommensurately heavier than the costs of doing too much.

V

An exponential increase in the power of any group of countries, occurring rapidly and initially at the expense of others, is never easy for an international system to absorb. Obviously, the nations fortunate enough to have major oil resources will be able, in any event, to maintain a greatly improved power status and to advance the lot of their people immensely in the years to come. Only the degree of change is now at issue, and with it the broader question of a lasting accommodation that will make the adjustment bearable to oil consumers—poor countries even more than rich—and that will evolve toward a world economy in which all may advance together.

Because of the interdependence of their trade and investment, the industrialized countries hold vast reciprocal power over each other's well-being. But a structure of economic, political, and security institutions governs the exercise of that power and makes its possession tolerable. No such structure exists between the oil-producing and oil-consuming states. Its creation will ultimately be in the interest of both producers and consumers: for the producers; because their dependence on the industrial economies is growing inexorably as they convert oil earnings into real imports and new industries; and for the consumers, because oil imports and oil-related financial transactions will play a major role in their economies, whether or not OPEC retains its capacity to set prices.

But for three reasons it is too early seriously to address the design of that structure.

First, we still do not know how rapidly and how forcefully the consumers will act to change the underlying market balance. In 1974 the industrial countries moved fast to draw the consequences of the embargo, establish a common strategy in the International Energy Agency, and draw up domestic energy programs. But by the time their response was ready at the start of this last winter, the recession had replaced energy as the dominant economic issue. The consequence has been to delay and to dilute energy action. As the industrial economies pull out of the recession and rising demand for oil creates conditions for new oil price increases, the politics of energy within the industrial countries will again change.

Second, it is not yet clear how far the producers will press their bid for leadership of the developing world. Should this become a permanent, dominant aim of their foreign policy, chances of successful negotiation of a new economic and ultimately a political framework between producers and consumers will be low.

Third, the future internal structure of OPEC is not yet knowable, for it depends on the way in which bargaining over production cuts develops. At one extreme would be a structure in which each OPEC member insisted that cuts be proportional to base-year output or capacity. In this case, Saudi Arabia and Kuwait would accumulate much of the OPEC financial surpluses, the industrial development of other OPEC members would be slower, and the cartel would be more fragile. At the other extreme, Saudi Arabia and Kuwait might take up most of the necessary production cuts, with the result that the industrial development of the group would accelerate, while the accumulation of financial assets by all OPEC members would be less. If developments approximate the first case, the real institutional problem between consumers and producers will be the management of the huge financial assets of a small number of countries. If events fit the second case, the problem will extend to all producers and cover a far wider range of economic and industrial problems.

The New Era in World Commodity Markets

C. FRED BERGSTEN

In this essay, originally published in the September-October 1974 issue of Challenge *magazine, C. Fred Bergsten, an assistant secretary of the treasury for international affairs on leave from the Brookings Institution, argues that the cartel formed by the oil-exporting nations is only the first in the new age of "commodity power."*

MANY COUNTRIES that produce primary products are now making intensive efforts to boost their earnings from these commodities. Increasingly, these countries have sought to maximize their market power by forming cartels. The success or failure of these "producers' associations" will have a major bearing on world economic conditions, particularly inflation, and on international political relationships for the foreseeable future.

THE EFFORT TO CARTELIZE

Joint action has now been taken by producing countries in at least seven major commodities since I first predicted this trend in 1973.[1]

1. The twelve leading oil exporters, operating through the Organization of Petroleum Exporting Countries (OPEC), have raised their returns by a factor of ten and, for a period, significantly limited world production.

2. The seven leading bauxite exporters formed the International Bauxite Association (IBA). Immediately thereafter, Jamaica forced a sixfold increase in its earnings. Other members are now beginning to follow suit, and further price rises may well be in store. Bauxite is, of course, the major raw material in the production of aluminum.

3. Six leading phosphate producers have tripled their prices,

[1]. "The Threat from the Third World," *Foreign Policy,* Summer 1973.

with further increases likely. Phosphate is a major input for fertilizers and detergents.

4. Four leading copper producers, through the Intergovernmental Council of Copper Exporting Countries (CIPEC is its French acronym), have announced that they will seize a greater share of the marketing of copper, expand the membership of CIPEC to increase its market power, and work directly with the producers of potentially substitutable metals to reduce the risks of cartelization to each.

4. The tin producers, through the International Tin Agreement, are seeking a 42 percent increase in the guaranteed floor price maintained by their buffer stock. These countries operated an effective producer's cartel before World War II.

5. The leading coffee producers, through a series of interlocking marketing companies and stockpile-financing arrangements have seized control of world coffee prices. They were confident enough of their success to let expire the International Coffee Agreement, through which they had previously sought the help of consuming countries to block price reductions.

6. Five of the leading banana producers, through the Organization of Banana-Exporting Countries, have levied sizable taxes on banana exports to boost their returns.

In addition, exporters of iron ore and mercury have been meeting regularly. The four major tea producers have sought to coordinate marketing and establish a floor price, and at least once reached agreement on production quotas. There are numerous other primary products, including tropical timber, natural rubber, nickel, tungsten, cobalt, columbium, tantalum, pepper and quinine, for which effective collusion among producing countries is distinctly possible. For some of these commodities, producer organizations, such as the Association of Natural-Rubber-Producing Countries and the Asian Pepper Community, already exist.

The primary producing countries have also taken several broad policy steps to support their commodity interests. Over two dozen of them have established ministries of natural resources. In an effort to legitimize their activities, they succeeded in including in a resolution adopted May 2 by the Special Session of the UN General Assembly, a call for "all efforts . . . to facilitate the functioning, and to further the aims, of producers' associations, including their joint marketing arrangements." To date, they have rejected all calls for new international rules to limit the use of export controls. And even Canada and Australia were most reluctant to accept the one-year moratorium on export controls encompassed in the "standstill agreement" on trade barriers agreed by the OECD countries in June 1974.

The measures employed so far by primary producers have taken many different forms—decreed prices, production cutbacks, selective embargoes, increased royalty payments, negotiated prices, direct market intervention, stockpiling, export taxes. Their objectives also differ: sharp increases in receipts from the commodity itself, protection against price declines, greater price stability, conservation of a depleting resource, more domestic processing, more local control over the industry, changes in the foreign policy of consuming countries. Some have clearly succeeded, at least so far (oil, coffee, phosphates); other have faltered at an early stage (bananas); for still others, it is too early to tell (bauxite, copper, tin). The importance of the products differs greatly; little sleep will be lost over a banana cartel, but many of the commodities are vital to modern industry and account for significant portions of consumers' market baskets. It is absolutely clear that such efforts are being made for an increasing array of products, and that more efforts are likely. What will determine their success?

THE SUCCESSFUL CARTEL

First, demand for the product must be relatively insensitive to price changes, that is, a higher price must neither excessively reduce final demand for the product nor trigger much substitution by alternative commodities. Second, supply of the product must also be relatively insensitive to price changes. This can occur because of actual physical shortages or technological monopolies, but such situations are quite rare. In virtually all cases, maintaining an artificially limited supply requires that most of the commodity be under the control of a small number of countries; it is even better for the cartel if a single country can dominate the market at the margin. The third requisite for success is that the potential colluding countries must be able to get along with each other.

These criteria appear to be met for a wide range of primary commodities. In the short run, demand for most metals and agricultural products is clearly very insensitive to price change. For commodities such as copper, aluminum, and tea, a price increase of 10 percent would reduce the amount demanded by only about 2 percent. A 10 percent price increase for coffee and cocoa would bring about a 4 percent drop, and for tin, about a 5 percent decrease in demand.

The opinion is widely held that demand is significantly more responsive to price changes in the long run. At best, however, the long run is very long indeed. It takes six to seven years, for example, to bring a new copper mine into production and as much as ten years for some other metals. But how do we get to the long run anyway?

Massive investments are necessary to generate an efficient expansion of supply, and they are very lumpy in nature. Because mines must be run near full capacity to be efficient, they will be developed only if the investors can count on a sustained level of high returns for the indefinite future. In purely economic terms, this is highly uncertain because of the traditionally very cyclical nature of demand for materials. In addition, there are other uncertainties which make it unlikely that these investments will be made as readily as in the past. New resource development often must be undertaken in countries which are likely to limit the freedom of the investing firm once the capital and technology are in place. And these countries include Canada and Australia as well as the developing nations. The host country may even take such extreme measures as expropriating the company's property or joining a cartel and limiting output. The difficulty in getting government insurance for such risky ventures deters investors even further. Finally, both within the United States and abroad, the high cost of environmental requirements, probable loss of previous tax advantages, and the likelihood of renewed price controls add greatly to the uncertainties.

The cartels themselves can further reduce the likelihood of major new investments in nonmembers, investments which could erode the cartel's position over time. To do so, their members must pursue subtle, and moderate, marketing strategies in raising their prices; and they must find that optimum price at which they can maximize their returns without triggering new investments. Indeed, if price rises are produced by cartel action rather than by underlying economics, there is always a strong possibility that the cartel will reduce its prices to choke off potential competitors. The fear of such "reverse dumping" is in fact a major deterrent at present to new investments in petroleum substitutes in the United States in the absence of governmental guarantees.

New cartels are in fact likely to adopt such strategies in light of the experience of OPEC. OPEC's actions clearly show that a cartel is likely to trigger a search for substitutes for its output if it pushes prices too far too fast (especially if it also demonstrates its unreliability as a supplier by cutting production and embargoing some buyers). So new OPECs are likely to adopt a more moderate and hence more successful approach.

In addition, the likelihood of substitution of alternative commodities for a cartel's product is sharply reduced if the prices of these commodities are rising as well. This has been the case in the recent commodity boom, either through natural market forces or parallel action by producing countries. For example, natural rubber suddenly became a candidate for cartelization when the price of synthetic rubber climbed dramatically in response to the rise in oil prices. It is thus particularly significant that representatives of IBA attended the latest meeting of CIPEC, since aluminum and copper are substitutable in many products from a technical standpoint.

The production processes for many end products are simply too fixed, both technologically and in terms of the proprietary interests of individual firms, to shift to new inputs without massive economic inducements. Even during World War II it took several years to develop synthetic rubber, and the efforts to produce substitutes for chrome and manganese, even of low quality and high cost, never did succeed. So, for a variety of reasons, it would be very risky to assume that the market will abort cartelization efforts even over the long run.

It should also be noted that some producers' cartels might not be deterred even if members foresaw long-term substitution. Iran is pushing hard for OPEC to maximize oil prices now precisely so that it can diversify its economy and reduce its vulnerability to such substitution. Jamaica's Prime Minister Michael N. Manley publicly based his action to boost bauxite receipts on that nation's "urgent" short-term needs and "reports [that] the time may not be too distant when technological progress will begin to yield substitutes for bauxite." Indeed, Harry Johnson long ago pointed out that it might be quite rational for developing countries to maximize in the short run even at the expense of future earnings.

As we noted, for a cartel to be successful, it must be able to limit the supply of its product. There are many cases where a few countries exert tight control over the supply of a basic commodity. The IBA countries account for about 75 percent of world bauxite exports. The four leading tin producers account for about 80 percent of non-Communist tin output, and an even larger share of exports. The CIPEC countries provide well over half of world copper exports and will probably expand that percentage by broadening their membership. Three countries provide 70 percent of world exports of tropical timber. These numbers, and the similar figures for other key commodities, are particularly impressive when we recall that they significantly exceed the shares of the four or five leading OPEC producers in world oil trade.

Furthermore, for a number of commodities, a single key country is in a position to exercise market dominance, as does Saudi Arabia in oil. Morocco is doing it in phosphates. Brazil is doing it in coffee. Malaysia could do it in tin and natural rubber, Nigeria in cocoa, and Jamaica can probably do it in bauxite. Similar situations exist for several commodities that are quantitatively less important, such as cobalt, for which the dominant producer is Zaïre, and columbium, mined principally in Brazil. Such capacity for price leadership by a single country simplifies the procedures needed to regulate a market.

As for the requirement that cartel members be able to get along, it is true that there are a few potential cartels which might be deterred by political differences. Three countries provide virtually all the world's exports of soybeans, but the United States, the People's Republic of China, and Brazil are unlikely to form a SOYBEC. The Soviet Union and South Africa are unlikely to collude overtly on platinum or chromium ore, though both are natural oligopolies. (Even in these cases, however, parallel market action could quite easily have similar effects.)

But there is little if any hostility among most of the key suppliers of heavily concentrated commodities. Indeed, many have no reason even to talk to each other except for their similar resources: Malaysia and Bolivia for tin, Chile and Zambia for copper, Jamaica and Australia for bauxite. The absence of a common enemy, as was Israel for the oil-producing Arab states, probably does rule out the use of new OPECs noneconomic purposes. But there is no political discord to block economic efforts by most of the potential cartels.

OIL IS NOT THE EXCEPTION

Contrary to my argument, there are those who assert that oil and OPEC represent a unique case which cannot be duplicated. This argument stresses the "shared political values" (that is, the enmity toward Israel) of the OPEC countries; the existence of monetary reserves large enough to permit them to take the risks associated with cartelization; the greater insensitivity of the demand for oil (and perhaps its supply) to price changes; the vertically integrated, oligopolistic market structure created by the multinational oil companies; the greater economic and strategic importance of oil; and the lesser susceptibility of the key OPEC countries to economic retaliation because of their small populations and hence small economic needs.

The Middle East politics ignited by the Yom Kippur War clearly prompted Saudi Arabia, the dominant oil supplier, to cut production temporarily. But the OPEC countries had more than tripled their 1970 earnings before the war broke out. And policy toward Israel had very little to do with the massive increase in oil prices last December—sponsored by Iran, which has been consistently pro-Israel, and Venezuela, which cares little about the Middle East conflict.

Most important, many if not all of these price hikes will continue to stick even though Saudi Arabia has restored its production to the pre-October 1973 level. And they will also stick despite the deep political hostilities among the Middle East oil countries over proper policy toward Israel, control of the Persian Gulf, and several key boundaries. The Yom Kippur War may have triggered the oil action that demonstrated to OPEC its own strength, but that genie is now out of the bottle and, in view of the massive economic gains to all member countries, is most unlikely to be capped again whether or not permanent peace comes to the Middle East.

Sizable monetary reserves do not distinguish OPEC either, although here again the initial Saudi move may have been influenced by its considerable wealth. But most OPEC members, including Iran, actually possessed very small reserves before they undertook the 1973 actions. In fact, the members of many other potential cartels (such as Malaysia and Brazil) are much stronger financially than were many OPEC countries, and much less dependent on the commodity in question.

Even more important, it is unclear that poverty breeds caution in this area. Jamaica has acted to boost its annual bauxite revenues by $180 million because its oil import bill has risen by a like amount and its reserves are low. Successful cartelization offsets low reserves, so the issue becomes how much risk is really involved.

A related argument is that production cutbacks in other primary products would generate unacceptably high unemployment, even if they were successful; such an outcome would supposedly differ sharply from the situation for oil, since the petroleum industry is capital intensive and the largest producers have small populations. But production of many other commodities is also very capital intensive, and the proceeds of successful collusion could be used to create many more jobs through the promotion of labor-intensive industries.

Economists simply do not know enough about the price sensitivity of supply and demand for different products to make firm judgments on the alleged difference between oil and other commodities, especially since all present estimates derive from earlier periods when both the structure of demand and the organization of markets differed greatly (as will be explained below). Some, such as Hendrik Houthakker, argue that the demand for oil is in fact quite responsive to price in any event. And there are certainly plenty of physical reserves of oil, so there is no reason to believe that the responsiveness of its supply in purely economic terms is less than for other commodities.

In addition, as indicated above, the responsiveness of many

other commodities appears very low in the short run and may even be quite low in any relevant long run. However, it is certainly true that stock-piles exist for a few commodities, though recently many of them have been run down. It is also true that recycling is possible for some commodities (though there is still not much known about the technology or the economics of the recycling process). Thus it may turn out that the supplies of some commodities may respond much more favorably to price increases than was the case for oil.

But if so, we cannot know it now. Market actions will, as always, be based on *ex ante* judgments rather than *ex post* analysis. In practice, the issue of cutting demand and triggering substitutes will probably turn on whether the new OPECs are wise enough to learn from OPEC's own major blunders (blunders, at least, from the standpoint of a maximizing cartel) in raising prices too far too fast, demonstrating their unreliability as suppliers by cutting back production and using their commodity power to gain influence over the foreign policies of their consumers. If they show such wisdom, new OPECs may succeed over the longer run far better than OPEC itself.

It is certainly useful for a cartel among nations to inherit an oligopolistic market structure from private industry. But oil is not the only product for which this kind of market structure exists; bauxite is a precise parallel. The producer country levies higher taxes and royalties on the firms, which in turn recoup these losses through higher prices to end users or diversion of revenues from the treasuries of consuming countries. In addition, there are many ways to implement oligopoly power other than through multinational firms. Again, the oligopoly is helpful but not necessary for success, and it is not peculiar to oil anyway.

Oil is certainly more important, both quantitatively and qualitatively, than any of the other commodities under discussion. Yet this would seem likely to trigger more resistance to OPEC than to its offspring, since any moves by the latter can be more readily absorbed or offset. The difference in importance has little impact on the nature of the action which is possible for different products.

Finally, it is certainly true that the oil-rich desert countries were peculiarly invulnerable to economic retaliation. But many of the key oil producers—Iran, Nigeria, Venezuela, Indonesia— were acutely vulnerable to economic retaliation. Even the desert countries would have been loathe to face the political consequences of economic countermeasures by the consumers, though the economic effects of such steps were limited. So their so-called invulnerability explains very little. Indeed, overt action by the rich and powerful against the poor and weak is probably politically infeasible in the 1970s and beyond, so that no producers' cartel need fear it.

Thus it is very doubtful that oil is different in any qualitative sense. Indeed, many other OPECs look much easier to organize and maintain. OPEC had to pool twelve countries to control 80 percent of world oil exports, but fewer countries are usually involved in production of other primary products. Most OPEC countries are heavily dependent on oil, and cartelization was especially risky for them. Other commodity producers are more diversified. OPEC could politicize oil and threaten the world economy; its successors will have an easier task because their products are less important. And economic and political differences among OPEC countries seem much sharper than those among other potential cartelizers. So new OPECs seem at least as likely as OPEC itself.

WHAT HAS CHANGED?

The new international situation does not involve physical shortages. The limits-to-growth projections of the Club of Rome are misleading, since physical reserves appear adequate for all important primary products for the relevant future. Instead, the new likelihood of producers' cartels is explained by changes in demand patterns, increases in the market power of producers, and increases in their perceptions of this power.

First, the advent of high rates of inflation, seemingly for the indefinite future, adds dramatically to the structural demand for commodities. Secular inflationary expectations generate higher, perhaps much higher, levels of business demand for inventories. The erosion of confidence in paper currencies triggered by rampant inflation, possibly accelerated by the widespread adoption of flexible exchange rates, has induced widespread shifts into real assets, primarily commodities (and land). Indeed, many of these commodities—particularly those traded on commodity exchanges —have now taken on a quasimonetary function. They have become more like gold and silver, which have always played both an industrial and a monetary role, and their prices will reflect monetary as well as industrial demand as long as inflationary expectations remain high.

In addition, rampant inflation spurs the investment demand for commodities. Real interest rates are rendered quite low by double-digit price rises, and that reduces the attractiveness of fixed-yield assets and makes credit to finance commodity purchases cheap. The plight of equities stemming from inflation has accelerated commodity investments.

These additions to demand have converted buyers' markets into sellers' markets for a wide range of primary products. Since the higher commodity prices further intensify inflation and vice versa, "commodity spiral inflation" may now have come to supplement price-wage inflation as a lasting feature of the world economic scene. Moreover, fears of new OPECs probably add to all these types of anticipatory buying.

Studies made at the National Bureau of Economic Research show that downturns in commodity prices have consistently led downturns in the economic cycle by one to five quarters throughout the postwar period (see Table 1), and that the average lead time of five to six months has been one of the more accurate indicators of coming slumps. This is why many observers began to predict a bursting of the latest commodity boom in early 1973 when the global economy began to slow down.

Yet commodity prices accelerated dramatically throughout 1973 and did not turn down, even temporarily, until the second quarter of 1974—about eighteen months behind schedule. They boomed even in the face of the first quarter's sharp reductions in GNP in the United States, Japan, and the United Kingdom, and very slow growth everywhere else. A lesser though significant deviation from the historical trend was also evident around the 1969–70 downturn. (The only previous such deviation occurred in 1951–52. It was much shorter than the recent one, and was even less than the deviation of 1969–70, which was almost ignored at the time.) So the explosion of prices of primary products in the

TABLE 1. *The Relationship between Prices of Nonfood Raw Materials and U.S. Economic Growth, 1948–74*
(lead −, lag +, in no. of months)

Growth Cycle		Wholesale Price Index (crude materials excluding foods)	
High	Low	High	Low
July 1948	October 1949	December 1947 (−7)	July 1949 (−3)
June 1951	June 1952	October 1958 (−8)	November 1951 (−7)
March 1953	August 1954	July 1953 (+4)	January 1954 (−7)
February 1957	May 1958	December 1955 (−14)	January 1958 (−4)
February 1960	February 1961	October 1958 (−16)	November 1960 (−3)
April 1962	March 1963	July 1961 (−9)	July 1962 (−8)
June 1966	October 1967	March 1966 (−3)	January 1967 (−9)
March 1969	November 1970	August 1969 (+5)	November 1970 (0)
March 1973		May 1974 (?) (+14)	
Mean lead or lag, excluding 1973–74		−6	−5
Correlation coefficients with leads in leading index, excluding 1962–63 and 1973–74 (all significant at 0.5 level)		.93 .82[a]	.52

[a] Highs and lows.
SOURCE: Geoffrey H. Moore, "Prices during Business Cycles," paper presented at a Roundtable on Inflation held by the Conference Board, Montreal, January 22, 1974.

recent past cannot be explained by the latest worldwide economic boom, though it obviously added significantly to the picture, nor can it be passed off simply as a recurrence of the Korean War experience. More lasting changes seem to be at work. At the same time, the likely increase of worldwide economic growth in the period immediately ahead adds to the probability that commodity prices will shortly resume their upward movement.

Market conditions thus provide an ideal setting for producers' cartels to improve their earnings still further. A world of inflation also increases the likelihood that countries will make every effort to collude so they can, in a sense, index themselves against increases in import prices through the best (sometimes only) means available to them. The many unsuccessful cartel efforts of the past are simply irrelevant; the present situation gives the producers more incentive and a far greater chance to succeed.

The second fundamental change is the success of OPEC itself. In economic terms, the dramatic increase in oil prices means that other countries will try to right their own terms of trade by forcing up prices of their commodities. As already noted, it is no coincidence that Jamaica will earn from its bauxite actions an amount virtually equal to the increase in its oil bill. This is the most direct form of international indexing against inflation.

The success of OPEC has dramatically raised the primary producers' perceptions of their market power. Indeed, it is almost impossible for a primary producing country in a position to try cartelization not to do so today in view of the success of OPEC, the burgeoning list of emulators, and the strident commodity rhetoric. How can Chile face Jamaica if CIPEC cannot equal IBA?

In addition, the oil situation shows that a concerted response by consuming countries is highly unlikely. The scramble for "special deals" by virtually all oil consumers continues to encourage OPEC efforts, a lesson not lost on OPEC's potential successors. Finally, there have been rumors that OPEC might help its offspring directly by buying commodities or financing producers' stockpiles—a rumor more likely to be true for products directly involving an OPEC country, such as Indonesia's tropical timber, or, shortly, Iran's copper.

Third, the producing countries are now in a far better position to pursue their own national interests effectively. In the past, both production and marketing were left largely to multinational firms or a market based on international rules and institutions created and maintained by the United States and other industrial countries.

Now, however, the postwar success of economic development throughout the world, particularly its emphasis on advanced education, has created cadres of exceptional indigenous talent in virtually all developing countries. OPEC was reportedly conceived in a bar in Cambridge, Massachusetts, and every country now has its full quota of graduates from prestigious institutions. The sizable resources of the firms can with impunity be forced to serve the host country rather than vice versa. Indeed, in oil and bauxite the firms have become tools of the producer countries. One result, as noted above, is the reduced likelihood of new investments which would undermine the cartel's prospects.

Concomitantly, the political leaderships in most developing countries are now well past the stage of nationalist rhetoric and political adventurism. They are focusing primarily on the hard realities of economic and social welfare and are looking to every possible device—like commodity cartels—to achieve it. Both the new capabilities and the current focus of national leaderships have sharply raised the market power of most primary producers.

At the same time, the rules and institutions which focused on market solutions to maintain the international economic order during the first postwar generation—and provided an eminently hospitable environment for large multinational firms—have largely eroded. The United States can no longer exert decisive leadership to that end. It can no longer effectively protect the rights of multinational firms, and indeed its policy makers have increasing doubts as to whether trying to do so would promote U.S. national interests anyway. In the resources industries, all these developments mean a much weaker position for the firms, much of whose leverage disappears once they sink their capital and technology into the foreign subsoil.

Thus there are structural changes which sharply tilt the balance of power in commodity markets. The producing countries have new capabilities. The firms are weaker. The consuming countries can no longer dictate either the structure of the system or its daily operation; and they are in disarray among themselves. Both the politics and the economics of commodity relations are now wide open.

RESOURCES DIPLOMACY

It is of course impossible to generalize about all primary products at every moment in the future. Firm judgments can rest only on intensive analysis of the economics and politics of each. Policy response must be based on assessments of the costs of possible cartel action compared with the costs of the possible responses by consumer countries.

But individual commodity developments, like all economic and political events, take place within a framework of broad and fundamental trends. The trends outlined in this article, many of which appear to represent lasting shifts in both the economic and political environments, suggest that "commodity power" and "resources diplomacy" will be with us for the relevant future.

If the cartels succeed—and, for a time, even if they do not—they will produce higher prices throughout the world. They can disrupt individual industries. They will raise the specter of interruptions of supply, deterring needed investments (at various stages of production as well as in the commodities themselves) and adding to the risk of political enmities in the already uncertain world. They will further impoverish the resource-poor developing countries, and add at least marginally to the balance-of-payments problem of some industrial countries as well. They could trigger more scrambles for position among the largest consuming countries and intensify the element of conflict in their relations. Hence they mark a major new factor in both international economics and world politics.

More Third World Cartels Ahead?

RAYMOND F. MIKESELL

Raymond F. Mikesell is W. E. Miner Professor of Economics at the University of Oregon. In this essay, first published in the November-December 1974 issue of Challenge, *he expresses the view that while other developing countries may try to follow the oil exporting countries in raising the prices of their raw material exports, the chances are that they will not succeed.*

THE FOURFOLD PRICE increase achieved by the Organization of Petroleum Exporting Countries (OPEC) quickly led the industrialized nations to assess their vulnerability on other raw materials imports. At the same time, OPEC's highly visible success spurred many countries exporting primary commodities to examine their existing terms of trade and pricing mechanisms. Concerns were not lessened any by the resolutions coming out of the special session of the UN General Assembly held last spring to discuss the problem of raw materials and development. That session ended with a call for developing countries to organize producers' associations so they could exercise "permanent sovereignty over natural resources." The developing countries have generally supported the price-raising actions of OPEC, even though they have suffered the most from increased fuel bills. They do not want to see petroleum prices fall; they want to achieve a similar rise for their own raw materials exports.

Even without collusion among governments, U.S. dollar prices of many primary commodities exported by developing countries more than doubled in 1973. Between January 1973 and April 1974, dollar prices of metals exported by the less developed countries increased by about 120 percent, while food prices rose by about 75 percent. In particular, the price of copper on the London Metal Exchange nearly tripled between January 1973 and May 1974 (although copper prices fell by half in the next few months). The question now is whether collusion can maintain or increase these already high prices.

In international trade, collusion is difficult. The success of any attempt to control the world market price will depend on how big the association's combined share of the market is, how easily nonmembers and producers of substitutes can increase their production, and how competitive the world market structure is. Each member's financial position, the political and economic orientations of the participating countries, and the cohesiveness and discipline of the members in carrying out joint policies are also important factors.

THE OPEC FORMULA

OPEC achieved control over the world petroleum market not by restricting output, but by taxing the international petroleum companies. (OPEC never limited output. The Arab members did in October 1973, but for political reasons.) The success of OPEC's tax policy suggests that, where mineral industries are vertically integrated and the market for the product is ruled by a few firms, taxation may be the best way for a nation to increase revenues.

Until OPEC's formation a decade ago, the world petroleum market outside the United States was controlled by several international firms that refined and marketed the bulk of their own production. This handful of companies did not sell their product on competitive international markets, but instead developed a system of "posted prices." These became the basis for calculating the royalties and income taxes paid to the host governments. When the oil companies attempted to reduce posted prices in 1959–60, the host governments reacted, banding together to form OPEC. OPEC's major function—one that it performed quite successfully—was to help members establish and maintain their own posted prices. OPEC's control over the world petroleum market was recently reinforced by participation agreements between the companies and the host governments. Under these agreements, the government receives a certain portion of the crude output (sometimes related to its share of the equity in the producing company). This crude is then sold—at a price set by the government—back to the company, which sends the crude downstream for refining and marketing. In this way, the OPEC members have been relieved of the task of marketing the output and making contracts for its sale. The international firms simply pass the increased prices on down the production line to the consumer. This task is made all the easier by the industry's tradition of price leadership, whereby an increase by one firm often triggers price hikes by the other companies.

OPEC has sought to standardize taxes among its members, but taxation has by no means been uniform. Indeed, Venezuela probably lost some of its market share in the 1960s because of its relatively higher per barrel taxes. When taxes are uneven, the international firm is likely to shift its output and investment to a lower tax country where it has facilities, unless other producer countries increase their taxes by roughly the same amount, or members of the producer's association take steps to keep the companies from expanding production in the lower tax countries. In 1966, for example, OPEC acted to prevent companies from shifting output from Libya, where firms were bucking an effective tax rise. Governments may also threaten expropriation. In some cases governments, by such a tactic, have actually gotten companies to increase their investment after a tax hike.

A market divided among just a few international firms was not the only important precondition of OPEC's success, for growth in world demand for petroleum (running in excess of 8 percent per year before October 1973) had been very rapid. In the face of such strong demand, Saudi Arabia—and a few other OPEC members in no hurry to increase their output—could easily support the present price of crude petroleum, and possibly even increase it. As long as the demand for petroleum is relatively unaffected by price hikes, Saudi Arabia—with or without help—can increase revenues, although OPEC members that do not go along with the production cuts (such as Iran) might reap much larger benefits.

PRODUCTION AND EXPORT CONTROLS

Even if OPEC could have achieved market control by a collusive agreement limiting production, other producers' associations would find production and export controls more difficult to maintain, particularly since the growth of demand for these minerals has not been anything like that for petroleum. Nearly all developing countries producing major minerals need foreign exchange income—and they need it urgently. Moreover, the high overhead costs that characterize the mining industry, and the large debt service associated with that overhead, make production cutbacks extremely expensive. This is true for both labor and capital costs, since, at least in the short run, labor tends to be a fixed cost.

Those seeking to control the world supply of primary commodities also face another problem: the reserves of most important minerals are rather widely distributed around the world. Although nonmembers may not be able to expand output significantly in the short run, over the longer run, export quotas will induce nonmember producers to expand capacity.

ESTABLISHING A MINIMUM PRICE

If the producers' association does control a substantial proportion of total world output (or exports), its members may agree on a minimum price. (All contracts will be negotiated at or above this minimum.) For this kind of agreement to be successful, each member must maintain what it considers to be an equitable market share, since any country losing a substantial share would be likely to break the minimum price agreement. Assigning market shares to maintain the status quo is no easy task, since the members historically have competed with one another. Usually each country has planned to increase capacity, and these plans are at various stages of completion. Thus, quotas based on recent performance may not be acceptable to all members. (Neither the OPEC nor the Intergovernmental Council of Copper Exporting Countries have ever been able to agree on export quotas.) Moreover, there is a natural tendency for members whose production is in the hands of private companies with downstream affiliates to win a market share from members with nationalized industries and relatively poor marketing organizations. This is especially true if purchasers prefer to negotiate contracts with international firms having several sources of supply. It is possible to maintain export quotas without production controls for relatively short periods of time. In the not-so-long run, however, export quotas must be accompanied by production controls, or the surpluses accumulating within member countries will make price shading increasingly likely.

Minimum price agreements without production or export controls are most likely to work when demand is rising as fast, or faster, than world supply. But it is not clear that a price agreement under these circumstances provides any significant advantage over competition.

BUFFER STOCKS

In general, price agreements will not work for minerals which are sold on international commodity exchanges, since exchanges provide alternative sources of supply. A producers' association could try to maintain prices by establishing a buffer stock. However, as with the International Tin Agreement, buffer stocks are generally useful only to reduce the amplitude of price fluctuations. To keep prices artificially high would require continuous purchasing—and that would necessitate large financial outlays, something developing countries cannot afford. The International Monetary Fund will finance buffer stock arrangements, but only if they are designed to smooth price fluctuations and include consumers as well as producers.

It has been rumored that OPEC countries might finance large purchases of copper from the members of CIPEC (French acronym for the copper council) to maintain high copper prices. Although such action is conceivable, thus far OPEC members have generally limited their investments to relatively liquid assets providing a reasonably high yield.

COMPETITION FROM SUBSTITUTES

A producers' association controlling no more than, say one-fourth of the world's supply of a mineral may hike prices in the short run, but in the longer run nonmember suppliers will increase output, thereby dampening prices.

There is a parallel in the case of substitute products, since increased production of a close substitute will also tend to erode artificially high prices. How much a rise in prices curtails demand for a mineral is partly a function of the time consumers require to adjust to substitutes. Once a consumer adopts a substitute for a certain use of a mineral, his switch is often permanent. For most minerals, demand is likely to be insensitive to higher prices in the short run, but highly responsive in the longer run. Producers are usually concerned about the relationship between the prices of their products and those of substitutes, particularly when the supply of a substitute commodity can be readily increased. CIPEC members, for example, are certainly aware that high copper prices may mean a permanent loss of market to aluminum. The association even charts the ratio between world copper and aluminum prices in its quarterly and annual reports.

Price increases could still occur. CIPEC and the bauxite producers could combine efforts and raise prices of both copper and bauxite. But bauxite prices would need to be raised substantially in order to have a significant direct effect on the price of aluminum. In a world of growing materials shortages, there is always the chance that an increase in the price of one commodity might induce a rise in the price of a close substitute, even without collusion between two producers' associations.

Scrap metal also provides an important substance for primary production in several minerals, and in the case of copper, scrap sometimes constitutes a third or more of the raw material. The potential supply of scrap and of recycled materials is very large for many commodities and supply is sensitive to price even in the relatively short run.

Unless the responsiveness of demand to price changes for a raw material is low, a rise in its price will not increase producers' export revenues and may even reduce them. According to a World Bank study, short-run world demand for CIPEC copper is so responsive to price changes that CIPEC could barely improve the export earnings of its members through an increase in price. And in the longer run, higher prices would actually reduce export earnings.

SOME POLITICAL CONSIDERATIONS

Needless to say, along with the economic forces underlying market actions there are the political ones. One of the strengths of OPEC has been the broad area of common interest among its members. But this community of interests is rare. The USSR, South Africa, Rhodesia, and Turkey produce the bulk of the world's chromium, but these nations would make strange bedfellows. Moreover, given South Africa's political and economic orientation, that country would be unlikely to force up the world chromium price by taxing chromium producers. Nor is South Africa likely to join with Gabon, Zaïre, and Brazil to raise the price of manganese. CIPEC members are currently in strong disagreement regarding the desirability of collusive action to raise copper prices.

ASSESSING THE CHANCES

Given the conditions necessary for a successful cartel among nations, what is the outlook for supplies and prices of those non-fuel minerals directly or indirectly important to U.S. interests? Let us review them one by one.

Copper · In 1972 CIPEC members accounted for 38 percent of the copper produced in the non-Communist world (including concentrates, blister, and refined). CIPEC's share of exports is even larger—amounting to 53 percent in 1971. If other Third World producers, such as Papua, New Guinea, and the Philippines, joined CIPEC, the association's share of exports would climb to almost two-thirds.

Clearly the CIPEC members could exercise a strong influence on the world price of copper. However, the OPEC tax formula would not be effective, since only a small portion of their output is taken by the affiliates of firms with substantial investment in CIPEC members. Among current members of CIPEC, well over half of the production—and almost all of the marketing—is in government hands. Contract prices are tied to those on the London Metal Exchange. No CIPEC member dominates the world market enough to negotiate contracts at a price significantly above that on the exchange.

CIPEC could gain market control through production and export quotas or a buffer stock arrangement. But each of the association's four members would apparently like to expand domestic production and capacity. Peru, the nation with the largest undeveloped reserves, is producing only about one-fourth as much as Chile or Zambia. Peru's policy makers are anxious to double or triple its productive capacity, and Chile is planning to double its output by 1980. These ambitions make any long-term agreement on production or export quotas unlikely. The CIPEC members have discussed establishing a buffer stock for controlling the London price. And there is the possibility that members could agree to a minimum contract price above that on the London exchange when the latter declined below a certain level. But that sort of an arrangement would be difficult to police.

CIPEC members, already concerned with the relationship between the price of copper and that of aluminum, copper's main substitute, would undoubtedly welcome the formation of an association among aluminum producers strong enough to raise prices of that commodity. We could even envisage short-term agreements for maintaining a certain ratio between the prices of the two commodities. In the longer term, however, such a ratio would be difficult to sustain, since the price of bauxite is only a small part of the total cost of producing aluminum.

Bauxite · Approximately 75 percent of the world's exports of bauxite and alumina is shipped from the seven countries in the recently formed International Bauxite Producers' Association. Excluding Australia (which accounts for 15 percent of world exports), all the members of the association are developing countries: Guinea, Guyana, Jamaica, Sierra Leone, Surinam, and Yugoslavia. Production of bauxite and alumina is largely controlled by vertically integrated international firms, except in Guyana, where Alcan properties were recently nationalized. While the vast share of bauxite reserves and production is in the developing countries plus Australia, nearly all of the aluminum metal is produced in the developed countries. The rate of growth in U.S. demand is relatively high (7 percent) and the growth rate for the rest of the world has been considerably higher.

This is perhaps the closest parallel to the OPEC situation, and member governments may be able to raise taxes, which companies would pass on to consumers in the form of higher prices. In May 1974 Jamaica, which accounts for 30 percent of world exports, proposed to raise taxes on the foreign companies by nearly eight-fold. If similar tax demands are made by other producing countries, Jamaica may achieve a severalfold rise in tax revenues without a significant loss of output.

There are, of course, important differences between bauxite and petroleum. There is a range of substitutes for aluminum, and most producing countries are sorely in need of foreign exchange. The crucial difference in terms of final prices is that four tons of bauxite costing a total of $36 to $60 are needed to produce one ton of aluminum ingots worth over $600. Doubling the price of bauxite would increase the price of aluminum by less than 10 percent. (By comparision, the value of refined petroleum products is ordinarily less than double the value of the crude input.)

Tin · Just four countries—Bolivia, Indonesia, Malaysia, and Thailand—account for 80 percent of the non-Communist world's production of tin and claim a somewhat larger share of world exports. Because of the high concentration of production in a few developing countries, there is some chance of an agreement on production or export quotas. However, there is a wide range of substitutes available for the important uses of tin. Moreover, the United States has a stockpile of the metal. Thus, producers are likely to continue using the buffer stock established under the International Tin Agreement as a mechanism for stabilizing prices. That arrangement, by the way, has the support of the IMF and all major consuming countries except the United States.

Chromium · Chromium is an essential ingredient for many metal products and, in the short term, demand is probably insensitive to price changes. Since most ferroalloys are substitutes for one another, however, demand is likely to respond to price increases over the longer run.

South Africa, Rhodesia, Turkey, the Philippines, and the USSR account for nearly 80 percent of world mine production of chromium and an even larger share of world exports. The structure of the industry and the differing political-economic orientations of the major exporters make the probability of collusion small. Nevertheless, if one of the major producers, say South Africa, should take the initiative to raise prices (by putting a special tax on exporters, for example), other producing countries might very well follow. The United States is wholly dependent upon foreign sources for chromium, importing approximately equal amounts from the USSR, South Africa, and Turkey. U.S. demand is growing at about 5 percent per year.

Manganese · The principal use of manganese is in steelmaking, where there is no satisfactory substitute. Even though demand has been growing by only 3 percent per year, the lack of a substitute probably means that demand would not be much dampened by a price increase. The Soviet Union, South Africa, Brazil, Gabon, and India account for over 80 percent of world output but a somewhat smaller share of world exports, since the Soviet Union consumes a large portion of its own output. The United States imports about 90 percent of its needs—chiefly from Gabon, Brazil, South Africa and Zaïre. The bulk of these imports comes from subsidiaries of U.S. steel firms, making increased taxation which would be passed on to U.S. consumers of steel a possibility. But a producers' association would have difficulty maintaining production controls, since much manganese is a co-product of the production of iron and other metals. Moreover, the diverse political orientations of the major producers would make effective collusion difficult.

Cobalt · Cobalt, like manganese and chromium, is used in the production of steel, as well as in certain chemical processes. Nickel is often a substitute for cobalt. World production and export of cobalt are dominated by Zaïre, but because the mineral is a by-product of copper production, its supply is insensitive to price movements. Moreover, there are very large reserves in Canada, New Caledonia, and Australia, so that any attempt to maintain very high prices would probably result in substantial expansion of sources outside of Zaïre.

Iron Ore · Iron ore production and reserves are widely distributed around the world among both developed and developing countries. Although some of the production is controlled by vertically integrated international firms, as in Canada, Brazil, Liberia, and Venezuela, much of the world's output in the developing countries has been nationalized. The Venezuelan government has recently announced its intention to nationalize the Venezuelan iron ore industry currently controlled by U.S. Steel and Bethlehem Steel.

The absence of concentration in reserves, production, or exports, and the wide differences in the political orientations of the major exporting countries would make effective collusion quite unlikely. The United States is currently dependent on foreign sources for about 30 percent of its iron ore requirements, and this dependence will increase over the coming decades. However, the United States could supply its own requirements with lower grade ores.

Lead, Zinc, and Other Minerals · On the whole, the world market structure does not appear conducive to collusion by either lead or zinc producers. The United States has the world's largest output of lead and the largest reserves; it also has large reserves of zinc and is the world's second largest producer. Although the United States is expected to be increasingly dependent upon foreign supplies for both minerals, most imports will probably continue to come from Canada, with smaller amounts from Australia and the Latin American countries. Vertical integration in the industry outside the United States is not substantial.

The United States is now heavily dependent upon foreign sources of nickel, potash, tungsten, and mercury, and in the future will become increasingly dependent on foreign sources of sulfur. Currently Canada is the major source of U.S. imports for all of these minerals, and in most cases collusive action among world producers would probably require that country's cooperation.

WHAT THE UNITED STATES CAN DO

The best candidate for world market control by means of OPEC-type action is bauxite; however, even a severalfold rise in taxes on bauxite producers would not have a major impact on the price of aluminum. Collusive action for raising copper prices seems remote given the divergent policies of the CIPEC members. Moreover, the financial position of the CIPEC countries precludes their being able to restrict exports over long periods or to accumulate large stocks. Collusion between bauxite and copper producers is likely to be of little help in raising or maintaining copper prices because of the minor impact on the price of aluminum. There is some potential for a sharp rise in prices of chromium and manganese through joint action, since output of both is heavily concentrated in a few countries and there are no readily available substitutes for their most important uses. Nevertheless, there appear to be political barriers to effective collusion on either of these metals. For most other minerals, either production and reserves are widely distributed or substitutes are readily available, or both. For a few commodities such as nickel, Canada would have to be included in any collusive association by developing countries.

We conclude with a recommendation. For every case of possible collusion, significant harm to the U.S. economy could be avoided by a stockpile of each commodity equivalent to one or two years' import requirements. Successful market control by producers' associations for periods longer than that simply does not appear feasible.

Toward the Integration of World Agriculture: Enlarging the Scope for International Cooperation

THE TRIPARTITE REPORT

In this report, economists in North America, the European Community, and Japan examine the need for international cooperation in agriculture among developed and developing countries.

EXPERIENCE demonstrates that agricultural trade will be the most difficult area for negotiating improvements in international economic relations. The reasons are apparent. Barriers to expanded international exchanges of farm and food products stem directly from domestic intervention and support policies. Typically, these domestic policies have taken precedence over general commitments to liberalization in international trade. As a consequence, comparative advantage has yielded to other considerations as a major determinant of the volume, composition, and location of agricultural production.

Among the shortcomings of this approach to farm policy are, notably, its failure to provide satisfactory incomes to those farmers who are most in need of assistance, its high cost to the taxpayer, and its inability to provide consumers with the benefits that could be gained by taking advantage of the substantial differences in agricultural productivity that exists among nations. Reform of these policies, therefore, is as much, if not more, a matter of meeting internal needs than of providing a more liberal trading environment.

That being so, there are several general principles that governments should follow in modifying agricultural programs to assist farmers in adapting to changing conditions. These are:

• Specific social and regional measures, not general agricultural policies such as price supports, should be used in dealing with the problems of rural communities.

- There should be positive policies to facilitate structural adjustment. These could include assistance in establishing viable full-time farms and changing production patterns, encouragement of part-time farming where this permits effective use of human resources, and help to those migrating from farms.
- The problems of low-income farm families should be alleviated through transitional direct income support rather than general product price support.
- Price support measures should be designed to expand consumption and to be anti-inflationary.
- Price relationships should provide additional incentives to produce those products that have a growing world demand and reduced incentives to produce products with a stable or declining demand.
- Price supports should include disincentives for unwarranted production, including a provision to place on farmers part of the costs of the additional output.

Domestic programs based on these principles would reduce costs to consumers and taxpayers, assist farmers who are in greatest need, and help transfer farm resources to the expanding sectors of agriculture. They should be adopted in pursuit of national self-interest as part of an effort to deal more effectively with domestic agricultural problems. At the same time, by permitting greater flexibility in agriculture, they would facilitate the negotiation of reductions in barriers to agricultural trade and thereby help to promote the more effective use of agricultural resources, both at home and abroad.

A useful link, therefore, exists betwen domestic and international agricultural policies. In view of the political sensitivities involved, these two aspects of policy can complement each other only if care is exercised in choosing the means and defining the goals of international agricultural negotiations.

No rapid changes are to be looked for in the farm programs that lie at the heart of the agricultural trade problem. Nor is progress likely if the international dialogue takes the form of aggressive confrontations between strongly divergent and doctrinaire views. Negotiations having as their direct objective the abrupt termination of, or a fundamental change in, national agricultural support policies are doomed to fail in the future as they have in the past.

What is required is a patient, long-haul effort that proceeds in stages: first, the external impact of national agricultural policies should be given more weight in internal debates; second, national agricultural policies should increasingly take into account the differences in international costs and changes in supply and demand developments on the world market; and third, national policies should be modified progressively to bring them into harmony with internationally agreed upon standards and objectives through specific and binding commitments.

This is not a dramatic process, but it offers the greatest promise. Hence, we would emphasize that the multilateral General Agreement on Tariffs and Trade (GATT) negotiations, if they are not to fail, must be only the beginning of this process of wider cooperation. Specifically, they should lead to significant progress in dealing with two interconnected issues. One is to bring down barriers to international trade in agricultural products; any real improvement in the use of the world's agricultural resources requires that the most disruptive restrictions on trade be reduced. The other is to provide assurances about the stability and security of supplies of the major traded commodities.

A variety of protective measures applies to agricultural trade. The most promising approach to dealing with them is to decide upon their actual restrictive impact and to agree on means for reducing it. In other words, the negotiators will need to focus on the effective margins of protection.

The security and stability of supplies will depend on the establishment of reserve stocks to meet fluctuations in the world market. The GATT negotiators will have the task of determining whether there can be international agreement on the financing and management of such reserves.

REDUCING MARGINS OF PROTECTION

It bears repeating that all of the industrial countries will have contributions to make to an agricultural trade negotiation. No country has a monopoly on free-trade virtue. None should be exempt from the effort to increase the proportion of the world's farm output that is produced under efficient conditions. Thus, negotiations in the field of agriculture should cover all farm products and should deal with all forms of protection and support, including domestic measures as well as restrictions at the border. This means that the negotiations should concentrate on the margin or degree of actual protection rather than on the means or technique used. In effect, the need is to build upon the *montant de soutien*, or level-of-support plan, which was proposed but not seriously pursued during the Kennedy Round.

A general formula to this end could be developed along the following lines:

1. Margins of support or protection would be determined against an agreed upon base price. The base for each product involved could be the average of the prices (including subsidies) received by producers in the major exporting countries for a recent period, such as 1969–72. Next, these averages would be adjusted by adding the appropriate transportation and marketing charges. The margin of protection would then be the difference between the base price and the intervention or target price in the importing country or region during the same period. It hardly needs to be emphasized that the price calculations undoubtedly would involve elements of judgment and negotiation; the principle, however, is clear enough.

2. The next step would be to agree to freeze margins of support, as these margins have been determined by agreement, and then to undertake their gradual reduction. A reasonable target might be an average reduction, covering all products, of 50 percent, to be achieved in stages over a decade.

3. In order to allow ample room and time for adjustment, the agreement might further specify that reductions in margins of support should not require reductions in nominal farm prices nor call for a reduction of more than 3 percent a year in the real prices (that is, after allowance is made for rising general price levels) received by producers.

4. It would be understood that agreed upon measures for social purposes, including programs for disadvantaged regions or low-income farm families, would not be included in calculating margins of support. As was noted earlier, governments would be responsible for designing social measures that would have minimum impact upon production.

This approach would have several advantages: It would exclude from the international base price the distortions introduced by artificial encouragement of output or by export subsidies. The base price would be recalculated each year to reflect actual returns received by producers in the major exporting countries. It would be above the world price for a commodity if exporters used export subsidies or paid subsidies to their producers. It would provide for gradual but progressive change. It would work against sharp year-to-year fluctuations in actual market prices. It would combine stability with flexibility. It would oblige governments to carry out farm policies with due recognition for the interests of other countries. Once embarked upon, change would be in the direction of adjusting production to meet changing consumer demands. The tolerable pace of change might well turn out to be considerably faster than had been expected, and this too could be accommodated.

SECURITY AND STABILITY OF SUPPLIES

For many years nations that have depended upon a substantial volume of imports of agricultural products have been concerned about the continuity of supply. A variety of bilateral arrangements has been used for particular products. However, the recent actions of most exporters in halting or rationing exports have created a great deal of uncertainty in world markets and, understandably, among policymakers in governments.

Importers can argue, with some force, that exporters should not expect them to open their markets unless there is some way of guaranteeing that adequate supplies will be available at reasonable prices. Exporters, in turn, have argued that importers in the past have failed to carry adequate stocks; consequently when supplies were adequate—or in surplus—the exporters had to bear all the costs of holding reserve stocks for the world.

It is time to consider a program of internationally supervised stockholding of major farm products. Three important objectives can be met by a stock policy for which responsibility is shared by the major trading nations. First, stocks can be held and managed so as to mitigate wide swings in prices and availabilities, such as occurred in 1972–73. Second, stocks can be managed so as to stabilize the volume of international trade in the face of fluctuations in output in both exporting and importing countries. Third, the industrial countries can help to finance strategic food stocks earmarked for the developing countries against the threat of famine. It is evident that had there been a crop failure in a large developing country in 1973–74, adequate food aid would have been difficult if not impossible to organize because of the lack of stocks readily accessible to governments and because large-scale purchases at this time would have pushed prices to extremely high levels.

The general principles that might govern an international arrangement for holding agricultural stocks can be stated simply: the costs of acquiring and holding stocks should be shared; and procedures for acquisition and disposal should be matters of international negotiation and agreement.

Stocks for Commercial Emergencies · These would be held by individual governments. The cost of acquiring and holding them should be allocated among participating governments on the basis of volume of production and of consumption, or some combination of the two. The size of the stocks deemed necessary for likely emergencies would be a matter for mutual decision. Acquisition of, and release from, stocks could be by mutual agreement under general guidelines decided in advance; or price could be the criterion. That is, in an emergency, stocks would be released for the market when the world price reached or exceeded a predetermined level and, in a situation of surplus, would be accumulated when prices fell below a predetermined floor.

Buffer Stock Operations · To meet the narrower objective of minimizing year-to-year fluctuations in the volume and value of international trade in major farm products, a commitment could be made to offset the effects of variations in supplies. For example, a country—either an importing or an exporting country—would be required to add to stocks when its output exceeded, say, the level of a moving average of its output over the previous four or five years. Similarly, unless it were agreed otherwise, a country would release stocks when its output fell below the same average. The share of excess production set aside for stocks might be, for example, one-half, with analogous provisions for those years when production fell short of trend.

As an alternative to a storage rule based on a relationship between current output and average output in the past, the requirement might be that stocks would be accumulated when an agreed upon international market price fell below a specified level and released when that price rose above a similarly specified level.

A buffer arrangement would establish an incentive for countries subject to wide swings in output to look for ways of decreasing these swings; or in the case of a product for which the market was growing slowly or not at all, the costs of holding stocks would tend to induce governments to modify support programs to hold down output.

A Strategic Food Reserve · Apart from stocks to cope with wide fluctuations in commercial trade and buffer stocks against smaller year-to-year swings in output, urgent consideration needs to be given to what may be called strategic reserves, established against the threat of sudden crop failures in the developing countries. As a practical matter, this would require financing of stock buildups in those developing countries that are unable to maintain adequate stocks on their own. It should be stressed that the size and costs of such insurance are not likely to be unacceptably large.

For a crude calculation, we may take as a benchmark India's cereal reserves of some nine million tons, the existence of which proved to be immensely helpful in bringing India through the difficult 1972–73 period. India uses roughly one-third of the total cereals consumed in the developing world, excluding China. Total reserves of twenty-five to thirty million tons might thus be assumed to be a reasonable target. All countries hold stocks to begin with. Some would be capable of financing any incremental amounts needed. So we may estimate that the added stocks to be held might be in the order of ten to twelve million tons. We may further suppose that these supplies could be purchased over a period of time at $100 a ton and that annual storage costs would be $10 to $15 a ton. An investment of $1 billion, and an annual cost of $100 million to $150 million, might thus be a preliminary guess as to the orders of magnitude involved.

If strategic reserves of this kind could be agreed upon, they should be placed, as far as is economically feasible, in the developing countries themselves. This would assure that supplies would not depend on the availability of international shipping facilities. But some earmarking of reserves in exporting countries might be necessary because of the high cost of storage in tropical areas.

A NEGLECTED LINK TO INDUSTRIAL TRADE NEGOTIATIONS

The problems of agricultural trade have become so specialized and complex that the agricultural negotiations will necessarily have rules that differ from those on industrial trade. At the same time, it should be emphasized that farmers have a substantial stake in the negotiations covering industrial products.

First is the matter of the protection afforded to the processing of farm products in the industrial countries. Although nominal tariff rates on these products are usually low, the effective protection given them is in many cases extremely high. This is because the raw products themselves usually carry no duty, so that the nominal tariff falls wholly on the value-added element in the final cost. It is not uncommon for the effective rate of protection, therefore, to reach 50 or 100 percent, or even a higher level.

These effective rates of protection discourage the establishment of processing industries in the developing countries and deprive those countries of the accompanying employment opportunities. Special attention should be given to drastic reductions in—or the elimination of—tariffs on processed agricultural products of interest to the developing countries.

A second issue relates to the prices of products the farmer uses in agricultural production. Farmers cannot compete on a fair basis in agricultural trade if they do not have relatively equal opportunities to purchase their fertilizer, farm equipment, and other agricultural inputs at the lowest possible prices. At present, prices of these products differ substantially from country to country. In part, this is due to monopoly practices and cartel arrangements, the strength of which depends on how individual governments enforce their antitrust statutes. Trade barriers, however, are also a factor influencing differences in the price of farm inputs. Consequently farmers have a strong interest in seeing that duties and other barriers to imports of farm inputs are eliminated as soon as possible in trade negotiations.

A Critical Survey of the New International Economic Order

MORDECHAI E. KREININ and J. M. FINGER

Mordechai E. Kreinin is professor of economics at the Michigan State University, J. M. Finger is director of the Office of Policy Research at the U.S. Treasury. In this essay, originally published in the November-December 1976 issue of the Journal of World Trade Law, *they express the view that the proposals made for the new international economic order would not appropriately serve the interests of the developing countries.*

INTRODUCTION

SINCE 1974 the developing countries have been voicing their increasing displeasure with the state of the world economy as it affects them. Calls abound for a "new world economic order," for a "better real for the developing nations," and for "increasing the rate of resource transfer" from the industrial to the underdeveloped world. A special session of the UN General Assembly was called in September 1975, to deal with these demands. It was followed by an ongoing Paris Conference on International Economic Cooperation between the developed and developing countries. And in May 1976, the United Nations Conference on Trade and Development (UNCTAD), with 125 member states, convened its fourth conference in Nairobi to implement "the essential elements of a new order."[1] The questions arise: What is all this fuss about? How much of it is new? How much of it is useful? How much of it is practical?

Most writings about the New Economic Order are concerned with means to obtain broadly defined objectives. The objectives are stated as: increasing LDCs' control over their economic destiny; accelerating the LDCs' growth rate; tripling the share

1. UNCTAD IV, "New Directions and New Structures for Trade and Development," Report by the Secretary General of UNCTAD to the Conference, TD/183, Nairobi, May 1976, p. 1.

of global industrial production conducted in the LDC, by the year 2000; and narrowing the gap in per capita income between the developed and developing countries. In turn, the proposed means invariably revolve around trade and aid relationships between the industrial and the developing countries. Thus, the form of the new order is defined in the basic UN documents[2] in terms of: (a) improved access into the markets of the industrial countries for manufacturing exports from the LDCs (b) changes in the marketing structure and the pricing mechanism of primary commodities; (c) revision of the international monetary system; (d) access by the LDCs to the technology and the capital markets of the developed countries; and (e) an increase in foreign aid or other forms of resource transfers to the LDCs.

This paper examines the elements of the program (the ones already in effect as well as those still in the debating stage), and assesses their effectiveness in attaining the objectives outlined above. Since the stated "means" refer exclusively to external economic relations, our survey will also be so focused. But, the concluding section attempts to "place matters in proper prospective" by emphasizing the importance of domestic transformation in the LDCs themselves if they are to accelerate their growth rate and attain the objectives of the new order. It will be argued that the external trade matters, which constitute the core of the "New Order" proposals, are at best of subsidiary importance. Yet domestic policies of the LDCs are mentioned only in passing in the basic documents of the UNCTAD Secretariat.[3]

The review deals with problems affecting LDCs as one cohesive unit, as they thrust themselves into the international arena. While it is recognized that on many issues the developing countries are polarized by region, level of development, and other characteristics, we overlook issues that affect only specific groups of LDCs. The following two sections are devoted to "North-South" trade issues in finished manufactures and primary commodities respectively. The third section deals briefly with the non-trade-

2. See for example, ibid, pp. 12–17.
3. Only at the end of the section entitled "The Essential of a New Order" (ibid., pp. 12–17) is there a one-paragraph discussion of internal development policies, and even that is devoted almost exclusively to income distribution.

related matters, while the concluding section offers an overall review and assessment.

A word about the authors' views and predilections is appropriate at the outset. We are in sympathy with the aspirations of the LDCs to improve their economic lot, and we take as given the goals stated above. The question we explore is whether the proposed means are likely to contribute to the attainment of these goals.

ISSUES RELATING TO FINISHED MANUFACTURES

Developing countries have not been full participants in the process of tariff reduction that has taken place under the General Agreement on Tariffs and Trade (GATT). Although tariff cuts exchanged by the industrial countries were extended to them on a non-reciprocal basis, these cuts pertained largely to products traded by the developed nations. This is a result of the *GATT* mechanism which is based on reciprocal concessions. The products that enter the bargaining process are those in which both sides to the negotiations have an interest. And because direct participation by LDCs has been limited at best, (as they offered little or no concessions to the developed nations), their exports were included in the negotiations only to the extent that they overlap with products produced in the industrial countries. The upshot of this mechanism is that LDCs' own tariffs remain very high and both tariffs and non-tariff barriers faced by their manufacturing exports remain highly restrictive.

Additionally the structure of protection (as against its level) in the industrial countries discourages the expansion of processing industries in the LDCs. For many products, tariff rates escalate with the stage of processing. Duties on iron ore are generally negligible, but rates on ingots and other primary steel products are quite steep. Hides and skins are admitted duty free into the developed countries, but tariffs imposed on leather imports are high. This means that effective rates of protection (i.e., protection accorded to the domestic value added) on products in advanced processing stages are much higher than the nominal rates, further accentuating the tariff escalation. Though processing activities tend to be labor intensive, and hence well suited to the resource base of the LDCs, the escalation of nominal and effective rates mitigates against these countries moving into such activities, i.e., against their exporting primary goods in processed rather than in raw form.

To gain freer access to industrial countries' markets, the LDCs have demanded tariff preferences for their manufactured exports; specifically, they wished to be charged no duty in the industrial countries while each developed country would charge the most-favored-nation (MFN) rate on competitive products from other industrial countries. This concept came to be known as the Generalized System of Preferences (GSP), under which LDCs would receive a margin of preferences equaling the MFN tariff in the developed countries. The GSP has been the thrust of LDCs' demands in the manufacturing field for the past 15 years. The proposed system was intended to be "general" in the sense of having identical treatment applied by all industrial countries to the export of all developing countries. A waiver from GATT's most-favored-nation clause (which prohibits tariff discrimination as between supplying countries) for such treatment has been secured on the ground that "unequals should be treated unequally."

Analytically, preferences are analogous to customs unions, for they give rise to two static effects on trade flows:

1. The trade-creation effect: Tariffs are reduced on imports from the beneficiary countries, which then displace some inefficient domestic production in the donor country.

2. The trade-diversion effect: The tariff discrimination embodied in the preferences results in imports from third countries being displaced by those from the beneficiary countries in the markets of the donor countries.

A recent study[4] suggests that across-the-board duty-free access (without exceptions or limitations) granted to the exports of the developing countries would be mainly trade creating. The structure of effective tariff protection on manufacturing industries in the developed countries is significantly and positively correlated with the comparative advantage of the developing countries, so

4. Z. Iqubal, "The Generalized System of Preferences and the Comparative Advantage of Less Developed Countries in Manufactures" (mimeographed), International Monetary Fund, April 1974.

that a comprehensive GSP would allow expansion of industries in which they have a comparative advantage. Conversely, effective protection in the developed countries was shown to be negatively correlated with their comparative advantage. Consequently, a truly generalized, limitation-free preference scheme would improve allocative efficiency in the developed countries as well. In so far as the output displaced is that of labor-intensive, technologically unsophisticated industries, the resources in the developed countries would be forced to move to more efficient industries. Unfortunately, internal political pressures in the industrial countries granting the GSP (donor countries) led to restrictions on the preferences which are invariably designed to limit their trade-creating effects.

Spurred by political pressures in the international arena, Western Europe and Japan introduced their GSP in 1971–72, while the U.S. GSP—part of the 1975 Trade Reform Legislation—became effective on 1 January 1976. But these schemes are a far cry from the GSP envisioned by UNCTAD in the past decade. Perusal of the fine print reveals that the schemes are not general, for they apply to a very limited list of products and also differ greatly as between donor countries. Nor do they contain substantial preferences—preferential access on the products covered is highly restricted. The European Community (EC) scheme is essentially a tariff quota. Under it, duty-free access of manufactures of export interest to the LDCs is subject to an upper limit. Once the limit is reached, further imports are subject to the full MFN tariff. Another restrictive provision is that the preferential imports of each product from any one developing country are not allowed to exceed one-half the total ceiling for the product. For sensitive products this "maximum amount limitation" is often limited to 20 to 30 per cent of the total. In the case of textiles certain important LDC suppliers are excluded from the list of beneficiaries. The rules of origin governing the GSP further restrict its value to the beneficiary countries. To qualify for duty-free entry, a product must be wholly produced in the preference-receiving country; if imported materials have been used, they must have been subject to "substantial transformation," the general criterion for such a transformation being that it must transfer them to another four-digit BTN (Brussels Tariff Nomenclature) heading. In addition, given the way the program is administered, much of the government tariff revenue given up by the scheme would be absorbed by the European importers rather than transferred to the developing countries' exporters, for in many cases the importers simply offer reduced prices for imports covered by the scheme.

Small as they are, the benefits conferred by the GSP were further diluted by the enlargement of the European customs union from six to nine countries, for two reasons. First, because upon their accession to the Community the relatively liberal British and Danish schemes were replaced by the more restrictive EC scheme. And second, because the attendant creation of a free-trade area in Europe by 1 July 1977, would eliminate the preferred treatment for LDCs in any part of Western Europe over any other European country. The only nonpreferred suppliers to Europe would be the United States and Japan, with whom the developing nations compete in only a very limited range of products, and the socialist states, who export largely the same products as the developing countries but who are likely to price their exports in such a way as to absorb the preferential margin and remain competitive.

The U.S. GSP suffers from a different set of restrictions. First, many commodities of particular export interest to the developing countries are excluded either because they are goods already subject to import relief measures, such as textiles and steel, or because they are politically sensitive items, such as footwear. Second, preferential treatment under the bill would not apply to imports of an article from a particular developing country if that country supplies 50 per cent of the total value of U.S. imports or $25 million of the article. Third, certain categories of LDCs are excluded from the list of beneficiaries. And finally, the "rules of origin" will bite into the product coverage of the scheme.

Several detailed studies[5] of the GSP schemes have placed an upper limit on their value in promoting LDCs' exports at $100 million a year. And this was before the enlargement of the EC.

5. Richard Cooper, "The European Community's System of Generalized Preferences: A Critique," *Journal of Development Studies,* July 1972; and Tracy Murray, "How Helpful Is the Generalized System of Preferences to Developing Countries?" *Economic Journal* 83 (June 1973).

These benefits are meager indeed. In fact, it has been estimated[6] that a relatively obscure provision in the U.S. tariff law results in greater expansion in LDCs' exports than the entire GSP. These provisions (tariff items 806:30 and 807:00) permit the value of U.S.-made parts to be deducted from the dutiable value of goods imported into the U.S. The tariff is thus applied only to the foreign value added. The label "offshore assembly provision" usually applied to these provisions is somewhat misleading in that any goods which contain U.S. parts can qualify, whether the foreign value added was a simple assembly process or a sophisticated manufacturing operation. Similar but less liberal provisions exist in the tariff codes of several European countries. Their provisions, however, are strictly overseas assembly provisions which restrict the foreign value-adding activity to the processing and assembly of components. Furthermore, while the U.S. provision is available to any foreign exporter in each European country, the provision can be applied only to goods reimported by a firm domestic to that country. To take advantage of the U.S. provisions, several LDCs such as Mexico, have established "'free-trade zones," where merchandise can move in and out without paying duty. That has attracted statewide corporations to set up processing plants and take advantage of the U.S. overseas assembly provisions. The advantages to the LDC concerned lie both on accelerated development through exports, and a guaranteed market for the products of these processing plants.

Not only has the GSP proven to be of very limited value; but there is considerable evidence that developing countries do not need preferences to compete. Both casual observations and formal analysis demonstrate that in a wide range of products they can effectively compete in Western markets in terms of both price and quality, when placed on equal competitive footing.[7] Indeed,

6. J. M. Finger, "Tariff Provisions for Offshore Assembly and the Exports of Developing Countries," *Economic Journal* 85 (June 1975): 365–72, and "Trade and Domestic Effects of the Offshore Assembly Provisions in the United States Tariff," *American Economic Review* 66 (September 1976).

7. J. M. Finger, "Effects of the Kennedy Round Tariff Concessions on the Exports of Developing Countries," *Economic Journal* 86 (March 1976): 87–95, and "GATT Tariff Concessions and the Exports of Developing Countries—U.S. Concessions at the Dillon Round," *Economic Journal* 84 (September 1974): 566–75.

an unpublished up-date of these studies estimates that in terms of 1974 trade magnitudes, the Kennedy Round tariff reductions added about $1 billion per year to LDC export receipts—about 10 times the estimated effect of the GSP.

The question arises: What should the LDCs press for in the area of finished manufactures? The issue assumes added significance in view of the ongoing round of multilateral trade negotiations (MTN) in Geneva. When the U.S. Trade Reform Act—the legislation authorizing American participation in the negotiations—was being debated, the LDCs felt threatened by any significant tariff reduction among the developed countries. For it would erode the margin of their preferences under the GSP. They went as far as lobbying against the MTN in Washington and Brussels. But in fact the developing countries may gain more than they lose from the next round of tariff reductions. Against the erosion of the highly restricted GSP there are potential gains from MFN tariff cuts: (a) on products restricted by the various GSP quota limitations; (b) on products excluded from the GSP; and (c) cuts affecting non-beneficiary (under the GSP) developing countries. These gains have been estimated at several times the potential loss on the GSP.[8] It must also be remembered that while the MFN tariff reductions are permanent in nature, the GSP has been granted for a ten-year period. Additionally, the MFN cuts are not subject to the various exclusions, quotas, and maximum amounts limitations. And finally, GATT's tariff concessions are subject to a "binding provision"; i.e., the new and lower tariff rates are bound against future increase. No such binding exists in the case of the GSP.

This argument in favor of non-discriminatory (MFN) tariff cuts as opposed to generalized preferences assumes that the LDCs will not succeed in liberalizing the GSP to any considerable degree. Indeed, the political winds blowing in the U.S., Europe, and Japan are protectionistic in nature, especially when it comes to granting non-reciprocal concessions and preferential treatment on labor-intensive products. The five-year history of the Japanese and EEC schemes which shows much "revision,"

8. See R. Baldwin and T. Murray, "MFN Tariff Reductions and LDC Benefits under the GSP," *Economic Journal* 87 (March 1977): 30–46.

but virtually no expansion[9] plus the five years required to gain congressional approval of a U.S. scheme, amply demonstrates this point. Consequently, the LDCs have an important stake in the success of the MTN. Non-discriminatory tariff reduction can benefit the developing countries, and LDC exporters can compete effectively with industrial country exports on a wide range of manufactured goods.

One argument against the usefulness of tariff reduction for expanding LDC exports is that tariff rates in the industrial countries are already so low that any further cuts would be insignificant. While this may be true for some rates, it is not true for a number of labor-intensive products which, as the LDCs protest, have been on the exclusions list in previous GATT rounds. Furthermore, though nominal rates may be low, effective rates are often high, especially on processed materials. For example, if Europe admits logs duty free, and sawing accounts for 20 per cent of the value of lumber, then a modest 8 per cent nominal rate on lumber amounts to a 40 per cent effective rate on processing. Reduction of the 8 per cent rate to 4 per cent would translate into a 20 percentage point reduction of the effective rate.

An additional point is that only the MTN (and not the GSP) may succeed in reducing non-tariff barriers, and thereby benefit the LDCs in an area of increasing importance.

What should the LDCs' position be in the multilateral trade negotiations? After solid staff work to identify precisely their common interests, the LDCs should press for one substantial outcome: inclusion in the tariff cuts of as many products as possible that are of export interest to them. Their precise strategy would have to depend on the mode of negotiations adopted. Should an across-the-border linear cut in rates be pursued in the MTN, the LDCs should pressure against placing their traditional and potential exports on the exception list (i.e., the list of products excepted from the linear cut). Alternatively, in the case of industry-by-industry negotiations, they should lobby for the inclusion in the bargaining process of products that are of interest to them.

Beyond that the LDCs should consider the possibility of offer-

9. Peter Ginman and Tracy Murray, "An Ex Post Evaluation of Tariff Preferences for Developing Countries," forthcoming.

ing reciprocal concessions rather than remaining strictly on the receiving end. They stand to reap a considerable welfare gain (on the import side) by simplifying and lowering their tariff rates as well as non-tariff barriers on reasonably sophisticated consumer goods. Consequently, what is a good strategy in negotiating with the industrial countries, may also be in their own best interests.

Another trade strategy that should be pursued with greater vigor is regional integrations among LDCs. That indeed is one of the more useful ingredients of the proposed New Economic Order. Past attempts at forming customs unions and free-trade areas have faltered over the issues of equal distribution of benefits and of polarization (i.e., the concentration of gains from integration in the most advanced cities or regions). If some redistributional schemes can be devised to overcome this problem, the integrating LDCs can enjoy the benefits of larger markets—crucial for any sensible policy of import substitution.

In summary, LDC trade policies currently being pursued emphasize preferences to the complete exclusion of other options. Indeed, the stress on non-reciprocity has become so strong that some LDC spokesmen seem to have rejected as tainted and unworthy any gains they might gather from reciprocal policy actions. But five years of revisions of the widely acclaimed GSP failed to liberalize it to any significant degree. This experience calls into question the validity of previous approaches and mandates a search for alternatives. Fortunately, the substantial contribution to LDCs' exports made by the Kennedy Round and the Offshore Assembly provisions suggest that such alternatives are available. Developing countries might better serve their own interests by searching out other areas of shared interest with the developed countries, within the MTN, rather than by insisting on non-reciprocal treatment by the developed countries.

ISSUES CONCERNING TRADE IN PRIMARY PRODUCTS

The "Problem" · An important range of issues addressed by the international economic order concerns primary commodities. Although the emphasis is new, the issues themselves date back to the early 1950s. Even before the creation of UNCTAD and the emergence of Raul Prebisch as an influential public figure, policy (and research) concern has focused on two allegations: (a) that the prices of primary products tend to fluctuate in the short run more widely than the prices of manufactured goods, i.e., commodity prices are less stable than prices of manufactured goods; and (b) that prices of primary products tend to decline, over the long run, relative to prices of manufactured goods, i.e., that there is a secular deterioration in the terms of trade of primary products versus manufactures and hence of commodity producing countries versus industrial countries.

Taking the issues in reverse order, the empirical evidence on the secular decline hypothesis is mixed. From as far back as the classical economists through the expert group convened by UNCTAD in 1975, researchers have verified the hypothesis for some commodities over some time periods, and rejected it in other cases.[10] Since the commodity terms of trade is a ratio between two indexes, the results depend on the base period chosen for comparison, and would vary accordingly. Thus, any empirical conclusion is necessarily arbitrary. In any case, it was long ago demonstrated that a country's terms of trade are a poor measure of its economic well-being. Whether the long-term trend of the market price of a particular commodity has been up or down is irrelevant to the pragmatic question of whether or not policy action can increase the revenues of exporters of that product.

With respect to short-run price fluctuations, available evidence indicates convincingly the commodity prices are more volatile than prices of manufactured goods, and that the export earnings of commodity producers are less stable than those of industrial countries.[11] However, there is no verification of the allegation that these fluctuations hinder economic growth.

10. The conclusions of the UNCTAD group are reported in "Idea of Growing Disparity in World Prices Disputed," *New York Times*, 25 May 1975, p. 1. References to earlier studies are given in Robert E. Lipsey, *Price and Quantity Trends in the Foreign Trade of the United States* (Princeton, Princeton University Press, 1963), pp. 17ff.

11. See Joseph D. Coppock, *International Economic Instability: The Experience after World War II* (New York: McGraw-Hill, 1962); G. F. Erb and S. Schiavo-Campo, "Export Stability, Level of Development, and Economic Size of Less Developed Countries," *Bulletin of the Oxford University Institute of Economics and Statistics* (November 1969), pp. 263–83; and B. F. Massell, "Export Instability and Economic Structure," *American Economic Review* 60 (September 1970): 618–30.

The Proposals · Most new economic order documents, such as the "Manila declaration" (the position paper of the Group of 77[12] going into the Nairobi meetings) stress the dual objectives of stabilizing and of supporting commodity prices. They frequently specify that the level at which commodity prices should be supported should be determined by indexing the prices of commodities to prices of the manufactured imports of the LDCs. While commodity agreements are proposed as the means for achieving these objectives, there are no specific proposals as to how, or through what economic instruments, commodity agreements should operate. The UNCTAD Secretariat's "Integrated Programme for Commodities"[13] does, however, make specific proposals. The basic element in this proposal is a common fund of $3 billion, which would finance commodity buffer stocks. Individual commodity agreements (such as the tin agreement, the cocoa agreement) would not be replaced by this fund. Rather, by providing a ready source of financing for their buffer stock operations, the fund is expected to encourage the negotiation of commodity agreements of each of the ten to eighteen commodities of export interest to the developing countries.

The Secretariat documentation does not explain why the common fund should finance the buffer stock operations of individual commodity agreements rather than itself operate as a collective buffer stock for the entire list of commodities. One can, however, speculate as to what their reasons might be. First, the merging of all buffer stock funds into one pool would probably be opposed by those commodity agreements already in existence. If the proposed common fund were established, the tin agreement, say, could borrow from the fund when it wished to do so, but would not see itself and its resources absorbed by a collective buffer stock. Second, countries would have the option of contributing to particular buffer stocks if they did not wish to contribute to the common fund. Finally, individual commodity agreements could operate other policy instruments, such as export controls, which

12. Third Ministerial Meeting of the Group of 77, 26 January–2 February 1976, "Manila Declaration and Program of Action," (77/MM[III]/49), 7 February 1976.

13. Secretary General of UNCTAD, "An Integrated Programme for Commodities," UNCTAD Documents TD/B/C.1/166 and TD/B/C.1/166/Supplements 1–6. All were issued in December 1974.

would be very difficult to operate through a collective agreement.

Behind the idea for linking buffer stocks together through a common financial fund is the hypothesis that as prices of some commodities are going up, prices of others will be going down. Thus when some buffer stocks will be borrowing from the common fund to finance purchases, those for other commodities will be selling, and obtaining funds with which to pay back their previous borrowings from the common fund. By taking advantage of such "complementarities" in commodity price movements, it is hypothesized that the total resource needs of a program to stabilize prices of several commodities will be less than the total resource needs of the same program if each of the individual buffer stocks was financed autonomously.

The Secretariat proposal includes three other elements not related to the common fund buffer stock proposal. They include a system of advance commodity purchase and sale commitments by governments, and the revision and expansion of the International Monetary Fund's (IMF) compensatory finance facility. Since the proposal for advance purchase and sales commitments would require what amounts to state trading by market economy countries, there seems little chance that it will be implemented. And because major changes in the IMF compensatory finance facility were announced in December of 1975, it is not likely that further changes will be considered in the near future.

The other element called for by the integrated program is the implementation of measures to diversify the economies of commodity exporting countries, both vertically into the processing of these commodities, and horizontally, into the exportation of other commodities, including manufactured goods. This element will be taken up in the concluding part of this section.

The means proposed by the Secretariat, buffer stocks, suggests that the objective is to reduce instability, rather than to attempt to change the secular trend of commodity prices. Buffer stocks can, if they are sufficiently large and are skillfully operated, reduce the volatility of commodity prices. But unless each stock was continually provided with additional financing, so that it could continuously buy and never sell, it cannot affect long-run price movements. To raise long-run commodity prices would require an instrument such as export or production controls.

Evaluation · 1. The question of supporting commodity prices. It is clear that the UNCTAD Secretariat has avoided the issue of price supporting agreements,[14] and has concentrated on proposals to stabilize prices. The reason for this was probably that price-support proposals would meet with strong objections from the developed countries, so that their inclusion in the program would prevent acceptance of the proposals to stabilize prices. While there are indirect references to "restrictions on supplies," there are no proposals as to how commodity agreements might, in the long run, support commodity prices above market-determined levels. It should also be noted that no such proposals were introduced at UNCTAD IV.

Except for the analysis of whether specific proposals to support prices would actually work, the issue of supporting prices has little economic content. Economic theory long ago established that direct transfers are a more efficient means than price supports for transferring income from buyer to seller. Furthermore, LDCs' sales to developed countries account for less than 25 per cent of the value of world production of commodities on the UNCTAD list. Hence, most of the income transferred by supporting the prices of these commodities would be transferred within developed countries. The issue for developed country participation in price-supporting commodity agreements is thus whether consumers-taxpayers will be willing to make (or can be fooled into making) transfers in this inefficient form which they are not willing to make in the direct form of foreign aid. Economic analysis can shed little light on this question, but the growth in the North of consumerism as a political force leads us to suspect that the answer is negative.

Perhaps the most constructive result of UNCTAD IV is that in not taking up indexation as a substantive issue, it may have set a precedent for leaving this issue an exclusively rhetorical one. No issue in the North-South dialogue has greater potential to divide. The South views indexation as a moral issue, while the North sees it as an inflationary economic instrument. These completely

14. There are occasional mentions of "equitable" prices, of "policing restrictions on supplies," and of indexation of commodities' prices to prices of manufactured goods (ibid., TD/183, pp. 31f).

different views leave little possibility for compromise. Further, the technical problems of implementation would be enormous, and could raise issues which would destroy the emerging solidarity of the Third World. Would indexation mean that increases as well as decreases of commodity prices would be eliminated? If, as indicated by the report of the UNCTAD expert group on the terms of trade, as many relative commodity prices increase over the long run as decrease, indexation would result in a transfer to commodity producers from other commodity producers. Another point is that if there is sufficient market power to control the price of a commodity, the producers of that commodity will seek to set the price which exploits this market power to a maximum. Only by accident would this price be equal to a price resulting from an essentially arbitrary terms-of-trade calculation. It seems then that progress on economic issues would be facilitated by continuing to leave indexation off the list of substantive (as opposed to rhetorical) issues.

2. Will the proposed stocks stabilize prices? Of the commodity agreements which are presently in operation, only the tin agreement has operated a buffer stock. Evaluations by Smith and Schink[15] and by Desai[16] agree that the tin buffer stock has had little, if any, effect on the stability (or the level) of the price of tin. Further, these studies conclude that the buffer stock has been much too small to stabilize prices effectively. Large-scale simulations of the world tin market indicate that to have kept price movements over 1956–73 to within ± 15 per cent a year, a buffer stock of some 120,000 metric tons (worth over $1 billion at present, low prices) would have been necessary. By contrast, the tin agreement buffer stock has never reached 20,000 metric tons.

Simulations of the world copper market also indicate that buffer stocks would have to be much larger than has been previously supposed. Such research[17] indicates that to maintain price movements within the range ± 15 per cent a year over the period

15. G. Smith and G. Schink, "International Tin Agreement: A Reassessment," *Economic Journal* 86 (December 1976): 715–28.

16. M. Desai, "An Econometric Model of the World Tin Economy," *Econometrica* 34 (January 1966): 105–34.

17. G. Smith, "An Economic Evaluation of International Buffer Stocks for Copper," U.S. State Department, Bureau of Intelligence and Research, Contract 1722–620008. (August 1975).

1956–73, a copper buffer stock of nearly 4 million metric tons, worth well over $6 billion at present depressed prices, would have been necessary.

Thus buffer stocks for tin and copper alone would require almost three times the $3 billion common fund which the Secretariat has proposed to finance buffer stocks for ten to eighteen commodities.

Available evidence indicates that there are small, if any, economies of scale to be exploited by an integrated program covering several commodity markets rather than autonomous, market-by-market, agreements. Labys and Perrin have examined the pattern of covariation of commodity price movements, and concluded, "When we turn to the ten [core] commodities selected by UNCTAD, the found pattern of price correlations again does not conform to initial expectations."[18]

The tin and copper market simulations referred to above also indicate that stabilization would sometimes require that the buffer stock remain on the same side of the market for five to six years. This does not constitute an economic argument against buffer stocks—it shows only that price cycles in these markets sometimes have unexpectedly long frequencies. But it does suggest that considerable political resolve will be necessary if buffer stocks are to perform their economic functions—sufficient to allow the buffer stock to continuously buy or continuously sell for long periods. If this economic necessity caused the commodity agreement to come apart politically, the net effect could be destabilization rather than partial stabilization.

There is another reason why the proposed program might destabilize commodity prices. Krause has argued that "too small" buffer stocks might destabilize commodity prices rather than partially stabilize them.[19] If a buffer stock were too small to prevent cyclical price movements, it would tend to provide speculators with a one-way bet, as is provided by a central bank which attempts to defend an exchange rate that the exchange market

18. W. C. Labys and Y. Perrin, "Multivariate Analysis of Price Aspects of Commodity Stabilization," Geneva, Graduate Institute of International Studies (1975), p. 10.

19. Lawrence B. Krause, "The Theory of Exhaustible Resources and International Commodity Agreements," paper presented to the Southern Economics Association Meetings, New Orleans, 14 November 1975.

considers inappropriate. Thus, even if political will holds strong, half a buffer stock may be worse than none at all.

3. Would stabilization contribute to the development effort? Even if the proposed buffer stock program would stabilize commodity prices it still does not follow that implementation of such a program is in the interests of the developing countries. Stabilization must be viewed not as an end, but as a means, designed to promote economic development. Yet extensive investigation has failed to verify the once conventional wisdom that export instability has a retarding influence on investment or on economic growth.

MacBean, who analyzed the experience of the 1950s, found no evidence to support that conventional hypothesis. Contrary to his own expectations, he discovered a statistically significant and positive relation between export instability and the rate of investment growth.[20] Similar results for different time periods have been published by Kenen and Voivodas.[21]

Knudsen and Parnes[22] also found that export instability correlates significantly and positively with the rate of investment growth and with the rate of growth in GNP. Their analysis indicates that export (and earnings) instability decreases the average propensity to consume; it thereby increases savings, and allows higher rates of investment and economic growth. Thus, not only do their results confirm earlier findings that the relation between export instability and economic growth is probably positive, and certainly not negative, but they provide a rational explanation of why this is the case.[23]

4. Conclusions. In sum, a substantial amount of empirical analysis indicates that export earnings stability does not contrib-

20. Alasdair MacBean, *Export Instability and Economic Development* (Cambridge, Mass.: Harvard University Press, 1966), Chap. 4.

21. P. B. Kenen and C. S. Voivodas, "Export Instability and Economic Growth," *Kyklos* 25 (Fasc. 4, 1972).

22. Odin Knudsen and Andrew Parnes, *Trade Instability and Economic Development* (Lexington, Mass.: D. C. Heath, 1975), Chap. 6.

23. Knudsen and Parnes, ibid., Chap. 1, as well as Harry G. Johnson, *Economic Policies toward Less Developed Countries* (Washington, D.C.: Brookings Institution, 1967), p. 143, point out that earlier work by Coppock, *International Economic Instability* and M. Michaely, *Concentration in International Trade* (Amsterdam: North-Holland, 1962) are consistent with these findings.

ute to economic growth, i.e., that export earnings stability is a luxury for government officials who manage the foreign accounts, not a necessity in the development process. It is therefore not in the developing countries' interests to allocate $3 billion to a program which has a good chance of not working, and even if it did, would probably have no effect on the development process Likewise, insisting that agreements be negotiated to transfer income by supporting commodity prices is an unproductive use of the political resources of the developing countries. If the developed countries were of a mood to make such transfers, more efficient means to do so could be found.

This does not mean that no progress is possible. As in the area of manufactured goods, there are many possibilities for reciprocal actions of mutual benefit to the developed and developing countries. The proposal made at UNCTAD IV by then Secretary of State Henry Kissinger reflected the developed world's interest in promoting investments in commodity production in the developing countries. Reservations have been expressed about the means Secretary Kissinger proposed, but even though there is disagreement over means, the potential of the mutual interest of the developing and developed countries in increased investment in the developing countries should be exploited. There is some evidence that diversification (the final element in the UNCTAD Secretariat proposal) tends to reduce export instability.[24] If the common fund were an investment fund rather than a buffer stock fund, and if it operated in such a way as to promote diversification, as well as expansion of LDCs' production, it might promote both the stabilization and the increase of LDCs' export earnings. In trading away their demands for commodity agreements, the LDCs would be giving up a means which does not have much to contribute to the development effort.

The developed countries' interest in promoting investment in the developing countries might also be linked with the developing countries' interest in reducing tariff escalation on processed goods. And if the developing countries could bring themselves to accept the considerable evidence which shows that they are competitive in international markets for a number of manufactured

24. B. F. Massell, "Export Instability and Economic Structure," *American Economic Review* 60 (September 1970): 618–30.

goods on which they themselves still have high tariffs, they might view reciprocal action at the MTN as an effective way to reduce tariff escalation on processed commodities.

NON-TRADE RELATED ISSUES

Although this survey is concerned primarily with trade-related issues it is of interest to review, albeit briefly, the entire spectrum of LDC complaints.

A long-standing concern of the developing countries has been the need to accelerate the transfer of resources from the industrial world. LDCs would like economic aid to reach the avowed goal (adopted by the United Nations) of 1 per cent of GNP of the donor countries, with the official aid component being at 0:7 per cent of GNP. Instead, official aid has declined to 0:3 per cent of GNP of the donor countries. LDCs also wish for the real value of financial assistance to rise by untying foreign aid from purchases in the particular donor country regardless of prices. Next, the large and rising amount of service payments on their foreign debt has become a real burden on their economies, as a substantial proportion of their foreign currency earnings, must be devoted to debt service. At the end of 1975, the official external debt of 88 non-oil producing developing countries added up to $90 billion, and their total external debt was estimated at $135 billion. More than a quarter of the total is held by private banking institutions. For all LDCs the cost of servicing the external debt is between 10 and 13 per cent of the value of their exports and for many of them it exceeds 20 per cent of their export earnings. LDCs demand either forgiveness of that debt or alternatively some long-term arrangement that would alleviate the servicing burden. But any action of that nature must be considered carefully, for it may undermine the credit standing of LDCs and hamper their ability to secure future loans on the private credit markets. In the last few years LDCs—especially the more advanced among them—have made extensive commercial borrowing, e.g., on the Eurodollar market. Holsen and Waelbroeck[25] estimate that without such borrowing the GNP of these

25. J. Holsen and J. Waelbroeck, "The LDC's and the International Monetary Mechanism," *American Economic Review* 66 (May 1976): 176.

LDCs would be 7 per cent lower than it is. No wonder these countries are reluctant to jeopardize their access to capital markets, and countries such as Brazil are opposed to negotiating the renunciation of all or part of this debt. Finally, the 25 countries identified by UNCTAD, on the basis of several criteria, as the least developed among the developing countries require special aid provisions to suit their own circumstances.

It is interesting to note that the OPEC countries, whose oil price increase had a devastating effect on the welfare and the development prospects of many LDCs, have not come under a sharp attack at the United Nations and elsewhere. LDC demands are generally directed at the West, which traditionally lent them more receptive ears, than either the Eastern block or the newly rich OPEC nations.

In discussing the international currency system, LDCs display a strong perference for a return to stable or fixed exchange rates among the currencies of the developed countries. Although most LDCs peg their currencies to that of a major industrial country (mainly the dollar) or to a basket of major currencies (such as SDRs), such pegging necessarily means that they float along with the pegged currency in terms of all other major currencies. These fluctuations add risk to their international transactions, and in the absence of well-developed forward exchange markets, their traders find it impossible to insure against such risks. Next, currency fluctuations affect the real value of their international reserves. And, in general, they lack adequate expertise for managing their affairs under, and taking advantage of, opportunities offered by a floating rate system. However, all these deficiencies can be remedied over time. Experts can be trained; forward exchange markets can be developed privately or the central bank can offer forward cover (as the Philippines did in winter 1975); and reserves can be diversified and managed so as to avoid losses in their real value.

Another reason for preferring fixed rates is the LDCs' hopes for a link betwen reserve creation and foreign assistance (secured by allocating to the LDCs a disproportionately large share of any new reserves created by the International Monetary Fund) which would insure an adequate amount of untied, non-political, economic aid. Since under floating rates little reserves need be created, any possible link arrangement would not result in large payments to the LDCs. However, considering the technical problems and especially the political opposition in the industrial countries to the link proposal, it is doubtful whether any meaningful arrangement would have come into being even under fixed exchange rates.

What the LDCs often overlook is the potential benefits to them derived from freeing the industrial countries from the balance-of-payments constraint. Under the fixed-exchange-rate system balance-of-payment deficits often led to political "solutions" such as import restrictions or curtailment of foreign aid and investments. The U.S. measures introduced in August 1971 are a case in point. Indeed, such restrictions often have a disproportionate effect on LDCs, because the industrial countries can exert more political and economic counter-pressure to prevent such measures from being placed on their exports.

In other areas, LDCs demand greater access to the financial markets of the West, and to Western technology. Both desires can best be satisfied by providing a welcoming climate to multinational corporations (MNC). For despite the recent heavily publicized abuses (which can and should be guarded against in the future) the MNC is the best vehicle for the transfer of technological and managerial knowhow, as well as of capital. Indeed, the visitor to many an LDC is struck by their own overwhelming desire for foreign investments. If the MNC is an instrument of exploitation, as it is sometimes alleged, then many LDCs are willing and even anxious victims. They must certainly be regarded as the best judges of their own interests.

CONCLUSION: PLACING MATTERS IN PERSPECTIVE

Most of the rhetoric about the new international economic order reduces to proposals affecting North-South trade and aid relations. It is a series of means designed to attain certain general objectives. But a close inspection of the proposals—executed with full sympathy to the aspirations of the LDCs for a better economic lot—leads to two conclusions. They are not revolutionary enough to deserve the flashy title ("New Order") assigned to them. And more importantly, in each case they are judged to be either economically ineffective or politically non-feasible in moving the world toward the advocated goals. The political problem arises from the fact that practically every ingredient of the proposed New Order—be it the GSP, the integrated commodity program, or increased foreign aid—depends exclusively on the economic altruism of the industrial countries. While the record of past performance indicates that this altruism does exist, this record also shows that it is not likely to be forthcoming to the degree desired by the LDCs. More critically, such policies would continue and intensify LDC dependence on the industrial countries, while one of the goals of the new economic order is to reduce this dependence. Yet in practically every case there are means available to attain the proclaimed objectives which are likely to be economically more productive and which would, in political terms, create mutually beneficial interdependence rather than one-way dependence.

But the proposals which are nowadays the center of global debate do damage in another important respect. For they center worldwide attention on the external sector of the LDCs (mainly on the part of that sector that relates to the industrial countries) and thereby divert attention from the far more crucial issue of internal development policies.

Economic development is essentially a process of internal transformation of society. It requires political stability, social mobility, economic incentives, and many other socio-economic characteristics that were prevalent in Western society during its industrialization. It also requires time—probably more time than the impatient Third World is willing to allow. Thus, for the most part, economic development is something that the developing countries must do for themselves. What the outside world can do for them —which is what the fuss is all about—is of peripheral importance. The important thing is for them to achieve self-sustained growth and to become better by producing more at home. Their final objective is, or should be, to support an acceptably high standard of living through their own productivity, rather than by continuous reliance on the infusion of foreign resources. Foreign assistance via the aid, investments, or trade route can render a temporary relief from poverty, but cannot by itself affect a fundamental change. All this is not to suggest that aid and trade are useless. They do add to resources available for development; they do contribute to technological transfer; they do tend to promote efficiency through specialization; and mere exposure to the international economy has a stimulating impact on development.

But it does mean that any foreign assistance can only be of secondary importance; that it can only supplement and spur on the internal efforts; that by itself it is of little value in bringing about permanent change to a point where the economy takes off on its own; and most emphatically, that the industrial world cannot be blamed for the failures of the developing countries to progress. It is indeed natural to find scapegoats and try to blame others for ones own failures. But in this case such an indictment is worse than being unjust. Looking for faults elsewhere means that the developing countries will do less than what is optimal to clean up their own houses.

Even in the trade and investment areas, the harm that the LDCs inflict upon themselves exceeds what the developed nations do to them. For example, very steep and highly variable import duties (as between commodities), designed to facilitate "import substitution to the hilt" cause gross misallocation of resources, discriminate against exports, and result in widespread production at negative value added. Having pursued such an import policy, LDC policy-makers proceed to wonder why the multinational companies attracted to invest in them have a strong preference toward producing for the (heavily protected) domestic market, as against the export market. Equally important waste results when an LDC establishes a final assembly plant as a part of an import substitution policy, and at a second stage proceeds to "deepen" the production process by producing intermediate inputs (to the final assembly) at home under heavy protection. For by doing so it lowers the effective protection on the final good, and makes its assembly unprofitable to operate.

It is doubly in the interest of the LDCs to lower their level of protection (and make it uniform across commodities). First it would facilitate at least a partial shift in their approach to development: away from extreme forms of import substitution and toward export promotion. That such a shift would be helpful has been demonstrated time and time again in studies comparing the experience of countries pursuing each approach. It is invariably shown that LDCs following the export-promotion approach develop faster than those bent on import substitution. (Although it is not our intent to advocate either of the two approaches in its extreme form.) Second, in the process of liberalizing their imports, the LDCs could offer concessions to the developed countries in exchange for which they would obtain reciprocal tariff reduction on products of interest to them. It is simply not in the LDCs' interest—on both sides of the trade equation—to remain on the sidelines of GATT negotiations. An active role in the reciprocal bargaining process would be to their advantage.

This discussion is designed to emphasize that the debate about a "New Economic Order" concerns essentially subsidiary issues, albeit important ones, in the development effort. However, while that may absolve the industrial West of responsibility for past failures in the development field, it does not mean that we should be oblivious to the plight of the other half. The Western democracies have a tradition of helping the poor, and being responsive to the needs of the developing world. It is indeed significant that the socialist states (and for that matter the OPEC countries), render very little assistance of pure economic value (as against military aid or political show-off aid), nor are they a major target of criticism from the developing world, partly because their response is likely to be short on action and long on political rhetoric. The West should continue the laudable tradition of being receptive and responsive to the plight of poor nations. But it should insist that the aid and trade measures be economically efficient in promoting LDC growth.

PART THREE: Foreign Investment and the Multinational Corporation

Problems and Policies Regarding Multinational Enterprises

RAYMOND VERNON

Raymond Vernon is professor at the Harvard Business School. In this essay, written for the Commission on International Trade and Investment, he examines ways and means for reducing tensions which the existence of multinational enterprises generates.

THE TITLE OF this paper requires a word or two of amplification. Problems, as is well known, are in the eye of the beholder; what is a problem from government's point of view is often an advantage from the point of view of the enterprises; and what is a problem from the enterprises' point of view may be a solution on the part of government.

The object of this paper is to define the problems as perceived by the various interested parties and to develop programs and policies that may be responsive. The proposals set out here are based on a number of fundamental propositions. The first of these is that the multinational enterprise has a substantial contribution to make to global welfare, if welfare is measured in economic terms. The second proposition is that many of the expressions of concern over the economic consequences of these enterprises, such as the views about their balance-of-payment effects and employment effects, are not supported by the facts. The third proposition, however, is that not all parties affected by the multinational enterprises' operations necessarily benefit equally, or indeed necessarily benefit at all; the sharing of economic benefits between the host country and the United States and between management, capital, and labor depends on the circumstances. Finally, the clearest problems generated by the existence of the multinational enterprise are political and psychological; they stem from the fact that the multinational enterprise, as seen through the eyes of those that have to deal with it, often seems threatening in its relative flexibility and strength. The challenge is to develop policies that deal with these problems effectively while leaving room for the multinational enterprise to make its creative contribution.

THE HOST COUNTRY VIEW

There is, of course, no single point of view on the part of host countries with respect to multinational enterprises. Some countries, such as Belgium and Thailand, seem reasonably comfortable with the presence of the foreign-owned subsidiaries of U.S. parents. Others, such as France and Japan, are much more uneasy at the possibility of a significant increase in U.S. interests. The generalizations that follow, therefore, need to be tailored to the individual case. Nonetheless, there are some generalizations that seem appropriate for host countries. And there are some differences between countries whose underlying causes seems fairly clear.

The Challenge of Elites · The subsidiaries of U.S. parent companies cannot move into an economy in significant number without affecting the relative position of various elite groups within that economy: government leaders, businessmen, and intellectuals. The impact on those groups has a good deal to do with the reactions encountered in different countries.

Consider first of all the situation in less-developed countries at the early stages of their growth. In those very early stages, foreign-owned subsidiaries have commonly been welcomed by the preponderance of the local leadership. The welcome was somewhat more unqualified before World War II than since. Its quality also was affected by the circumstances—often accidental and idiosyncratic in character—under which the country received its independence. Ex-colonial powers which gained their independence by struggle have tended to be chary of foreign-owned investments, while countries that acquired their independence more peacefully tended to be less resistant to foreign investment. Countries that chose "socialism," following the charisma of their first post-independence leaders, have been rather less forthcoming toward foreign investors than others; witness the case of Guinea and Tanzania versus that of the Ivory Coast and the Congo. At any rate, if the country concerned did extend some sort of welcome to the foreign investor in the early stages of its existence, that welcome gradually tended to become more equivocal and more qualified with the passage of time. Among the reasons for this shift was the changing position of various elite groups.

During the early stages of the development process, there were few among the local elite to whom foreign investors seemed threatening. Among government leaders, the need for help in launching the process of development generally transcended other considerations. Among local businessmen, the opportunity to become the provisioners or customers of the foreign enterprise were more important than the threat of confronting foreign competitors.

The positions of the government elite and of the industrial elite, however, changed in the course of time. Government officials gradually became unhappy as their needs for revenue exceeded the amounts being generated by the foreign-owned ventures, and as their sense of dependence seemed to grow. Local businessmen, meanwhile, came to acquire ambitions that extended beyond the role of mere provisioner and customer, to the role of partner and competitor.

As for the intellectual leaders outside of government and business, in the less-developed countries, their disposition to welcome the appearance of foreign-owned enterprises was generally more qualified from the very first. Even when local official and local business attitudes were cordial, an undercurrent of dissent among the intellectual often existed. The role assumed by leaders of the university and of the press in many less-developed countries was the role of the outside critic. From the opposition viewpoint, the appearance of the foreign investors represented a force that could well entrench the government and its supporters. The intellectuals could generally be counted on, therefore, to resist the entry of foreign investment.

Today, there is scarcely an underdeveloped country in which intellectuals have not raised a voice of strong dissent against foreign investors as a class. Significant protests have appeared in Ghana, Nigeria, India, Chile, Mexico, Brazil, Malaysia, Turkey, Pakistan, and the Philippines, among others. The reaction is not confined to the less-developed world, however; it is to be found also in Canada and many countries of Europe. There are a few countries in which the prevailing mood in intellectual circles does not run strongly in this direction; but they are only a few, including Britain and Holland, for instance. Even in such friendly countries, however, there is some wistful or purposeful speculation over the possibilities of converting multinational enterprises to structures that are more local in character without losing the benefits of multinationality.

The Challenge to Ideologies · It is not easy to draw the line between a threat to personal position and a threat to a deeply held ideology. Some of the resistance of elites in host countries, especially those in underdeveloped economies, may well be more ideological than personal.

The ideological basis on which foreign-owned investment is resisted goes back a long way. Some of it is Marxist-Leninist in its underpinnings. Much more, however, is nationalistic in nature, even when it uses the language and concepts of Marxist ideology.

The ideological assertions regarding the impact of multinational enterprises tend to change over time, in order to keep abreast of changes in the multinational enterprises themselves. In Latin America, for instance, it was generally assumed until the mid-1950's that foreign investors were interested solely in the exploitation of raw materials and could not be persuaded to invest extensively in manufacturing facilities. Because of that assumption, it was easy to link the drawbacks of foreign investment to the drawbacks of raw material exporting. These links were provided by the well-known propositions of the Economic Commission for Latin America and of Raul Prebisch, according to which countries that specialized in exporting raw materials suffered from deteriorating terms of trade, immiserating growth, and so on.

When it became evident in the late 1950's that foreign-owned investment was going extensively into the manufacturing industries, the ideological rationalization shifted. The argument against the foreign-owned investment then began to take the form of a protest against the exploitation or the low-wage situation of the country. Subsequently, when it became clear that as a rule foreign-owned investors paid more than prevailing local wages, the argument was developed that these excess payments were being used to buy out the industrial working class and to abort their proper role as members of a revolutionary proletariat. In addition, there was growing protest that the local partners in joint ventures were becoming indigenous Robber Barons in their respective economies.

The assumption in most quarters during the late 1950's also had been that foreign-owned manufacturing subsidiaries could only be persuaded to engage in import-substitution for the local market, and could not be persuaded to export. Today, as it is beginning to grow clear that foreign-owned subsidiaries are exporting manufactured products in some volume, the argument is shifting once again. It is pointed out that the exported products, being standardized and price-sensitive as a rule, have many of the economic characteristics of raw materials and hence are poor media for improving the long-run export position of the less-developed countries.

There are various lessons to be drawn from this recital. One of them is that the tension generated by foreign-owned subsidiaries is to some extent independent of what it does; that the overt rationalizations for the existence of the tension will shift as the function of the subsidiary shifts. One must probe beneath the overt rationalizations, therefore, to find more deep-seated causes of the tension.

The Clash of Cultures · Part of the tension, it may well be, has deep-seated cultural roots. That possibility is better illustrated in the case of a number of advanced countries, where extensive studies of the cultural background offer rich materials on which to test this general proposition. Let me illuminate the point by reviewing briefly some of the differences in business-government relations between the United States, the United Kingdom, France, and Japan.

In the case of the United States, there have been a number of persistent threads in the long history of business-government relations which distinguish this country from most other advanced economies.

The first of these is the relatively high social status of businessmen in U.S. society; as the Horatio Alger novels attest, the theme of the successful businessman as a folk-hero has been exceedingly strong in U.S. culture for a very long time. On the other hand, in classic Hegelian contradiction, there has been a deep-seated mistrust in the United States toward the concentration of economic power that big business was thought to represent. This mistrust has manifested itself in numerous ways in U.S. political history, from the passage of the Sherman Act and the Clayton Act on the one hand, to the promulgation of the Public Utility Holding Company Act on the other.

Against this background, the general U.S. approach toward the regulation of business transactions has been either to leave them alone or to prohibit them. Although some areas of business activity have been subjected to detailed regulations, the regulatory approach is a good deal less important in the United States than it is elsewhere. Where regulation does exist, the regulatory style of U.S. government agencies, is mechanistic, nondiscriminatory, and arms' length, as compared with the style of other countries. All of these elements are important, but the arms' length quality is especially so.

It would be reckless to attempt to explain the arms' length quality of U.S. administration in cultural terms. For present purposes, it is only necessary to point out that U.S. businessmen confront a governmental apparatus that is extraordinarily fractionated and diffused, as compared with most other modern states. All three branches of the U.S. government have some power to legislate, adjudicate, and execute. That fact, coupled with the distribution of relevant powers between the states and the federal government, makes it exceedingly difficult for the public and the private sector to collaborate on a very broad basis. There are some rather obvious exceptions, of course: the regulated industries such as the airlines; the major defense contractors, such as the airframe producers; and to a more limited extent, the major oil companies. By comparison with other countries, however, these exceptions do not cover a very wide area.

There is a widespread notion, both at home and abroad, that a close collaboration exists between U.S. industry on the one hand and U.S. government on the other, forming collectively an expensive force bent on gaining control of the world economy. That impression is grossly at variance with the actual facts. But from time to time the policies of the United States have lent support to this widespread perception: by the landing of the marines in distant countries once or twice every decade; by the passage of legislation such as the Hickenlooper Amendment; and by various other measures that would be consistent with the collaboration theory. Even a small amount of collaborative behavior between business and government can be frightening to other nations, if the collaboration is undertaken by such great powers as the U.S. government and U.S. business overseas.

Business-government relations in the United Kingdom display some obvious similarities to those in the United States. The capacity of the United Kingdom to tolerate U.S.-controlled investments without much tension may stem in part from those similarities. True, there are marked differences in such relations as well; but these differences are small as compared with most other countries.

The British, for instance, share some of the U.S. distaste for privilege and monopoly on the part of business. True, their responses to problems of this sort have been later, milder, and more equivocal than those of the United States. When eventually they began to appear in a series of enactments beginning with the Restrictive Practices Acts of 1948, they reflected a much less doctrinaire view of the nature of "undesirable" restraints of trade and "undesirable" monopolies. But they represented a view that was shared on both sides of the Atlantic.

In one fundamental respect, the British environment and the U.S. environment are nearly identical. In both cases, there is a basic presumption shared by both business and government that governmental regulatory powers will normally be applied on a non-discriminatory basis—that discrimination, preference, and the chosen-instrument approach represent the exceptional case, not the preferred state. This approach sits well with the arms' length habits and expectations of U.S. business.

One difference of some significance between the British approach and the U.S. approach to business-government relations is the greater reliance of the British on voluntary schemes of business regulation. The British are conditioned to the view that any class of enterprise which for a long time has exercised some kind of prerogative in the economy, whatever the basis for that prerogative, presumptively ought to be allowed to continue to practice its acquired rights. On the other hand, there is a constraining proposition which accompanies this approach: the view that anybody that has such rights should not abuse them. As a result, "voluntary" controls schemes are much more common, more feasible, and more effective in the British environment than in the United States.

The differences between U.S. practice and U.K. norms are especially marked in one field—in that of external relations. Here the long British tradition, under which the flag has tended to follow trade, still seems to have some vestigial influence. In any event, the degree of collaboration between British business and British government outside of Britain is very much closer than that in the case of the United States.

Moving from the British case to the French case, the similarities with the United States decrease while the differences grow large. In this instance, the U.S. businessman encounters a set of relationships that are almost wholly foreign to his experience.

In France, both the concept of an arms' length relationship and the notion of non-discrimination in the exercise of governmental power evaporate. To be sure, businessmen have rights; but they are rights that depend upon an explicit and formal grant from the state, not upon any general presumption in favor of non-interference or non-discrimination. Moreover, until recently, innovation and change were not regarded as a virtue when initiated by businessmen. Quite the contrary. The emphasis was on harmony and stability, rather than on growth and profit. A great deal of that sentiment still remains, as part of the background of relations between French business and French government. When initiatives were forthcoming from the government in order to induce change, as has commonly been the case, resort to the use of chosen instruments has been perfectly easy and natural, violating no deeply held convictions to the contrary on the part of the French public.

In the range of country cases considered here, Japan sits at the far extreme from the United States. Reams have been written about the outstanding characteristics of contemporary Japanese culture. That culture incorporates some concepts that have proved extraordinarily useful in an industrial society, including a widespread commitment to goal attainment and a concept of shared responsibility within any group assigned to achieve a given goal. The limits of "the group," however, are much more readily visible to the Japanese eye than to that of the outsider. Sometimes the group is a family; sometimes an industry; and sometimes—especially in matters that relate to negotiations with foreigners—the whole of the Japanese economy.

The line that is drawn between the public and the private sector in Japan is not nearly as clear as in many Western countries. From the very first, economic tasks assigned to the two sectors have been determined pragmatically, rather than on the basis of some deep-seated ideology. Business leaders have readily become ministers in government; and ministers have easily returned to business. This process has not been accompanied by any of the soul-searching and the conflict-of-interest questions that arise when similar events occur in the United States.

Today, as is well known, the policies of Japanese business and Japanese government are coordinated largely through two institutions: the banking system and the Ministry of International Trade and Industry (MITI). For external purposes, MITI puts up a common front, on the basis of policies that are worked out with Japanese industry. Once that front is created, it is exceedingly difficult for any foreigner to negotiate independently with any Japanese entity.

There are a number of generalizations to be drawn from these brief observations. The capacity of each of these cultures to tolerate outsiders runs in the order in which they are presented: from the United States to the U.K. to France to Japan. The Japanese find it particularly difficult to tolerate the existence within the Japanese society of someone who is not a part of "the group." The extent to which governments are selective in their treatment of business firms runs in roughly the same order. The United States is least capable of being selective in its handling of business, while the Japanese are probably most capable in engaging in such selectivity. There is a similar ranking in the degree to which nationals are monitored by their respective governments when such nationals engage in major activities outside the boundaries of their country. In this case, again, the United States is at the low end of the monitoring activity, while Japan is at the high end of such activity.

In sum, the tension generated by the presence of U.S. enterprises seems highest where the differences between the norms of the local culture and the U.S. are greatest. As long as those differences persist, as they surely will, tension may be the normal state of being.

CONTROL AND JURISDICTION

So far the emphasis has been on the special issues that generate tension in the host countries. But the tension that follows in the trail of multinational enterprise operations is not limited to host countries. It also appears from time to time in the United States. What are these more general sources of difficulty?

Loss of Control · The multinational enterprise is perceived by those that deal with it as an entity with an extraordinary capacity for flexibility and choice. It is thought capable of choosing between different locations for the establishment of production and research facilities, for the allocation of markets, for the storing of its surplus funds, and so on. Stated another way, the multinational enterprise is thought of as mobile between national economies, while those with whom it bargains—including government and labor—are fixed to a particular piece of national real estate. The perception of mobility is probably exaggerated by those that do not share it; but there is not much doubt that such mobility does exist. Indeed, this element of choice is one of the major strengths of the multinational enterprise as a contributor to global welfare.

Nevertheless, this aspect of the operations of multinational enterprise adds to the unease not only of interests in the host countries but also of interests in the United States. Take some of the reactions of U.S. labor to the multinational enterprise. Labor economists are presumably well aware that the effect of freezing U.S. jobs in existing job patterns would eventually reduce U.S. incomes, pushing them toward the levels existing in other countries; that the essence of any U.S. strategy for maintaining the world's highest per capita income is to shift constantly out of the lines in which others can compete into those in which they cannot. It is one thing to accept that ineluctable proposition in the abstract; it is another however, to confront the business decision-maker across the bargaining table who seems to be charged with deciding when the shift will take place. Irrespective of the inevitability—even the desirability—of the shift in the long run, the short-run negotiating advantage that the representative of the multinational enterprise may appear to have is exceedingly difficult for any negotiator to endure.

The sense of uneasiness over the seeming options of multinational enterprise is not confined to American labor, however. It is also to be found in the reactions of other governments, with a degree of intensity that depends upon the capacity of the government to tolerate uncertainty. Accordingly, the Japanese and the French—who put heavy emphasis upon control and predictability in the economy—find the presence of the multinational enterprise less tolerable than, say, the British and the Dutch. There are some signs that the U.S. government itself from time to time feels uneasy over the operations of multinational enterprises, sensing the limits on its own control over their operations. These indications of uneasiness appear from time to time in the usual fields: antitrust, trading with the enemy, and capital movements.

The capacity of the multinational enterprise to choose among alternative locations generates a particularly acute form of uneasiness in connection with the rivalries of member countries that form part of a common market area. In the European Economic Community, for instance, the French have been particularly disturbed over the operations of multinational enterprises because of their fear that such enterprises, if discouraged from establishing themselves in France, would simply set up business in Belgium or Italy. In a similar vein, the Mexicans have been greatly concerned over the possibility that multinational enterprises might penetrate the Latin American Free Trade Area by subsidiaries established in, say, Colombia. The same kind of strain is visible from time to time in the Central American Common Market.

This special concern is a realistic reflection of the fact that multinational enterprises take the potential opportunities of free trade areas a good deal more seriously than do the national firms of the constituent countries. The reasons are evident: a U.S. firm that is setting up a subsidiary in the European Community has less reason for rejecting a location in, say, Sardinia than would a French firm that is already nicely settled in Lille or Nancy. By the same token, U.S.-owned enterprises that are setting up subsidiaries in foreign countries are much more responsive to local programs that offer subsidies for settling in backward areas of the country. As a result, governments find themselves paying embarassingly high proportions of their subsidy funds to foreign-owned subsidiaries.

The Problem of Jurisdictional Conflict · Every international transaction has two sides and, having two sides is subject to the reach of two different sovereigns. A state is unlikely to surrender control over its end of an international transaction, unless it is also prepared to accept the consequences that go with relinquishing control over the transaction.

The result is that governments are frequently involved in conflicts with regard to international transactions—transactions that one sovereign may want to promote and the other sovereign want to prevent. When the United States is one of those sovereigns, the measure of nervousness and resentment exhibited by the other side is greater than usual, given the relative size and strength of the U.S. economy. This issue, of course, is not one that is unique to the multinational enterprise. Its relation to the multinational enterprise is generated by the fact that such entities account for so high a proportion of international transactions.

There is another problem of overlapping jurisdictions, however, in which the multinational enterprise plays a very special role. From time to time, the U.S. government tries to influence the behavior not merely of the U.S. parent but also of other entities in the multinational enterprise structure, including overseas subsidiaries. In essence, that is what the United States was trying to do when it imposed capital export controls on overseas investments. In this case, the instructions issued to the parent were instructions that were intended to govern the behavior of the overseas subsidiary in such matters as the declaration of dividends, the remission of cash, the generation of imports, and so on. Much the same could be said with respect to the trading-with-the-enemy policies of the U.S. government; in these cases, the object was to oblige overseas subsidiaries to refrain from undertaking transactions with the enemy even when these transactions were perfectly acceptable to the host government. Another well-known illustration of the same problem has had to do with the antitrust laws. The U.S. government has found itself constantly reaching into the jurisdictions of other countries in order to influence the behavior of U.S.-controlled subsidiaries in those countries.

The antitrust laws have proved particularly irritating because at times the reach of the United States government has gone even further, seeking to affect the alleged foreign co-conspirators of U.S. firms, whatever the ownership of the co-conspirators might be. Although this effort at the extension of national jurisdiction is not in violation of accepted principles of international law, its application by the United States was deeply resented by other countries. That resentment was especially great on the part of those countries which thought of private agreements as desirable in the interests of stabilizing or rationalizing industrial activities within their borders.

Summing Up · The list of governmental concerns that have been elaborated in the last few pages could no doubt be matched by an equally persuasive list enumerating the advantages of multinational enterprises and the advantages of the consequences flowing from their existence. Although the presence of the U.S.-controlled subsidiary may represent a challenge to some of the elite groups in the host country, it also generates support for other elite groups; although the activities of the multinational enterprise may clash with some ideologies, it lends support to others; although it may be inconsistent with some strains of European culture, it may be helpful to others; although it may create impediments for rationalization policies in some European countries, it contributes to a more vigorous competition in other countries and other sectors. In a world that weighed benefits against costs on some objectively calibrated basis, it may be that governments would tend to take a more relaxed view toward U.S.-controlled enterprises. But reality is something else again. The presence of a large, imperfectly controlled foreign element, associated with considerable strength and flexibility, constitutes a source of psychic pain that is so strong in some countries as to overwhelm and cancel out any perceived benefits.

GOVERNMENT MEASURES

The measures that governments take in response to their perceived problems are the source of many of the grievances of multinational enterprises. Some governmental measures, of course, generate a larger sense of grievance than others. Practically all of them, insofar as they represent a narrowing of choice or a competitive burden for the foreign investor, constitute a source of grievance on his part.

One response of governments consists of excluding foreign-owned enterprises from certain areas of activity. Practically all countries, including the United States, sharply limit the right of foreign-owned subsidiaries to participate in industries such as ordnance and aircraft, public broadcasting, coastal shipping, banking, and minerals exploitation on public lands. France and Japan, among others, go much further. In the case of France, foreign-owned oil companies have been limited in their activities for nearly 50 years; and all foreign-owned enterprises have been systematically screened for the past 10 years. In Japan throughout its national life, drastic limitations were placed on foreign rights of entry; the recent trend toward liberalization in this regard has been undertaken with the utmost reluctance and has involved a series of very false starts. Even Britain and Germany, though associated with a relaxed attitude toward foreign-owned enterprises, have been exhibiting occasional misgivings over the intrusion of such enterprises in "sensitive" industries. That sensitivity occasionally manifests itself in the United States as well.[1]

Apart from prohibiting foreign investment in specified areas of activity, governments have commonly laid down conditions governing foreign investment in other areas. One common condition has been that the foreigners should take on local partners in joint ventures. The motivations for that condition have been mixed. In part, it has been assumed that joint ventures would function in the interests of the local economy more surely than wholly owned subsidiaries; but in part, the motivation has been to benefit members of the local industrial community by helping them acquire equity at bargain rates. The other requirements that have been placed on foreign-owned subsidiaries have included commitments to avoid the use of local credit, commitments to produce certain stated quantities of product, commitments to export a certain proportion of goods, commitments to train local labor up to management positions, and so on.

Official requirements that lay special conditions on foreign-owned subsidiaries are rapidly increasing in scope and character. As advanced nations have begun to develop explicit policies for the development of new industries, they have begun to dispense grants and subsidies in support of those policies. For example, subsidies have been dispensed in support of industrial research. In that case, understandably, governments as a rule have not been anxious to subsidize the research of U.S.-owned subsidiaries; accordingly, they have been careful to channel their funds to national enterprises that were locally owned. The same general policy has been followed with respect to the extension of credits for modernization and improvement of plants. It is quite clear, for instance, that the Industrial Reorganization Corporation in Great Britain and the Institut de Developpement Industriel in France would be loathe to direct their assistance to enterprises that were not indigenously owned.

More generally, the disposition of public agencies to favor locally owned producers is being formalized and strengthened in

1. Indeed, a leading U.S. congressman has expressed concern that, in view of the British government's large minority stock ownership in British Petroleum, the company's acquisition of Sohio in the United States could create a Trojan horse in the U.S. economy ("Europeans Irked by U.S. Trust Role," *New York Times*, October 13, 1969, p. 71).

many countries. This is especially evident, for instance, with regard to procurement polices, especially when the procurement involves advanced products. The United Kingdom and France discriminate overtly in the procurement of products such as computers and nuclear plants, while Japan goes a great deal further and excludes foreigners from supplying practically anything to government agencies. This policy is not to be confused with the U.S. "Buy American" policy, a policy which is directed at imports of foreign goods, not at those produced on U.S. soil. In the European and Japanese cases, the preference is extended to exclude domestic goods, if such domestic goods were produced in foreign-owned plants.

The disposition on the part of governments to distinguish between national corporations that are foreign owned and those that are locally owned goes even further in some cases. In the United Kingdom, it influences the views of the Monopolies Commission regarding the tolerability of monopolies in the local market. If the monopolies are local in ownership the tolerance of their existence is greater than if they are foreign owned.

Many of the countries that engage in practices of the sort just described have undertaken treaty commitments to grant national treatment to U.S.-owned enterprises in their jurisdictions. Some of these practices no doubt are inconsistent with such treaty obligations. But the pressures that are pushing governments in the direction of distinguishing foreign-owned corporations from those locally owned are too strong to be resisted on such grounds.

There is one more line of governmental action that generates a sense of grievance among multinational enterprises. This is the situation in which two governments, each eager to bend the activities of the multinational enterprise to serve its needs, issue directly conflicting demands to the management of the enterprise. A classic case was one in which the headquarters of a multinational enterprise received a communication from the U.S. Department of Commerce and one from the U.K. Board of Trade urging it simultaneously to increase its exports in both directions across the Atlantic.

But there are more serious cases of a similar sort. One has to do with conflicts among the states as to what constitutes taxable income. In some instances, these conflicts can generate levies upon a given source of income that are close to confiscatory levels.

Another instance, already suggested, involves action in the field of antitrust. There is no serious difficulty with cases in which U.S.-owned subsidiaries abroad are explicitly being directed by foreign governments to engage in some kind of restrictive action. The difficult cases are those in which the U.S. management knows that undertaking measures that would be pleasing to the host government runs the risk of generating an antitrust suit in the United States; or, conversely, that conforming to the pressures of the U.S. Antitrust Division would be displeasing to their overseas host governments. Finally, there is the case of capital export controls. Although I am not yet aware of any such case, I confidently anticipate the day when, by formal action, a foreign government will prohibit one of the U.S.-owned subsidiaries in its jurisdiction from conforming to the requirements of the U.S. government controls.

In sum, the concept that corporations acquired by foreigners stand in a different position under local law from corporations that are indigenously owned is gaining greatly in strength in many countries of the world. That concept is not altogether new, but the scope and variety of applications of the distinction are going very fast. If there is any element in the international situation that may yet lead the management of U.S.-controlled multinational enterprises to search for a new modus operandi, it will be the continued growth of this tendency.

RESPONSES TO THE PROBLEMS

The Question of Timing · All the main factors that have generated the problems associated with multinational enterprises promise to grow over the years. As transportation and communication improve in quality and decline in cost, enterprises will continue to expand their horizons; business opportunities and business threats will be more readily visible from long distances and will lead to quicker and more frequent international responses. Meanwhile, nation-states are likely to find themselves increasingly frustrated by the growing entanglements between their national economies and those of other countries, and by the limitations on their ability to control the forces that determine their economic and political future. Over the long run, therefore, the disposition to search for some new basis to regularize the activities of multinational enterprises promises to grow.

Over the shorter run, the proposals appear somewhat different. For the present, the less-developed countries are much too suspicious of the intentions and motives of the United States to engage in any joint efforts at regularizing the position of the multinational enterprises, except perhaps in terms of regional schemes for their control. And Europe is so preoccupied with broadening and developing the structure of the European Communities that it may seem for the present to have little time for much else.

The history of U.S. negotiations with the European Communities, however, suggests that their very process of internal negotiation will improve the conditions for external negotiation; that the problems they encounter in their internal deliberations will at times suggest the desirability of negotiation on their external relations. This could well be the case with regard to company law, taxation, and capital movements during the next few years. The question is whether the U.S. itself will then be in a position to know its own mind, to sense the opportunity for action, and to frame the necessary initiatives.

Reducing Tension: The Fair-Conduct Code · If the multinational enterprise is to have a chance to express its creative potentials fully in a global society, the tensions that are generated by its presence will have to be contained. There are numerous ways for trying to achieve that objective.

If there is any view common to the U.S.-controlled multinational enterprises regarding the appropriate line of response, it is the view that sensible businessmen can be relied upon to avoid business behavior that might prove itself destructive in the long run. Governmental action may be necessary to deal with a few special problems, according to this view; but agreements such as the long-standing International Convention for the Protection of Industrial Property or bilateral treaties to avoid double taxation are quite enough, according to this view, to deal with the intergovernmental aspects of the problem.

When spokesmen for U.S. business have deviated from this

general line, they have sometimes proposed that multinational enterprises might agree to adhere to a "code of fair conduct," including a commitment to adhere carefully to the provisions of local law, to respect local custom, to train local workers for responsible jobs, to support local social projects, and so on. The attraction of accepting such a code, from the viewpoint of many businessmen, stems from the fact that it fairly well describes their present behavior and requires few changes in practice or outlook. As a response to the tensions that have been described earlier, however, it is inadequate. Its inadequacy, of course, stems from the fact that it fails to see the problem as others see it.

Reducing Tension: The Divestiture Issue · Another approach, commonly espoused by host governments in less-developed countries and by some sources in the advanced countries, contemplates the eventual divestiture by multinational enterprises of their interests in local subsidiaries. The general assumption behind their proposals is that multinational enterprises perform a useful function at the time at which they set up any of their subsidiaries, but that the function declines over time. On this assumption, the object is to ensure that the multinational enterprise separates itself from the subsidiary at the time at which its net contribution to the host country begins to disappear.[2]

The facts regarding the operations of multinational enterprises abroad are not inconsistent with the assumption that benefits may decline over time. The trouble of course, is that a conclusion of this sort is much too simple. As long as multinational enterprises continue to broaden, deepen, and complicate their role in the subsidiaries that they establish in those countries, their contribution to those economies may be unending. A program of divestiture that cuts off this process could be hurtful to the governments that were demanding it.

2. A. O. Hirschman, *How to Divest in Latin America and Why?* (Princeton: Princeton University Press, 1969), Essays in International Finance, no. 76; P. N. Rosenstein-Rodan, *Multinational Investment in the Framework of Latin American Integration,* Report presented at the Round Table of the Board of Governors (Bogota, Colombia: Inter-American Development Bank April 1968), pp. 66–78. For a more qualified endorsement of the approach, see C. F. Carlos Diaz Alejandro, *Direct Foreign Investment in Latin America,* Center Paper no. 150 (Yale University, Economic Growth Center, 1970) pp. 334–36.

Another fundamental problem that reduces the practicability of a divestiture program is the great gap that often exists between the value of a subsidiary as part of a multinational enterprise system and the value of that same entity when separated from the system. An automobile assembly plant that is part of a multinational system may be of great value so long as it is attached to the system, but of little value once it is separated. This means that any effort to establish an appropriate price in connection with the divestiture will lead to major difficulties.

Still another question is whether any significant number of enterprises could be expected to set up their subsidiaries if they faced the possibility of eventual divestiture. It seems plausible to assume that in circumstances of this sort the foreign investors who went ahead would be those with the strongest penchant for quick profits and those with the weakest desire to enlarge the functions of the subsidiary.

But these are problems that are more appropriately the concern of the host country than of the multinational enterprise. It is for host countries to reckon whether the relaxation of tension associated with the prospect of ultimate divestiture is worth the economic cost that such a choice may entail. Even if the arrangements are hurtful in economic terms, the fact that they are between consenting adults has a bearing. And if they reduce political tensions, the economic harm they do may well be worth the cost.

As a practical matter, an investor who was prepared to contemplate an ultimate divestiture at the outset of his operation would probably demand undisturbed possession of the subsidiary on the order of twelve or fifteen years. Moreover, the arrangement, instead of contemplating inevitable sale, could better be in the form of an option on the part of local interests to buy at the end of the period; this would provide some protection against the possibility that, by the time the end of the period was in sight, the local government might prefer to extend the option rather than to exercise it, given the alternative uses it would have for investment funds at that time and given the nature of the foreigners' operations. The Agency for International Development (AID) might even give some thought to how it could use its extended-risk insurance program in order to guarantee prospective investors against the risk that the host government might fail to perform in accordance with the provisions of the agreed option, or against the risk that the investor might not receive some minimum upset price under the terms of the option.

Reducing Tension: The Tax Issue · One subject that contributes to the levels of tension associated with the activities of multinational enterprises is the question of taxes. Until recently, such enterprises were fairly free to allocate their costs, adjust their transfer prices, and arrange their affairs, in order to minimize the aggregate burden of national taxes. That freedom is gradually being curtailed. Government authorities are becoming slightly more sophisticated and more aggressive in tax matters. The use of tax-safe-haven companies is being somewhat curtailed. The tendency toward a greater tax pinch is growing, a fact that should predispose multinational enterprises to consider seriously whether they are prepared to accept a different kind of international regime in the tax field.

Heretofore, cooperative governmental action in this area has been confined to bilateral tax treaties. It could well be, however, that this approach will prove inadequate. In any event, inadequate or not, the approach could well be replaced by another that might contribute to a decline in the level of tensions.

One such approach is the development of a set of multinational principles applicable to all tax jurisdictions, governing the calculation of profit for tax purposes. Such principles could cover problems in the field of transfer pricing, problems involving the use of debt in lieu of equity, and problems relating to the allocation of costs. These rules, like the rules of bilateral tax treaties, could conceivably reduce the possibility that multinational enterprises might be caught between the scissor blades of two taxing jurisdictions. At the same time, however, it would increase the assurances to governments that such enterprises were not slipping between the national tax jurisdictions.

There is a more fundamental and more ambitious approach that might be considered. This is an approach based on the principle that the operations of the individual subsidiaries of multinational enterprises are inescapably interrelated and that the assignment of the profits to each of them unavoidably involves large elements of the arbitrary. The assessment of tax liability in any jurisdiction, therefore, ought to be based upon a pro-rationing of the consolidated profit of the multinational enterprise as a whole.

It will be recognized at once that this is the principle generally followed by the several states of the United States. The analogy to the U.S. interstate system, however, indicates how profound the proposed change would be. Such a change, for instance, would require the United States and other countries to look upon profits generated abroad in a wholly new light. These profits would be taxable to all jurisdictions as earned. At the same time, the rules for the calculation of profit would have to be harmonized in some measure, local deviations being kept within bounds. The odds are that this approach could only be followed in the first instance by the advanced countries collectively; it would be some time before many of the less-developed countries would see it in their interests to proceed on these lines.

Reducing Tensions: The Sorting Out of Jurisdictions · Perhaps the most flamboyant source of the tension that goes with the operations of multinational enterprises is the occasional overlap and clash of national jurisdictions. The tax issue is a familiar manifestation of that problem, but there are more difficult and more sensitive areas in which the problem appears. If real progress is to be made on this issue, several different kinds of agreement would have to be achieved simultaneously.

In the first place, countries engaged in any collaborative effort in this area would have to begin by accepting a set of self-denying ordinances. They would have to be prepared to give up the precious right to reach into the jurisdictions of others in order to influence actions affecting their national interests. The areas in which they gave up such rights would probably have to be explicitly specified. The obvious candidates include the field of restrictive business practices and mergers, trading-with-the-enemy regulations, and the control of capital movements. On subjects such as these, governments would undertake not to try to shape the behavior of the overseas subsidiaries of their national companies by means of direct injunction or by coercion of the parent.

Commitments of that sort would not be forthcoming, however, unless at the same time there were also provisions for some continuous efforts at the harmonization of national policy in these fields. Such efforts need not lead to identical national policy. The United States has long since learned that it can live comfortably alongside friendly countries even if they refuse to pursue precisely the same policies in these sensitive fields. But countries would be loathe to give up their rights to reach outward if they thought that there were no possible means by which very large differences in national policy could be somewhat narrowed. Accordingly, the self-denying ordinances would probably have to be accompanied by a mechanism for the harmonization of policies among the nations concerned.

If overseas subsidiaries are to lie beyond the reach of the governments of their parent companies, the corollary principle is that they should be looked upon unambiguously as the nationals of their host governments. That corollary, which underlies the well-known Calvo clause in American diplomatic history, has always been bitterly resisted by the United States. In essence, the Calvo clause provides that the local subsidiaries of foreign-owned enterprises will be treated on the same basis as any other national in the host country, and that such subsidiaries will lose any rights of access to the diplomatic support of foreign governments.

One of the difficulties of the approach, of course, is that "national treatment" in most-jurisdictions of the world carries no connotation of non-discriminatory treatment. Unlike the presumption in U.S. jurisprudence, most other nations operate under domestic systems that permit the selective and discriminatory treatment of enterprises in their jurisdiction. The use of chosen instruments, of approved and disapproved firms, and similar devices is normal rather than exceptional in most countries. A commitment by such countries to national treatment is no guarantee against systematic discrimination.

Besides, there are numerous instances in which the foreign-owned subsidiary bulks so large in the economy and occupies so unique a position that there is no norm by which to determine whether the enterprise is in fact receiving non-discriminatory treatment. It would be hard to say, for instance, just what non-discrimination meant if applied to Southern Peru Copper in Peru or to Aramco in Saudi Arabia.

Nevertheless, difficulties of this sort can be partially bridged.

Minimal standards can be developed in treaty form and provision for appeal to some international authority can be developed. Here again, the odds are that the less-developed countries would be exceedingly hesitant to enter into agreements of this sort. Once again, therefore, realism suggests that early advances in this field would probably have to be confined to the advanced countries.

Observe the relationship between this set of recommendations and those made earlier regarding international capital movements. In the disentangling of national jurisdictions, one could readily contemplate that the countries concerned would jointly agree not to impose any restraints on the export of capital for foreign direct investment, subject to the usual GATT-style caveats relating to balance-of-payment difficulties and national security. In addition, as part of the undertaking to extend equitable treatment to foreign-owned subsidiaries, countries would be committed not to discriminate against such subsidiaries in establishment rights. As a consequence, the freedom that multinational enterprises enjoyed in establishing new activities would probably exceed the present situation. Would this increased freedom reduce the tension associated with their operations; or would it add to that tension?

The Heart of the Problem · The question serves to remind us that some of the toughest problems still remain. A great deal of what concerns host governments, local elites, American labor, and others is the strength, suppleness, and flexibility of such multinational enterprises, at least as perceived by those that must negotiate with them. Tension from that source could be allayed at the margin by substantially better disclosure on the part of the multinational enterprises covering the whole of the operations. Indeed, the tax proposals made earlier have the incidental virtue of requiring such disclosure.

But disclosure provisions, experience suggests, can only do a little in allaying the tension. A second step, therefore, might well be to set up a procedure under which major locational decisions on the part of multinational enterprises, such as decisions to locate additional production facilities, might be subject to a process of challenge and review. Such a process could either be national or international in scope. This sort of approach would be of special interest to labor unions, of course, since it relates to their desire to stop "runaway plants."

From the viewpoint of many multinational enterprises, a proposal of this sort opens Pandora's box; it is important, therefore, to be clear at once on just what such a procedure would be expected to achieve. A review procedure would be destructive if it blocked multinational enterprises from proceeding with their plans where those plans were consistent with the achievement of increased efficiency. Proposed projects that could be blocked, therefore, would be those based upon government subsidies, government restrictions, or government threats. Decisions that could be traced to private cartel agreements or decisions based on the firm's ignorance of more attractive alternative opportunities might presumably also be prevented. But efforts simply to arrest change would be destructive; in any case, they would probably suffer the fate of King Canute.

Each of the possibilities suggested in these last few pages requires considerably more development and elaboration. None of them sits easily in the framework of our present thinking. The justification for proposing them at this time stems from two facts: from the fact that the multinational enterprise itself is a revolutionary institution that may in the end generate revolutionary responses; and from the further fact that the capacity for governments to accept change is so much greater than it was a few decades ago. Indeed, there is a considerable possibility that the multinational enterprise problem will find itself shortly merged in a very much larger issue: how advanced nations can live side by side in a world in which physical and cultural space is so rapidly shrinking. This issue involves not only the multinational enterprise but all forms of international movements, of goods, of capital, of people, and of ideas. It may be that in dealing with the overwhelming problems that are arising from forces such as these, the problem of the multinational enterprise will have been solved as well.

American Multinationals and the U.S. Economy

THOMAS HORST

Thomas Horst is professor at the Fletcher School of Law and Diplomacy, Tufts University. In this essay, first published in the May 1976 issue of the American Economic Review, *he analyses the impact of American multinational firms on the U.S. economy as regards international trade, taxation, and antitrust regulations.*

TRADE ISSUES

THE IMPACT OF American investments abroad on U.S. exports and imports is certainly a controversial issue. Whatever interest it may hold in its own right is overshadowed by its implications for the export of American jobs, the distribution of income between American labor and capital, and the balance of payments. In approaching this complex issue, we focused on the microeconomics of foreign trade and investment rather than on the general-equilibrium linkages. An American multinational chooses—explicitly or implicitly—whether to supply its foreign and domestic markets with goods manufactured at home or overseas. When a company like International Business Machines (IBM) decides to manufacture its computers for its European customers in Europe, it displaces its own exports of computers from the United States. While data on the exports, imports, and foreign affiliate sales of individual American investors are exceedingly hard to come by, industry statistics are comparatively easy to find and seemed altogether appropriate for demonstrating the substitution of subsidiary production for American exports.

While this notion of direct substitution has obvious intuitive appeal and is implicit in the labor unions' charges that American investors export their jobs, we had no success whatsoever in demonstrating statistically that it was a major factor in shaping the flows of U.S. exports and imports. If one industry's exports and foreign subsidiary sales are compared to another's, one often finds that the industry which exports more also produces more overseas. This simple correlation does not imply, however, that exporting stimulates foreign production or vice versa. Often one industry is more technically sophisticated than the other, and its technical capability assists its exports and its foreign production. What surprised us was that when we used common statistical procedures to correct for differences in technical sophistication and other spurious factors, we still could not demonstrate any clear or obvious tradeoff between exporting and foreign subsidiary production. There was no evidence that an increase in foreign subsidiary production was normally accompanied by a reduction in U.S. exports or, for that matter, an increase in U.S. imports. In fact, there was some evidence that a modest amount of foreign investment might be prerequisite to exporting. But ignoring that and focusing on the industries with substantial exports or overseas markets, we found no statistically significant relationship across industries between foreign investing and U.S. exports or imports.

What conclusion should we draw from the absence of any such relationship? That our exports are never displaced or our imports never enhanced by foreign production? That tariffs, transport costs, international differences in labor costs and exchange rates have no impact on the location of a multinational's production? Most certainly not. But our negative findings do suggest that the implications of subsidiary production for U.S. exports or imports have been overstated and/or that the ways in which foreign affiliate production may complement U.S. exports have been underestimated. Although economists often ignore the sort of market imperfections on which the complementarity may be based, the histories of multinational corporations or industries are more revealing. When American firms invest abroad, they not only produce goods which hypothetically might be produced in the United States, but they also undertake a wide variety of non-manufacturing activities to expand the foreign market for their products. Direct selling, advertising, wholesale and even retail distribution, adapting American products to local market conditions, follow-up maintenance and repair all play an indispensible role in broadening the market for the firm's products. In labeling these activities "ancillary" when they are performed by an American manufacturer, it has been all too easy to ignore their significance.

Our conclusions are simple. Published foreign investment statistics reflect a heterogeneous combination of manufacturing and nonmanufacturing activities, and while the foreign manufacturing may be an alternative to American production, the nonmanufacturing activities tend to promote U.S. exports by expanding the market for U.S. goods. We would not risk belaboring this point were it not for the regretable tendency of such distinctions to be the first casualties of public policy debates over foreign investment. The Burke-Hartke Bill, which was supported by the AFL-CIO and finally rejected in 1973 by the Congress after a long and bitter debate, proposed to repeal the foreign tax credit for all foreign investment. By subjecting foreign investment income to double taxation, the labor unions hoped to slow down or reverse the export of jobs. We conclude that such a policy in failing to discriminate between one type of foreign investment and another could easily do more harm than good to the U.S. trade balance. The depreciation of the U.S. dollar did far more to reverse the export of jobs than the Burke-Hartke Bill ever could have.

TAX ISSUES

Under current United States tax policy, foreign investment income is subject to the corporate income tax, but not until that income is formally paid as a dividend to the American investor, and then a tax credit is given for foreign income taxes. Even if this policy has had an ambiguous impact on U.S. exports and imports, it has had two unfortunate side effects. It has allowed foreign governments to collect the lion's share of taxes on foreign investment income, a phenomenon which is highly significant in any reckoning of the national gains from international investment. Secondly, it has encouraged American investors to undercharge their foreign affiliates for intra-company exports and for mutually beneficial research and development programs and other joint expenses. In the end the United States has little or no share in the taxes paid on the income generated by American investments abroad and may even lose some tax revenues on domestic income to overseas governments.

As an aid in evaluating various tax reforms, we have constructed a microeconomic model of a multinational firm and used various estimates of the model's parameters to simulate the multinational's response to possible changes in United States tax policy. In Table 1 we show our estimates of the impact of eliminating deferral for manufacturing investors in 1974. Without the deferral of foreign investment income, we estimate that the total assets of foreign manufacturing affiliates would be reduced by $3.2 billion, which is 2.3 percent of their estimated total value. The total domestic assets of the multinationals might rise by $2.4 billion, which is only 0.7 percent of these firms' domestic assets. That domestic investment rises by less than foreign investment falls reflects the loss of investable funds through higher tax payments to the U.S. Treasury. The primary reason why eliminating deferral has so small an impact on foreign and domestic investment is that foreign governments collect income and withholding taxes amounting to 45 percent of foreign investment income. If deferral were repealed, the total taxes imposed on foreign investment income would not exceed 48 percent, the statutory U.S. tax rate. If repealing deferral adds only 3 percent to the total taxes

TABLE 1. *Estimated Impact of Eliminating Deferral for Manufacturing Firms, 1974 (millions of dollars)*

Variable Affected	Impact Assuming No Change in Intra-firm Financial Practices	Estimated 1974 Value	Percentage Change
Total domestic assets	2,436	338,400	.7
Total foreign assets	−3,216	140,400	−2.2
Intra-firm financial transfer	−11,046	28,080	−39.3
Consolidated after-tax earnings	−755	43,123	−1.8
U.S. Income Taxes[a]	1,233	28,815	4.2
Foreign income & withholding taxes	−433	9,569	−4.5

[a] U.S. income taxes include taxes paid on parents' domestic income.

on foreign investment income, the impact on the location of investment is apt to be small.

But this is not to say that the United States has little to gain by eliminating deferral. Far from it. We estimate that the total taxes paid by American investors to the U.S. Treasury (including taxes on domestic income) would rise by $1.2 billion, a 4.2 percent increase in those taxes. Eliminating deferral has a comparatively larger impact on U.S. taxable income and tax payments than on domestic investment (a 4.2 percent gain versus a 0.7 percent gain). This striking difference reflects our presumption that the elimination of deferral would encourage American investors to finance more of their overseas investment with locally borrowed funds than they now do. If the subsidiaries borrow in local capital markets, the interest is deductible from their taxable income and not from their American parents' domestic income. The gains from encouraging American investors to refinance their foreign operations constitute a major incentive to repeal deferral.

The tax gains of this particular reform do not end here. Deferral encourages firms to undercharge their foreign affiliates for research and development programs undertaken in the United States. Although American investors often spend as much as 5 percent of their domestic sales receipts on research and development programs, only a small portion of the total cost is charged back to the foreign affiliates. In 1973, for example, total royalties, management fees, rentals and all other such charges amounted to only 1.1 percent of manufacturing affiliates' sales. If repealing deferral encouraged firms to raise these charges by another 1.1 percent, the tax gain for the United States in 1974 would have been almost $1 billion—a gain over and above that shown in Table 1.

So while we favor the repeal of deferral, we believe that the primary benefits are quite different from those stressed by earlier writers. The principal gain derives from the tax benefits of encouraging American investors to alter the capital structure of their overseas affiliates and to increase the portion of taxable income allocated to the U.S. parent. The more familiar gains—the more efficient pattern of international investment and the additional U.S. taxes collected on subsidiaries retained earnings—may pale by comparison.

ANTITRUST ISSUES

As Stephen Hymer, Raymond Vernon, Richard Caves, and several other authors have noted, American multinationals are anything but the atomistic competitors envisaged by classical economic analysts. Multinational firms tend, if anything, to be the largest firms in their industries, and those industries are distinguished by high advertising, high research and development spending, substantial economies of scale, and other wellsprings of monopoly power. The primary connection between multinationalization and monopolization is simple: the technological and marketing advantages which allow a few firms to dominate the market also serve as a springboard for entering foreign markets.

Our interest was not in reconfirming this primary linkage between foreign investment and market power, but in determining whether foreign investment reinforces or entrenches the multinationals' market position in the United States. Our suspicions were aroused not by the opportunities a multinational may have to use its foreign earnings to finance predatory attacks on its domestic competitiors (as Richard J. Barnet and Ronald E. Müller argued in *Global Reach*), but by the possibility that the underlying sources of market power—patents, brand differentiation, vertical integration—would be augmented by foreign investment.

A prima facie case for this hypothesis is easy enough to make— the multinational companies themselves often claim that only through their large, global operations can they afford the substantial research and development programs they undertake. The fruits of their research efforts help them fend off foreign competition when they enter foreign markets while enhancing their premier positions in the United States.

Whether the contribution of foreign investment to domestic market power is large or small is a much harder question to answer. We have examined Internal Revenue Service statistics on the domestic rates of return for firms of different sizes and in different industries. Industrial organization analysts reason that firms will be able to earn consistently higher profits than average only if they are protected in one way or another from new competition. A summary of our findings appears in Table 2 where we have cross-tabulated firms' domestic returns on capital according to whether they were "multinational" or "domestic," whether they spent heavily on advertising or not, whether they employed many scientists and engineers or not, and whether they were large or small. Comparisons are made for 1966, a good year, and 1970, a bad one. By reading up and down the columns, one can see that firms spending heavily on advertising consistently showed higher rates of return than firms which advertise less. The advantages of technological effort are less striking, but apparent nonetheless.

TABLE 2. *Cross Tabulations of Domestic Returns as a Percent of Parents' Total Assets, 1966 and 1970*

	Multinational Groups	Domestic Groups
1966		
High advertising	17.0	13.8
Low advertising	13.0	11.4
1970		
High advertising	14.3	10.8
Low advertising	8.1	6.6
1966		
High technology	16.7	13.2
Low technology	12.6	11.5
1970		
High technology	11.0	5.7
Low technology	8.7	7.1
1966		
Large firms	14.9	11.6
Small firms	13.8	11.7
1970		
Large firms	9.7	6.2
Small firms	9.6	7.3

NOTES: Domestic net returns equal net income before taxes plus interest paid on debt less foreign dividends and tax credits. Multinationals were those industry-size-class groups whose foreign dividends and tax credits exceeded 1 percent of parents' assets; high advertisers were those groups spending amounts more than 5 percent of parents' assets on advertising; high technology industries were those whose 1970 employment of scientists and engineers exceeded 5 percent of their total employment; large firms had more than $250 million in total assets. The "groups" of American corporations consisted of all firms of a given size class (e.g., $50–$100 million in total assets) in one of seventy-five "minor" industries (e.g., meatpacking). SOURCES: Internal Revenue Service, *Sourcebook of Statistics of Income, Corporations, 1966* and *1970*, obtained from the National Archives in machine-readable form.

Large firms do not, however, consistently earn more than small firms do.

The more interesting relationship, so far as we are concerned is apparent in reading across the rows. Now we are comparing firms spending comparable amounts on advertising, employing comparable numbers of scientists and enginers, or of comparable size to determine whether those with foreign operations earn higher returns on their domestic investments than those without overseas investments. What is striking about these hoizontal comparisons is that for high advertisers and low, large and small employers of scientists and engineers, and large firms and small, the multinational groups earned significantly higher domestic returns than domestic groups in 1966 and 1970. (The relationship also held for each of the seven years 1965–71.) The possibility that foreign investment significantly increases the domestic monopoly power of multinational firms clearly should not be dismissed out of hand.

Unfortunately, this sort of monopoly power hits American antitrust policy right where it is weakest. Antitrust policy has had its greatest success in undoing price-fixing and market-sharing arrangements among would-be cartels and in preventing horizontal and vertical mergers among large firms. Its greatest failures have come in attacking market power inherent in economies of scale, technological knowhow and other basic elements of industry structure. These failures may be due in part to a lack of legal resources or political support for antitrust prosecution of large firms, but are also a reflection of a troublesome tradeoff between competition and economic efficiency. Even if the Justice Department or the Federal Trade Commission can prove that a technologically advanced firm has illegally monopolized a market, judges are often reluctant to split the company into several smaller, independent competitors for fear of sacrificing the substantial economies of scale the firm achieves in production or in developing new technology. Foreign investment tends to reinforce domestic market power in those very cases where antitrust authorities are least willing and able to act.

Every cloud has its silver lining, and this one is no exception. In trying to find an effective remedy for this type of monopoly power, antitrust authorities often look for natural ways to split dominant firms into self-sufficient entities, just as a jeweler looks for a natural way to split a diamond. In this search we would hope that antitrust authorities would not overlook the obvious opportunities to split the large and more sufficient foreign subsidiaries from their American parents. Although these subsidiaries are not current participants in U.S. product markets, they are often credible entrants. Is IBM Europe not a credible contender in the U.S. computer industry? Is General Motors, Canada, not a potential entrant in the United States auto industry? In fairness to the American parent, we presume that it would be allowed to compete with its erstwhile affiliates in overseas markets, just as they would compete with their erstwhile parents in the domestic U.S. markets. In ordering the cross-licensing of critical patents and otherwise fashioning an effective remedy, the objective should always be to promote competition, not to emasculate one national firm or the other. Multinationals may thus derive competitive advantages over their domestic competition from their foreign operations, but those foreign operations may be a solution to, and not just a cause of, the problem of market power.

Problems and Policies Affecting Labor's Interests

In this essay, first published in the May 1974 issue of the American Economic Review, *George H. Hildebrand critically examines
the proposition that investments abroad by U.S. companies would
have compromised the interests of American labor. The author is
Maxwell M. Upson Professor of Economics and Industrial Relations at Cornell University.*

IT IS TEMPTING to draw a parallel between the spread of American
industry south and west after, say, 1830 and the spread of multinational enterprises throughout the world, particularly in the
past quarter-century. One calls to mind immediately visions of
runaway shops, legions of low-paid new nonunion workers, old
high-cost plants in declining regions, and the difficulties of extending collective bargaining and common labor standards to
remote groups and places. And to be sure, there are similarities,
but also some sharp differences.

Perhaps the best way to begin is to set up a conceptual framework with which to examine these questions. First, we should
distinguish between the interests of labor organizations in
negotiating and enforcing wages and standards of employment
and the interests of individual workers, for some union members
have interests that do not always parallel those of their organizations and other workers do not belong to unions at all.

Second, we have to consider these interests in all of their
geographical complexity: workers and their organizations in a
source country for direct foreign investment capital, such as the
United States; in the host countries to which the capital is applied; and third, in countries whose workers and their organizations have economic interests that can be either competitive with
or complementary to those in the host countries. Here I find it
useful to distinguish four admittedly rough categories: the United

States itself, the industrial economies of Western Europe and Japan, the developing industral economies of Asia—Taiwan, Singapore, Hong Kong, and South Korea—and a grab bag of primarily natural-resource-oriented countries, such as Saudi Arabia, Peru, Chile, and Australia. The only brief for this classification is that it helps one perceive the limitations of the runaway-shop model as a basis for looking at direct investment overseas and realize the obstacles to effective extension of union power beyond the seas.

Third, it is safe to assume that capitalistic firms expand abroad to maximize profits. This motive finds concrete expression in different ways. One is the perennial search for cheaper raw materials, for example, richer deposits of oil and copper. Closely related is the desire to take advantage of lower costs of production and distribution, as it were by substituting foreign investment for export sales of manufactured goods. In some cases this phenomenon may involve Raymond Vernon's cycle of overseas expansion, where there exists a joint motive to cut costs and enlarge total sales to overcome saturation problems at home. However, in other situations the purpose may be oriented mainly to cost-savings, for example, low-cost assembly of television components in Taiwan for re-export to the United States. Then again the motive may be to penetrate a foreign market that is closed to imports by a variety of possible barriers—a demand-oriented expansion that may also involve economies of scale as well (export of components, spreading costs of central management, lower prices for inputs purchased in larger volume).

Finally, the objective may be to secure the profit-yielding advantages of vertical or horizontal integration, for example in the vertical case to get favorable cost differentials for raw materials or to obtain an assured supply or, on occasion, even to shut off competitors' access (borates in 1899, bauxite before 1942). In the horizontal case the goal may be to make possible a strategy of shifting production from struck plants (probably overrated) or to get rid of a troublesome competitor or even to reduce the vigor of import competition back home. But horizontal integration may also involve none of these things and, instead, simply may emerge from expansion abroad to improve the rate of return through larger sales and lower costs.

Let me consider first the impacts of direct foreign investment (DFI) upon the interests of workers as individuals. Wherever the investment goes, of course, the overall effect is to increase the stock of capital relative to the labor force, increasing employment and, depending upon elasticity of supply of industrial labor, real wages. In relatively undeveloped raw materials countries, the accompanying infusion of advanced technology and managerial skills can make a strong and continuing contribution to the training and upgrading of the local labor force with beneficial spin-off effects for the whole economy. In time, serious political issues may emerge from this invasion by foreign capital and its representatives, whether it be from capitalist or Communist countries, and there exist cases of both types. However, I am limiting myself here to purely economic effects.

Of somewhat greater interest, I think is the effect of the process upon individual workers in the source country, in this instance the United States. The freedom both of capital and of commodities to move internationally operates continuously to shift the participating economies toward specialization according to comparative advantage. Depending upon the case, the home effects may be favorable or unfavorable, complementary or competitive. Funds sent out to develop an oil field in Indonesia will aid the employment and real wages of refining and distribution employees back home, although they may be adverse to the interests of workers in high-cost domestic fields. U.S. investments in radio, computer, and television plants in the Asian group or in the Mexican border zone will at least slow the rate of expansion of employment in the collateral domestic branches of these industries and may well reduce it absolutely. However, the lower production costs may also have favorable effects in the other domestic branches of the same industries. The migration of New England textiles southward was a similar process.

Before leaving this topic, let me record my belief that progressive overvaluation of the dollar during the two decades prior to the adoption of floating exchange rates in 1973 has had a great deal to do with both the volume and the nature of DFI from the United States. As with the United Kingdom in the 1920's, the effect was to impose a cost-scissors upon domestic industries and their workers, discouraging exports and attracting imports. At the same time, fixed dollar parities were a standing invitation to send capital abroad in place of goods and services. As the whole process went on and its consequences worsened, we began to hear that the United States would eventually be driven out of hard goods production and would become an exporter primarily of computers and managerial talent.

I think we are now able to see matters in better perspective. The evolution of our export and import patterns in these years reflected dollar overvaluation as well as longer run factors of comparative advantage. The cheap labor and runaway shop arguments will continue to be with us, but the forces provoking them should be less severe.

Let me turn now to the impacts of DFI upon unions, using a three-way geographic classification: host country, source country, and "third party" countries. As a general rule we may follow John R. Commons and say that the ability of a trade union to extract gains by bargaining with employers depends ultimately upon the completeness of its control over the relevant product market. "Taking wages out of competition" means eliminating competing uncontrolled sources of product supply, so that differences in wages and benefits do not yield differences in unit costs and that strike strategy may be fully effective.

If the host country for DFI is, for example, an industrial country in Western Europe, then the infusion of private capital is likely to pose different problems for a trade union from those that would emerge, say, in Zambia or Saudi Arabia or within a country of the Asian group. In the European case, if the capital is used to acquire an existing firm, the immediate problems are to control the labor policy of the new owners and very possibly to cope with a multiplant technique for combating strikes. If, instead, the investment is directed to a new plant, the basic problems are likely to be the same, plus the added one of organizing the new work force.

Continuing with the United Kingdom-West European setting, DFI in either form in any one of these countries is likely to make the problem of product substitution far more acute all around. Within the host country, the unions will be compelled to look to their fellow organizations for international cooperation against competing employers in the industry. Likewise, these organizations will be furnished with the same incentive. Here there would seem to be three main choices for policy. One is to try to extend the reach of organization, to form genuine international unions to achieve a common policy as regards negotiations, strikes, settlements, and wage and employment standards. Short of this difficult goal, the affected organizations might attempt to form bargaining and strike coalitions, as it were to achieve horizontal integration of the relevant labor markets for both offensive and defensive purposes. Third, they might seek the establishment of "fair" international labor standards for wages, hours, and working conditions, through bodies such as the International Labour Organisation. With this last approach, the problem of what Arnold Weber calls the "mediation of interests" of diverse worker-groups becomes even more formidable.

Consider, next, the case where DFI is directed to light manufacturing and assembly in the so-called Asian group of developing countries. Here technology, skill requirements, and predominance of final sales in the United States all enforce a certain commonality and substitutability as among plants within the group. In consequence there is some similarity with the Western European case. However, there are differences: unionism is much more unevenly distributed. Where found, the organizations are local and tend to be weak. Distances among competing sources are great, there are ethnic and linguistic barriers, and fraternal ties are usually not close. Taken together, these factors do not make for near-term cohesive action through internationalization of unions, international coalitions, or pursuit of common labor standards. Thus we can conclude tentatively that, whereas in the United Kingdom-Western European region the forces making for cohesive labor policies are strong and growing, dispersion and fragmentation now characterize the Asian group.

Last among the receiving countries for DFI are those in the natural-resource-oriented group. These nations are scattered far and wide over the globe. Formally, of course, the country suppliers of petroleum, or copper, or iron ore, for example, are interdependent, but unification of policies on an international scale, where it has occurred at all, has been the consequence of cooperative action by states, not of trade union bodies. On the one side, physical distances are great while competitive disturbances from opening up a new deposit are small. On the other, where independent unionism is found at all, it has neither the power nor the incentive to strive for international lines of action. Everything favors an inward-looking concern for organizing and policing the foreign-owned extractive company, and this is where the practical pay-offs are to be had. Put a little differently, the problem for organized labor typically is to capture and exploit the local resource base, not to reduce the possibilities for substitution of foreign for domestic labor as among far distant locations.

This brings us to the impacts of DFI for labor unions in a capital-source country such as the United States. With unimportant exceptions, the outflow of capital to develop new sources of raw materials has not constituted a problem for union policy. Rather, the problem—viewed here as a composite of wages, jobs, and bargaining effectiveness—has asserted itself in two main ways: the loss of export markets, when investment abroad has been substituted, and the substitution of imports for domestic production. From the union standpoint, loss of export sales hurts because of the old principle that capital is more mobile than labor. The same handicap has asserted itself probably even more strongly through import substitution. Impacts here have been felt in apparel, specialty fabrics, footwear, automobiles, fabricated steel, calculators, typewriters, radios, and television sets. To be sure, the effects have been diffuse. In some cases the displacement of workers in particular places has been concealed by overall growth of the industry. In others, the problem appears as slackened growth rather than absolute decline. But for a labor union, significant specific job losses, together with a failure of membership to grow, are serious weakening agents as regards organizational effectiveness.

Interestingly enough, the principal source of these problems seems to be the Asian group and the "twin plants" problem along the Mexican border. I have neither time nor opportunity to examine the statistical evidence, hence must confine myself to a few observations.

One of them is that the products involved require large amounts of unskilled and semiskilled labor. This means a high elasticity of substitution as between the domestic and foreign labor groups involved—always a difficult problem for a labor union. Another consideration is that the competing foreign sources are very unevenly unionized—a version of the open-shop problem. Still another is that all of these countries tend to fit W. Arthur Lewis's model—they have excess supplies of labor, and these exert significant downward pressure against wage increases. This long-distance factor cripples the bargaining effectiveness of domestic unions in the same field.

And finally, while it is cold comfort at best, I suspect that the chief explanation for this phenomenon of sharply increased product-market competition from the Asian group has been simultaneous overvaluation of the dollar and deliberate undervaluation of the yen. Overvaluation limited exportation while promoting a soaring expansion of imports. So far as the United States is concerned, undervaluation made Japan a particularly formidable competitor. How, then, was a domestic producer of, say, television sets to endure against the mortal thrust of Japanese competition? So long as the dollar was firmly pegged and official policy favored liberalized trade, the only way to survive was to have light fabrication and assembly performed in countries that could put the Japanese producers in the same squeeze.

In my view, these are the main situations that have made DFI an adverse force for the American unions, a force deriving more from Asian than from European sources.

Obviously one kind of response would be the internationalization of unionism itself—directly or through coalitions. Alternatively, unions could seek "fair" international labor standards. But, with the notable exception of the United Auto Workers and the Japanese auto unions, expansion outward has not been tried. If anything, the American labor movement in recent years has been reducing its ties to its foreign counterparts. As for international economic relations, the line taken has been to support the Burke-Hartke trade bill in all of its intricate protectionist apparatus—import quotas, restrictions upon DFI, and restraints upon the diffusion of American technology abroad.

The explanation seems to be that the American unions, like their sister organizations abroad, orient their policies to the interests of their incumbent employed members. Until the last two decades, foreign trade and international movements of private capital offered no significant threat to the position of incumbent jobholders in the organized sections of American industry. With the progressive overvaluation of the dollar and the enormous outflow of private capital, now exceeding $90 billion in cumulative total, certain U.S. unions began to feel the pinch—in slackened growth of their industries, in specific job losses, and in diminished bargaining effectiveness (higher elasticity of derived demand for production labor).

As these pressures mounted in the 1960's, they began to impose some hard policy choices upon the American labor movement. Extension of unionism beyond Canadian affiliates to places such as Taiwan or Hong Kong in the Orient, or to Italy and West Germany in Europe, was a manifest impracticality: the organizational requirements were too difficult while the necessary incentive on the side of the prospective foreign members simply was not there. As a second-best alternative, international coalitions offered the American unions even less advantages while the organizational problems were equally difficult. Why, for example, should unions in Hong Kong seek wage parity with their American brethren just to relieve the latter from the competitive rigors of what they would term runaway shops based upon cheap foreign labor? Workers are just not that naive about the negativeness of demand elasticities for their services.

The solution, then, was to turn to measures such as Burke-Hartke because the goal of making secure the interests of incumbent American members seemed easier to obtain given the political power requirements involved.

There was still another alternative, but it was never tried: to press for an end to the Bretton Woods system of fixed parities so that the dollar could attain a competitive position in the world economy. Here was the means to relieve the pressure of imports and to restore the strength of our export industries at one stroke. With the progressive abandonment of administered prices for the dollar in foreign exchange over the last two years, the American unions have gained more for their members than internationalization or Burke-Hartke could ever be expected to provide them. Perception of this economic truth may well explain the almost total silence now enveloping both of these proposals in the United States.

What, then, can be said regarding the overall significance of private international investment from the standpoint of labor as a factor of production?

First, DFI is a vehicle for the diffusion of capital, technology, managerial skills, and occupational training over those regions of the world that are hospitable to the process. As such, what is involved is an increasing international division of labor. In essence the process is no different from westward expansion within the United States itself, except that, at least in its earlier period, that expansion did not entail branch-plant enterprises to the extent that it later did and that development of multinational corporations does today. But this is a question of organizational forms: probably the real significance of the multinational device in this respect is that it simplifies and accelerates the transmission process.

From the standpoint purely of economic welfare, that portion of the world's consumers that falls within the ambit of the process is clearly benefited by its extension. As these consumers are preponderantly workers, the latter are beneficiaries of the increased efficiency in resource use that DFI makes possible.

Second, the consequential effect is a widening of the product market and of the number of competing sources of supply effectively within it, although the multinational device works to hold down the number of independent suppliers at the same time that the market itself is widening and expanding.

From the labor standpoint, there are those who gain and those who lose. All workers gain as consumers, most of them as producers, and some lose through the displacement effects of broader competition. Because the unions speak mainly for incumbents on the job and not for consumers or for newly employed workers in lands often far away, the dominant theme in their reaction is hostility to both DFI and liberalized international trade. Yet there is reason still to accept what Alfred Marshall taught us more than half a century ago: that on the whole the relationship of capital to labor is far more complementary than it is competitive. Increased employment and higher real wages are the main consequences to be looked for. To search, therefore, for ways to obstruct the export of capital is to look for inefficient and inequitable methods to redistribute income, paradoxical as this may seem.

Looking far ahead, however, the continued spread of the multinationals does presage a shift in the power balance as between the free world's employers and its labor organizations, an emerging gap that the sovereign state, acting alone, seems unable to fill. Indeed, the situation in rough ways is a replica of the United States in the 1920's. The business enterprise has proved fully capable of extending its organizational reach literally all over the world. The world's labor movements have not demonstrated anywhere near as much flexibility and adaptability. As DFI proceeds, this gap in the power balance will increase. It is difficult to believe that it will proceed unchecked and unchallenged from the labor side over the decades to come.

Foreign Investment in the United States

An influential congressman and chairman of the Subcommittee on Foreign Economic Policy, John C. Culver examines the issues related to the alleged threat of direct investments in the United States by oil-exporting countries. This essay was published in the Fall 1974 issue of Foreign Policy.

IN 1972, NO one would have predicted that foreign investment in the United States would attract a great deal of congressional interest. At that time, when the Burke-Hartke bill was freshly minted, the talk was all about the flight of U.S. capital overseas and the extent to which "runaway industries" could and should be checked. My own Subcommittee on Foreign Economic Policy responded by holding hearings and drafting legislation (incorported in the pending trade bill) to overhaul the administration of trade adjustment assistance as an alternative to excessive protectionism against imports. People who testified did not voice concern about the import of foreign capital; it was not even a potential issue.

What a difference two years can make! By 1974, dollar devaluation had taken hold, and this combined with depressed stock prices made U.S. companies look like very attractive acquisitions. Some of the more dramatic takeovers—Texas Gulf by the Canadian Development Corporation, for example—received extensive press treatment. Concern was expressed as well about the impact of geographically and sectorally concentrated investments by foreign interests and about the trends of foreign direct investment in land and agricultural and mineral resources. It even became a bad joke: Will we put a camel instead of a tiger in our gas tanks?

More and more insistently, we heard questions like: Is the

dramatic increase in Japanese investment in Hawaii disruptive enough to the local community to warrant some action by the government? How much of the timberland on the West Coast and in Alaska has been purchased by non-U.S. citizens? Is there a level at which the national interest might be jeopardized? Are the expressions of concern in the Midwest over reports of foreign purchase of large agricultural tracts and transportation facilities legitimate or fanciful? Is it appropriate that foreign banks are allowed to establish branches in more than one state, contrary to the restrictions on domestic banks, and that their U.S. operations fall outside the jurisdiction of the Federal Reserve System? What about the entry of foreign brokerage houses into the new national exchange system in the spring of 1975?

These questions spell out a latent domestic political issue with both national and international implications. They were not ignored by Congress. Several bills were introduced to prohibit foreign ownership in certain designated industries and to limit such ownership in publicly held companies.

The importance of devising an appropriate policy response was underscored by the enormous increase in 1924 in foreign government earnings from oil production—the so-called "petro-dollars" which now overhang world financial markets. It was estimated that there were some $50 billion in annual oil reserves that were excess to the producing governments' normal investment and expenditure capabilities. Downstream U.S. investments by these governments in "Flying Camel" refineries and service stations would benefit our balance of payments, but where else may such investments go? And what of the long-term implications of swollen foreign oil exchequers? Are we mortgaging a significant share of U.S. industrial growth to foreign capital?

To explore such questions, our House Foreign Affairs Subcommittee on Foreign Economic Policy held a series of hearings on foreign direct investment in the United States in January and February 1974. We ran into an immediate and fundamental obstacle: The information base on which to construct any meaningful policy conclusions was wholly unreliable. We heard from the Commerce Department that cumulative foreign direct investment at the end of 1972 was $14.4 billion, of which $10.4 billion was in manufacturing, mining, and petroleum. An independent study,[1] however, placed the figure for the latter three industries alone at $38 billion, almost four times the Commerce figure. Government witnesses were unable to reconcile the two computations. As a further illustration, the Commerce Department list of foreign-controlled plants in the United States indicated that there were only two in my own state of Iowa, whereas an admittedly unsatisfactory search through state records by the staff of the Iowa Development Commission identified twenty-eight companies that appeared to have some degree of foreign ownership. Such was the state of our information on direct foreign investment in manufacturing, mining, and petroleum—and there was almost none available on real-estate holdings or on the farm-production and food-processing industries.

It was against the background of such fragmentary and inconsistent data that the Nixon administration, acting through the Council on International Economic Policy (CIEP), testified to the subcommittee that no basis had been established for departing from the traditional U.S. policy of neutrality toward foreign investment in this country. As a matter of pure macroeconomic theory, this policy of benign neglect may have been entirely rational. Prevailing theory suggests that the free movement of capital benefits society in the same way as the free movement of goods. However, this holds only for the overall impact and tells us little about the economic and geographic effect on specific sectors of the country. A foreign investment in manufacturing or mineral resources might increase domestic employment, introduce new technology, or add a competitive spur to efficient production, whereas an acquisition of a financial institution or an agricultural enterprise might remove scarce resources from domestic consumption. Different concerns are implicated in each case.

GROWING FEARS

Whether or not the administration's policy was correct, it did not address itself to widespread and growing fears. The failure to do so risked not only the withholding of political consent but,

1. By Professors Jeffrey Arpan of Georgia State University and David Ricks of Ohio State University.

far more gravely, the emergence of narrowly protectionist reactions that could seriously thwart the formulation of a balanced and coherent policy. Any study of current U.S. practice must conclude that present policy exhibits little coherence.

The one area in which the administration conceded a need for vigilance was that of national security. Yet present laws addressed to this exception are nothing more than a random patchwork. For example, foreign interests may not obtain licenses to operate facilities for the utilization or production of atomic energy; but the Atomic Energy Commission has allowed 50-50 joint ventures with foreign concerns for this purpose. So also, development of hydroelectric power sites on navigable rivers and streams is restricted to U.S. corporations; but foreign control of such corporations is not prohibited. Aliens cannot acquire or exploit mineral lands owned by the federal government, but they can control domestic corporations entitled to hold such leases. if their country allows reciprocal rights to U.S. citizens.

The incoherence of policy is compounded in the area of state restrictions and incentives. Only six states permit operations by foreign banks. The various states have different laws regarding alien ownership of land, from a strict ban to a certain number of acres to no limit at all. Limitations on land ownership are apparently honored mostly in the breach. Similarly, the various states have different incentives to attract industry (domestic or foreign), ranging from tax advantages to financial assistance to special services, such as free land, R and D assistance, and job training. Twelve states, in fact, have established representative offices in Europe and/or Japan to attract foreign investment.

If we need codification at home, we should also pursue a multilateral approach to foreign investment guidelines in the Organization for Economic Cooperation and Development (OECD) and, insofar as practicable, an international approach in the United Nations. The OECD Code of Liberalization of Capital Movements is one of the principal underpinnings of efforts to promote an open, nondiscriminatory, and fair international economic system. This code, however, is merely a statement of principle—that the signatories should pursue a liberalization program in their international finance and investment policies—almost an idyllic statement of a goal lacking enforceability. Agreed upon in 1961, the code has been riddled with reservations and exemptions, which are permitted at the discretion of each nation. Restrictions must be justified before a Committee on Invisible Transactions, which has yet to deny a request. Praiseworthy as the code's objectives may be, it is, in practice, a weak support for arguing that the United States should unilaterally and in all cases follow a policy of "national treatment" of foreign investment.

Without clear and solid support in either domestic or international practice, the administration's policy necessarily rested on the presumed benefits of a free-market system, with the concomitant efficient allocation of resources. Again, reality did not reflect theory. For one thing, that theory ignores the fact that many countries have adopted policies, designed either to attract or to deter the entry of foreign capital, which distort the free market system. The invisible hand has less to do when so many highly visible hands are so actively at work.

Second, the rise of the MNC has itself had undoubted effects on the operation of any possible free market system. This is not the place to rehearse all the arguments about the impact of MNCs on the international economy. Suffice it to say that their highly skilled battalions of lawyers, accountants, and financiers are quick to spot the slightest variations in national tax and other regulations and to turn them to corporate advantage by such maneuvers as swift relocation of assets. Although the energy crisis may have demonstrated that the international petroleum companies do not have complete self-mastery, it also demonstrated their ability to move petroleum supplies without the full knowledge of governments. At times, the U.S. government was clearly unable to influence the actions of American companies. This experience highlights the absence of internationally agreed upon rules of behavior and demonstrates the foolhardiness of not keeping a close tab on the free-market system.

WHAT ROLE DOMESTIC INTERESTS?

The above is not intended as an argument for restrictions on foreign investment in the United States; it is intended to point out that critical questions have not been answered and to warn both government officials and the international business community that ignoring the concerns of various groups can be continued only at great risk.

The message to policy-makers both in Congress and the Executive is that domestic interests must be taken into account when setting foreign economic policy. At one time many such decisions were made on the assumption that international economic developments did not materially affect the United States and that foreign economic policy could be divorced not only from domestic considerations but also from international security and political interests as well. These various elements are part of a seamless web and must be treated as such. Otherwise, similar behavior in the future could harm the interests of various groups within the United States and their narrowly conceived reactions would jeopardize a rational foreign economic policy.

The answer is not for the United States to move in the direction of the Andean nations—clamping strict requirements on foreign investment—nor that of Canada—screening and limiting foreign investment. Our situation is different, with foreign investment still a small portion of a much larger economy. However, it does mean we must find answers to the hard questions. The necessary first step in that direction is the collection and regular updating of complete and accurate information. Appropriate disclosure requirements must be levied on foreign investors so that both federal and state governments can gain a thorough grasp on the trends of foreign investment and its sectoral distribution. The data must be brought together and subjected to systematic, policy-oriented analysis, rather than being left in a raw form segmented among numerous governmental agencies. Valid information is essential, not just for the use of policy-makers in setting policy, but in allaying rumor-fueled suspicions such as have periodically assailed various parts of the country since 1972.

Leadership in this and related areas, furthermore, will require the elevation of foreign economic policy decision-making to a higher level within the U.S. government. Foreign policy in this country has too long been wedded to straight balance-of-power considerations and to conventional definitions of security interests. Foreign economic policy attitudes and formulation in particular have too often been a reflex reaction to sudden shock:

witness the hasty 1968 balance-of-payments regulations or the sudden lurch into the reforms of August 1971. Just as it is time to cease preparing for the last war and crisis, so it is high time to recognize that in international relations, economic issues have attained ascendancy over political and security matters. Some small steps in this direction have been taken—the creation of CIEP and the expansion of the number of economic positions in the Department of State—but CIEP has not proved to be the focal point for foreign economic policy that had been hoped, and State has not as yet taken a lead role.

These two steps—information gathering and structural improvement—will not by themselves answer the concern of the farmer who sees a soybean processing plant taken over by foreign interests and who wants to know what it means for his crops and his prices and his access to transportation facilities. But they will help us develop the right answers, and allow the Congress to push the Executive to share and meet such concerns.

The Future of the Multinational Enterprise

John H. Dunning is professor of economics at the University of Reading and was a member of the Group of Eminent Persons appointed by the secretary-general of the United Nations in 1973 to study the impact of the multinational corporations. His essay was originally published in the July 1974 issue of the Lloyds Bank Review.

THE MULTINATIONAL ENTERPRISE is approaching a crossroad in its development in the world economy. After an unparalleled and almost unchecked expansion in its activities in the 1950s and 1960s, its future role in economic development is being increasingly questioned. Not so long ago, it was being confidently predicted that, within the foreseeable future, the 300 or 400 largest companies with foreign direct investments would account for 60 to 70 per cent of the world's industrial output outside the centrally planned economies. In the economic and political environment of the mid-1970s, this prediction seems highly unrealistic. Over the course of the last five years, in particular, quite dramatic changes have occurred which suggest that the international economic order might be substantially reshaped in the years to come.

This article traces the forces making for the growth of the multinational enterprise since 1950, and speculates a little about its prospects. It begins by discussing certain parallels between trade and foreign direct investment as forms of international economic involvement, arguing that they have much in common and provoke similar reactions by governments. It then highlights the main determinants of international production under three broad headings: the general economic and political environment; the attitudes and policies of investing (home) and recipient (host) countries; and the goals, capabilities, and strategies of multinational enterprises. Finally, I describe how changes in these conditions have affected the flow and pattern of international production in the last two decades and how changes now taking place, or likely to take place, will affect it in the future.

WHAT IS A MULTINATIONAL ENTERPRISE?

First, however, it is important to be clear what we mean by a multinational enterprise. A multinational enterprise is one which undertakes foreign direct investment, i.e., which owns or controls income-gathering assets in more than one country; and, in so doing, produces goods or services outside its country of origin, that is, engages in international production. Multinational enterprises may be publicly or privately owned. Of the leading 211 manufacturing companies with sales of over $1 billion in 1971 listed in the UN document *Multinational Corporations in World Development*, all save a few engage in international production but at least 12 are state owned. I anticipate that the number of state-owned multinationals may increase in the years to come, particularly as more socialist-inclined and less-developed countries spawn multinationals of their own.

Like animals in a zoo, multinationals (and their affiliates) come in various shapes and sizes, perform distinctive functions, behave differently, and make their individual impacts on the environment. The skills and know-how provided by multinationals are different in resource-based industries from those provided in manufacturing industries. The control mechanisms of multinationals which adopt an integrated production or marketing strategy towards their affiliates are not the same as those which treat their affiliates as largely autonomous units. Large multinationals from powerful developed countries, operating in small developing countries, in which there is little or no indigenous industry, pose quite different problems from those of their smaller counterparts which compete alongside established producers in advanced markets. Moreover, the extent to which an enterprise engages in international production may be neither its most important characteristic nor the major cause of its impact on the economies in which it operates. Any analysis of multinational enterprises must take account of these structural differences, and any generalizations about their activities should be treated with great caution.

FORMS OF INTERNATIONAL ECONOMIC INVOLVEMENT

International production, financed by foreign direct investment, is one of many forms of international economic involvement. A country may be said to be internationally involved wherever at least some decisions over the way its resources are used are taken by institutions (including governments) or individuals in other countries or by regional or international bodies. Such involvement introduces an element of openness and interdependence to the participating economies, and produces certain costs and benefits, the balance between which depends both on the form of international involvement and on the conditions under which it takes place. Trade, for example, may bring benefits arising from a more efficient allocation of the world's resources and the opening up of new markets. It may also bring costs, or potential costs, most of which stem from a loss of control of participating countries over their own resources.

Partly because of these costs, completely free trade has not existed for many years; nor are the conditions under which the benefits of free trade were first promulgated often present in the modern world. In retrospect, it is possible to distinguish between a number of phases through which trade has evolved during the last two centuries. The years following the Industrial Revolution were the golden era of free trade, particularly for Britain, its main beneficiary. But, even for Britain, this period was, for a variety of reasons, short-lived. Initially, by means of tariffs and other import controls and, later, by the abandonment of the monetary system underpinning free trade, this form of international involvement became regulated by governments.

Until the Second World War, attempts to control the volume and terms of trade were undertaken largely unilaterally, with each country seeking to protect its own interests. However, such measures often provoked retaliation and proved to be self-defeating. Efforts were then made to conclude bilateral treaties on trade between countries and/or by groups of countries with respect to particular commodities. It was not until after the Second World

War when the International Monetary Fund (IMF) formed the basis for the international monetary system and the General Agreement on Tariffs and Trade (GATT) the basis for international trade, that a multinational machinery was created for an orderly system of trade; this, while far from being perfect, avoided the worst features of free trade on the one hand and unilateral import restrictions on the other.

Since countries do not find it in their interests to engage in free trade, it is understandable why they may wish to exert some control over other forms of international economic involvement which have similar effects. Here, we are interested in the openness and interdependence introduced by the operation of one country's enterprises in that of another country; sometimes as a substitute for trade, sometimes as a complement to it. Where foreign direct investment provides resources to a host country which enable it to produce goods more cheaply than could have been imported (exclusive of tariffs or other import duties), then it acts as a superior substitute for trade. This will be the case whenever there are natural barriers to trade, e.g., transport and marketing costs, or barriers to entry of indigenous producers to necessary knowledge (technological, managerial, marketing) or to the economies of scale and integration possessed by the foreign enterprises.

On the other hand, the terms on which these resources are provided and the control over the way in which they are actually deployed may impose a cost unacceptable to host countries. In such cases, countries will seek either to obtain these resources in other ways or to control the amount, direction, and terms of international production. How much and in what form control is exerted depends on the estimated cost/benefit ratio of free international production, compared with that of regulated international production or of obtaining resources provided by multinationals in alternative ways.

It is worth recalling that international production as an important form of international economic involvement is fairly new. Though the multinational enterprise has a long heritage, even at the eve of the Second World War the value of international production was only one-third that of international trade in general. In the mid-1950s and 1960s, the growth of foreign production outpaced that of trade, in spite of trade liberalization, and by 1970 had exceeded that of trade in total. In the case of the leading international direct investor (the U.S.), foreign production is four times as great and, in the case of the second largest (the U.K.), it is more than twice as great, as their respective total exports.

A second feature of international production concerns its geographical origins. Even in 1971, two-thirds of the foreign investment stake was of U.S. or U.K. origin, although these same countries accounted for just over one-fifth of all exports. This is an interesting fact in itself. Trade implies economic interdependence, as, normally over the long run, a country's exports and imports are fairly evenly balanced. This is not so with international production, where the flow of direct investment may be only one way. The majority of countries in the world are, in fact, substantial net importers of foreign capital; thus the dependence effect of foreign investment may be, and usually is, much greater than that of trade.

But, over and above these general consequences of openness, international production has other effects. These arise mainly because, while trade normally takes place between independent economic agents, international production, financed by foreign direct investment, involves no change in ownership. In trade, buyers and sellers have competing goals; in international production, producing affiliates seek to meet the goals set by their parent companies. These differences are likely to be most pronounced wherever international production gives rise to substantial economies of integration and where its ownership is concentrated in the hands of a few large firms.

DETERMINANTS OF INTERNATIONAL PRODUCTION

There are many factors which influence the level and character of international production. These may be considered under three broad headings: the general international and national economic and political environment; specific policies and attitudes towards foreign direct investment and multinational enterprises by home and host countries; the character and organizational strategy of multinational enterprises.

The General Economic and Political Environment · Given a
neutral policy towards foreign direct investment and the multinational enterprise, the general economic and political environment is perhaps the most important influence on international
production. Most firms have some choice of what and where to
produce, and some influence on their patterns of growth. International production is one option which may be considered as an
alternative to production at home, either to supply the domestic or export market. Both domestic and international economic considerations influence this choice, as they do the goods
to be produced. In particular, the choice between supplying a
foreign market from a domestic or foreign base will be influenced, *inter alia*, by exchange rates, transport costs, tariff and
nontariff barriers, relative input costs, size of markets, and the
technology of multiplant operations. On the other hand, the
ability of foreign affiliates to compete with local companies will
depend on the extent to which their advantages of being part of
a larger foreign firm outweigh the additional marketing and other
costs of international production.

The determinants of these choices are most often shaped by
technological factors and government policies. Advances in com-
munications technology, for example, may make it easier for enterprises to operate geographically separate plants; advances in
enterprise-specific knowledge which can be effectively exploited
only by large firms give multinationals in research-intensive
industries an advantage; tariffs and other import controls induce
international production in place of trade, and an overvalued
exchange rate of the exporting country does the same thing;
policies promoting regional integration may encourage both
trade and investment; the discovery of new sources of energy,
a changed bargaining position between raw material producers
and consumers, and policies towards industrialization may each
influence the terms of trade between the developed and less-
developed nations. All of these, and other factors, including the
role of international trading and monetary organizations, may
vitally affect the environment in which foreign direct investment
takes place.

Some of these environmental conditions are specific to particular countries; and it is not difficult to establish which countries

are attractive to multinational enterprises or which spawn multi-nationals. Some affect particular industries or forms of investment; others are common to all forms of international economic involvement.

Attitudes and Policies towards Foreign Direct investment · Policies towards international production are, in fact, rarely neutral. Most host and home countries have introduced specific measures to regulate the activities of foreign affiliates in their midst. These include the screening of new investments; controlling the conditions of production by foreign affiliates, or procurement behavior policies, e.g., with respect to their pricing practices, their exports, dividend remissions; ensuring the benefits created by foreign direct investment and the share retained by host countries are maximized; and various devices to harmonize the decisions of foreign affiliates with the interests of host countries.

Foreign affiliates may also be treated differently from indigenous firms with respect to more specific issues: access to local capital markets, competition policy, regional incentives, and measures taken to improve the balance of payments. Home governments may also use their power to affect the behavior of their own multinationals: by capital controls, taxation of foreign income, extraterritorial legislation, and so on.

The Character and Strategy of Multinational Enterprises · There are many specific factors which make for more or less international production. These are related essentially to the financial, managerial, marketing, and technological capabilities of firms; their size; and their organizational strategies. Not only is it possible to indicate particular industries in which multinational enterprises operate or countries which are net capital exporters; so particular types of firms tend to be pace-setters as international producers. In a manufacturing industry, for example, the single-product firm will be more likely to engage in international production when transport costs are high, scale economies of the plant are low, local customer requirements vary between markets, product differentiation is marked, and the national barriers of entry to indigenous producers are formidable.

For the multiproducts or multiprocessing producer, there is a choice whether to set up in other countries. In those areas where differences in costs and productivity promote trade, so too will they make for specialization by multinational enterprises and within such enterprises. Since most of the larger multinationals in manufacturing are diversified as regards products or processes, and factor costs do differ more between countries than within countries, there is plenty of scope for this kind of specialization.

Besides technological and size factors, the style of management may differ between companies. As a company's international involvement grows, so its organizational structure changes. Personalities may also play an important part. At the same time, control patterns differ between functions. For example, while decisions on capital expenditure, research and development, and the allocation of export markets may be centralized, those on personnel policy and industrial relations may be localized.

DEVELOPMENTS SINCE 1950

It is by analyzing the changing conditions for international production that one can best understand what has happened in the last twenty years and what may happen in the next two decades. I believe that, like policies towards trade, those towards international production have followed a fairly distinct evolutionary pattern and that, together with environmental conditions and changes in the organizational structure of the multinational enterprises, they have brought this form of international involvement to a point corresponding to the interwar years in the development of trade. At the same time, attitudes towards international involvement *per se* are themselves undergoing change. Let us consider what has happened in the last quarter of a century, since 1950.

The Honeymoon Period: 1950 to Mid-1960s · The precise timing of this phase differs between countries, but it is distinguishable by the especially favorable environment for international production, and particularly that undertaken by U.S. firms. During these years, the U.S. dominated international production as the U.K. had dominated trade a century and a half earlier. It was the honeymoon period between host countries and multinational enterprises, during which the benefits of foreign direct investment were widely acclaimed. Western Europe, for example, starved of capital, knowledge, and human skills and desperately short of foreign currency, had no option but to acquire them from the U.S. which, in 1950, was technologically far and away the most advanced country in the world. American firms were especially welcome for the new resources they provided. In rich developing countries, like Canada and Australia, the need was no less pressing. It was for money and human capital to develop indigenous national resources and to supply products which, because of their small markets, could not be economically produced by their own firms. The poorer developing countries, particularly those with untapped mineral resources, were just beginning to appreciate their own economic potential but, again, were crucially short of the organizational skills and capital by which they could translate this potential into actual wealth. Since the import of goods or technology was not possible because of the shortage of foreign exchange, and as most countries did not have infrastructure or institutional framework (as did Japan) to rely on licensing, foreign direct investment had a flourishing environment in which to operate. These were the years in which the technological and managerial gap between the U.S. and the rest of the world was at its widest.

Besides these "pull" factors, there were "push" factors in the leading capital exporting country: the U.S.A. By the mid-1950s some of the steam had gone out of the domestic economy. Institutional constraints inhibited domestic expansion by merger. Rates of return on capital and growth prospects seemed more promising in other countries. Scale economies and technological developments were favoring the larger firm; the production of knowledge, often financed by government support, was becoming more enterprise-specific and more difficult to assimilate by those who had not produced it; to finance expensive innovatory costs, large markets were necessary; and, towards the end of the period, the dollar became overvalued relatively to other currencies.

Within this broad economic environment, international production by American firms flourished. Import protection and the need to exploit new markets also encouraged U.K. investment in the same period. Because, too, of the need for the package of resources which the multinational could provide, host countries were willing to adopt very generous policies to inward investment. Some attempted to influence the direction of investment or to ensure that it was in conformity with the more pressing national goals—e.g., improving the balance of payments—but most imposed few constraints. The cost/benefit ratio was rarely calculated, as the benefits were taken for granted. Little attention was paid to obtaining the resources provided by multinationals in other ways.

For the most part, the strategy of multinationals during this period was simple and straightforward. Most affiliates in manufacturing were set up to supply local or other markets in place of imports. The affiliates operated largely independently of each other and were closely identified with the interests of the local economy. Few firms had yet evolved an integrated or global strategy. Though most decisions, especially those taken by newly established affiliates, were controlled by parent companies, they were usually geared to advance the prosperity and growth of the affiliate. There was comparatively little intragroup trading or product or process specialization within the multinationals. Branch plants were offshoots of parent companies and in only a few countries, e.g., the U.K., did affiliates do much exporting.

Partly for these reasons, partly because so little was known about the effects of foreign affiliates, and partly because their involvement in local economies was generally small, some of the costs of foreign investment were discounted or not even considered. There was little xenophobia. Free international production seemed to be the order of the day, the equivalent for the multinational enterprise of the free-trade era.

Counting the Costs: Mid-1960s to Mid-1970s · In this period, attention switched to the cost of, and alternatives to, international production financed by foreign direct investment. The report of the UN Study Group[1] on multinational corporations identifies these costs. Although it acknowledges the benefits, it recognizes that the multinational enterprise is under criticism. The honey-

1. Report of the Group of Eminent Persons on the Role of Multinational Corporations in World Development and International Relations (United Nations, 1974).

moon period is over. In spite of impressive research evidence that, on balance, the economic welfare of host countries has been advanced by foreign direct investment, its net benefits are being increasingly questioned. Bad news often makes the headlines more than good news. This certainly has been the case with multinationals, and public opinion about them has been much colored by incidents in recent years of a disturbing character, as in Chile, for example.

How has this change in attitude come about in such a remarkably short period of time? Will it last? What does it foreshadow for the future? How has it been reflected in government policies towards the multinationals?

On the first question, there are many reasons for the increasing concern about multinationals. Perhaps the most important lies simply in their significance both in domestic economies and in the world economic scene. Currently, more than 20 per cent of the world's industrial output outside centrally planned economies is supplied by multinationals. In almost every country, affiliates of foreign firms have increased their share of the national product; in more than a score, they now account for over one-third of the output of manufacturing industries. In some sectors, they have acquired a dominating position. Among these are the high-technology industries of the late twentieth century: computers, industrial instruments, pharmaceuticals, and so on. In less-developed countries, they own or control many vital raw materials: oil, copper, aluminum, zinc; and in service industries, they are, or have been dominant in insurance, banking, and tourism.

Second, with this growing international involvement has come a change in the management style and organizational strategy within multinationals. In the very industries in which international production has grown the fastest, product or process specialization is the most widely practiced. In consequence, in these industries, at least, foreign affiliates have become less rather than more like their indigenous competitors, for example, in how they behave and react towards domestic economic policies.

Third, the rapid growth of international production has occurred at a time when most governments have become more aware of the need for centralized economic planning. This was already well in evidence in the 1950s and 1960s but it has accelerated and spread in the last decade. Both in developed and developing countries, the state is participating increasingly in economic affairs. Not only has this been undertaken for the usual Keynesian reasons, but on a much broader front—e.g., long-term economic planning, urban redevelopment, environmental control, preservation of raw materials—governments now exert much more influence on the way resources are used. It follows, then, that anything which reduces their ability to control the behavior of foreign firms, without having to resort to special measures, is regarded as a challenge to their economic sovereignty.

From the viewpoint of developing countries, the situation has changed even more dramatically. As countries have become politically independent and are searching for their own identity, they have often tended to reject the ties of the past, including direct investment by foreign companies, which they regard as a form of economic imperialism or colonialism. They have also become more aware of the value of the resources they possess, while, at the same time, their knowledge of how to control the use of these resources has increased. Their contacts with the outside world, particularly through education and contacts with international agencies, especially the United Nations, and the technical aid received from such bodies, have made them conscious both of their economic power and of the wider implications of inward investment. They have become better equipped to evaluate the effects of such investment and of the alternatives to it. As they have formulated development plans, their perception of the contribution of multinationals has widened. Not only are they interested in their impact on technology, employment, or the balance of payments, but also in how they affect consumption patterns, cultural goals, and the distribution of income.

This process of reorientation in outlook has not always been accompanied by the most sensible policies on the part of host countries. All too frequently, the multinational has been made the scapegoat for the failure of host governments to manage their economies properly. Though some developing countries still adopt a liberal approach towards inward investment, most have introduced stringent control procedures on types of investment permitted and conditions of production. In some cases, nationalization and expropriation have been resorted to; in others, there has been insistence upon local majority ownership and a gradual disinvestment of assets.

Developed countries, too, have attempted to reduce the costs of and increase the benefits from foreign direct investment. In Europe, the fear has been that American direct investment, particularly in research-intensive industries, would lead to technological dependence on the U.S. The main weapon used to forestall this has been to encourage "countervailing power," both by the rationalization of domestic firms and by mergers between European and/or European and U.S. companies. Similarly, there has been concern about the effects of foreign investment on the balance of payments and competition policy, and whether the share of the benefits accruing to the local economy was as much as it should have been.

Home countries have been no less concerned about the impact of foreign investment by their own multinationals on their own balances of payments, employment, and competitive positions. In the U.S., in particular, various efforts are being made by labor and other interests to control the flow of American direct foreign investment.

In part, this reaction against the multinational enterprise has nothing to do with its multinationality as such. Nor is it as widespread as may be thought. Those who are most vocal often represent special interests or have particular political axes to grind. There is much less outcry from the man in the street, to whom the benefits of foreign direct investment are more immediately obvious than its costs. Moreover, the multinational is caught up in a general disquiet about bigness in business, and in the developed countries in at least a questioning of economic growth as an end in itself. Greater attention is now being placed on income relatives and on the widening gap between rich and poor countries; on the environment, the depletion of natural resources, protecting energy supplies, and so on. At every turn, the multinationals seem to be involved and are an easy target for complaint. The present climate of opinion towards them must be interpreted in this broader context.

How have the targets of attack reacted to these views and to the efforts made to regulate their activities? As yet, the statistics would suggest the multinationals' operations have been affected only marginally. The pace of new investment is slowing down, but it is still impressive, at least within the developed world. How long this will continue, if present attitudes to foreign investment persist, is another matter. In recent years, the general environment facing the world's largest companies has been much less favorable to growth. As a result of the realignment of currencies, U.S. companies find foreign investment less attractive than previously. Inflation has produced difficult cash-flow situations. Disengagement may be the order of the day, particularly in the uncertain environment of developing countries. The alternative is for companies to adapt their involvement to meet the particular needs of host countries, a course being actively pursued by some of the smaller multinationals, particularly those of Japanese and Continental European origin.

REPORT OF THE UN STUDY GROUP

It is my belief that we are at the beginning of a fairly fundamental reappraisal, both by countries of the role of multinationals in their development and by multinationals towards the form and direction of their international involvement. The present situation, with few exceptions, ranges from one of uneasy alliance to one of open hostility. Even where the attitudes towards foreign direct investment are still welcoming—e.g., in much of Southeast Asia—one wonders how long they will last.

Policies so far adopted towards multinationals have been largely unilateral, and only occasionally bilateral in character. Just as the incentives to investment were originally of this kind, so now are the regulations and constraints. As these constraints multiply, there is a real danger of international production seizing up—as did international trade in the 1930s—to the disadvantage of all nations. Indeed, there is some evidence that such a retrenchment has already begun.

It is at this point that the Report of the UN study group on multinational corporations is particularly pertinent. It rejects both the view put forward from some quarters that the nation-state is dead and that the world is moving to economic interdependence and unhampered trade and international production, and also the opposite view that economic nationalism will become the order of the day and international trade and production will be severely constrained.

The group takes as its starting point the need to approach the control of international production from a multilateral viewpoint. It observes that, while at present there are organizations such as GATT and the United Nations Conference on Trade and Development (UNCTAD) which help to create orderly conditions for trade and, to a certain extent, influence the terms of trade, such institutions are necessary to regulate the flow of international production. In its report, the group proposes that consideration should be given to the conclusion of a General Agreement on Multinational Enterprises (GAME) between governments, which would identify and set out the general conditions for international production. These might include, *inter alia,* the harmonization of investment incentives, double taxation agreements, antitrust legislation, competition policy, controls on capital flows and dividend remissions, and questions relating to extraterritoriality. I believe this is on the right lines, although, rather than to focus attention on particular institutions, which possess many characteristics other than that of multinationality, I consider that it should be "issue"- or "problem"-oriented and that a General Agreement on International Production (GAIP) would be a more appropriate nomenclature.

While acknowledging the benefits of international production, the group's report concentrates on the problems which it may cause countries, or may seem to cause. It seeks to identify these and concludes that some are inherent in the nature of multinationality, while many are due to unsatisfactory terms of international production agreed on at the point of entry, resulting from inadequate bargaining power of host countries *vis-à-vis* large international investors. It argues that, for the good of all parties, the terms of entry should be fair and seen to be fair; that companies should know exactly what is expected of them by host countries; that, as far as possible, foreign affiliates should identify themselves with the local economies in which they operate; and that countries should not take discriminatory or retroactive measures against multinationals, which have led to so much bitterness and misunderstanding between companies and countries in the past.

Finally, the group argues the need for harmonization of policies of host countries towards international production. Initially, this might be done by the conclusion of voluntary agreements or codes of conduct, in which respect the multinationals themselves can play an important role, or by bilateral treaties on certain aspects of international production. Eventually, over the years, a more comprehensive mechanism is needed to tackle international production, to avoid distortions and to make possible orderly production, while allowing flexibility to countries in particular situations.

As an immediate step to this end, the group proposes the establishment of a permanent Commission on Multinational Enterprises responsible to the Economic and Social Council of the UN, to whom it would make an annual report. This commission would have a variety of functions[2] and it is proposed it should be supported by an information and reserch center whose job would be both to collect and to analyze data relating to all aspects of international production. The group also felt that the technical advisory services of the United Nations should be strengthened to assist governments, particularly in developing countries, in their dealings with large multinational enterprises. All these functions are designed to improve the economic environment for direct investment and to get more data about its consequences, including questions relating to income distribution, appropriateness of technology, consumers' welfare, and so on.

This approach of the group, directed to creating more harmonious conditions for international production, will most certainly have its critics. To some, it will be felt that the sovereignty of states has been insufficiently protected; that there is nothing proposed which could reduce the dependency of developing countries on foreign capital and entrepreneurship or to improve

2. These include providing a forum for the presentation and exchange of views of governments, intergovernmental, and nongovernmental organizations about the impact of multinationals on world development; undertaking work leading to the adoption of specific agreements in selected areas relating to the activities of multinationals; conducting inquiries, making studies, preparing reports, and organizing panels for facilitating a dialogue among the parties concerned; and promoting a program of technical cooperation, including training and advisory services, aimed, in particular, at strengthening the capacity of developing countries in their relations with multinational corporations.

the balance of economic power between developed and less-developed countries. Here nothing less than a revolution in the whole system and institutional mechanism by which resources are allocated would suffice. On the other hand, those who are looking for a vindication of the existing system of resource allocation can take little comfort either. Though a careful reading of the report will show that the group was cautious not to generalize about the behavior of all multinationals from its knowledge of a well-publicized few, there was some unease that the economic power of many of the larger multinationals could be used against the interest of countries or particular groups. It felt that, although some conflict is inevitable, because of the differences in goals of companies and countries, unless something is done to create a better understanding, the relationships between multinationals and countries and other interests will deteriorate to the disadvantage of all concerned. One's judgment is, of course, clearly clouded by the way in which one thinks the world economic system ought to be arranged and how in the foreseeable future it is likely to be arranged.

FUTURE PROSPECTS FOR MULTINATIONALS

In all this, I believe that a distinction should be drawn between the future of multinational enterprises in developed and in less-developed countries. Concern is greatest where the countries in which foreign production is undertaken are most different—ideologically, politically, and economically—from those making the investment. An investment by a powerful industrial nation, with a belief in the free-enterprise economy, made in a small centrally planned developing economy, where there is little indigenous competition and where cultural and other goals are different, may bring far more tensions than where the same investment is made in a similar environment. For these reasons, I foresee that there may be fewer problems connected with trans-Atlantic investment in the next few years than with that made by advanced countries in less-advanced countries and that, in the future, the development of foreign investment may take two quite separate courses.

So far as direct investment between developed countries is

concerned, apart from closer economic integration in Europe, the environment for international production is unlikely to change much. The main problems arising from it will essentially be those normally posed to industrial societies by powerful companies, but in an international context.

A good guide to the approach of the European Communities (EC) Commission is contained in its document *Multinational Undertakings and Community Regulations*. Basically, the concern of the commission is to ensure that the monopolistic power and flexibility of foreign multinationals are not used against the interest of host countries in the community. There is also some concern lest a lack of harmonization among individual countries on tax, competition, and regional incentive policies may induce foreign companies to play one European country off against another. There is, however, less fear than once there was that Europe will be economically dominated by U.S. firms, particularly as, in the next decade, European direct investment in the U.S. is likely to grow faster than U.S. investment in Europe and as the technological and managerial gap may narrow further. Nevertheless, the commission believes that a united European policy towards foreign investment will strengthen the bargaining positions of individual countries. One is less sanguine about their efforts to promote indigenous competition in some of the high-technology industries.

So long as there are proper safeguards, it would seem that foreign (=mainly U.S.) enterprises will continue to be given a qualified welcome to invest in Europe; there seems little pressure among EC countries to encourage other forms of arrangements with foreign firms. One may expect more public involvement in some industries—e.g., oil and motor cars, computers and pharmaceuticals—in which foreign companies are actively concerned. A rather more cautious treatment may be accorded to Japanese investment, but as yet this has not created a serious problem.

So far as investment between developed and developing countries is concerned, the situation is very different and there are reasons to suppose that the role of the multinational may undergo substantial change. First, the environment which shapes the economic relationships between the developed and less-developed world is changing. We can illustrate from recent oil developments, where the developing nations are making concerted efforts to improve their bargaining position and terms of trade *vis-à-vis* consuming countries. This is also happening at a regional level, as seen, for example, by the efforts of the Andean Pact countries. When the supply of basic commodities vital to the prosperity of consuming nations is threatened, governments of these nations inevitably become involved; and this could mean that in place of market forces bilateral governmental agreements may determine the conditions and terms of trade. It may well be that international agreements on the supply of a variety of commodities may set the future framework within which multinationals operate. If this is so, the role of multinationals in resource-based industries may be much less decisive than in the past.

With respect to specific attitudes by developing countries to foreign direct investment, even when its advantages are undisputed there is a dislike of foreign ownership. This, then, leads countries to consider alternatives to multinationals. In the belief that they can rid themselves of foreign control over their economies, host countries either encourage divestment or, by "unwrapping the package" of foreign investment, attempt to buy the individual ingredients from separate sources. In some cases, this may not be difficult to do: capital and many kinds of knowledge can be bought on the open market. But such a policy can be successful only if the local economy has the necessary technological expertise to choose exactly what is needed and, once acquired, is able to assimilate the resources and to use them productively. But as many countries are finding to their cost, the replacement of international production by production undertaken under foreign licence or management contract is not necessarily less costly; nor does it always lessen economic dependence. Knowledge still has been imported; and, because of imperfections in the diffusion of knowledge and technology, on the one hand, and lack of local capabilities, on the other, the key components of dependence—at least at the firm level—still remain.

At the same time, the sources of the main ingredients of foreign investment are widening. Already, much new capital is flowing from the oil countries; technology is being exported from the centrally planned economies; and in the 1980s more advanced developing countries may become suppliers. There is some suggestion of a technological convergence among the industrial powers. If this is so, the developing countries will no longer be dependent on the traditional sources of knowledge, nor be bound by the traditional ways of obtaining it.

With political attitudes as they are, with a growing bargaining power of developing countries, and with alternatives to such investment becoming available, one might expect the multinational enterprise to invest rather less in developing countries in the future. On the other hand, in some kinds of activity involving centralized decisions they may invest more. The exodus of some firms from high-cost countries to take advantage of lower costs and to concentrate labor-intensive parts of their international operations may well continue and intensify. At the same time, there will be pressure from trade unions and others for a gradual upgrading of the type of work delegated to developing countries.

There are other reasons to suppose direct investment might grow in developing countries. As they become wealthier and their markets grow, developing countries become more attractive to foreign companies. Pressures in the oil-producing countries for more petroleum-processing activities may offer great prospects for foreign petro-chemical and plant equipment companies. As their governments become more stable and expert at managing their economies, the riskiness of foreign investment declines; firms may then be prepared to accept a lower rate of return. As these countries are seen to accord fair treatment to foreign companies, the incentive to invest will increase.

Host countries, undoubtedly, have much to learn about the costs and benefits of direct investment, which is made all the more difficult in developing countries as they struggle to identify their goals of development and the best way to achieve them. In this respect, the advisory services of professional bodies and international agencies can help. So can the multinationals, by a more sensitive understanding of the aspirations of developing countries. The international community can also play its part, by considering whether or not, in the light of international production, existing machinery needs to be modified. Very often, the multinationals have made people in rich countries more aware not only of some of the problems existing between rich and poor countries, but of the inadequacies of existing machineries to deal with them.

I would make one final point. I believe that the immense resources of multinationals are not being fully harnessed and that they are able to help governments to reach their goals. They often possess the very capabilities necessary for development but, as yet, they have been used to meet largely commercial demands, mainly in the developed countries. These are not the priorities of developing countries. Since these cannot be satisfied entirely through commercial markets, some cooperation with governments is necessary. In food and agriculture, this has been started with the Industrial Co-operative Programme of the Food and Agriculture Organization of the United Nations, in which many leading multinational companies are involved. Cooperation with governments in social infrastructure, e.g., for electrification and irrigation schemes, exploration of the sea-bed, and similar schemes, is also needed.

Given a world which recognizes the benefits of multilaterally regulated international economic involvement, and provided that the machinery to accomplish this is adequate, I believe that multinational enterprises still have a vital role to play in world development, but that the nature of this role will change. In general, I believe that direct investment will be a relatively less important channel for the transfer of knowledge; instead, there will be more nonfinancial investment, e.g., in knowledge and human skills in developed countries, which will then be supplied to the developing countries on a contract basis. This means that, in place of investment in equity capital—for which the reward is profits—there will be a package of services supplied by one firm to another or to governments—for which the reward will be a management or licensing fee. To the country, for direct investment by ownership will be substituted a contractual relationship of a limited duration, with ownership left in national hands. To the firm, its foreign earnings will take the form of fees for services rendered; and, already, such fees are rising at a faster rate than profits.

The years up to 1914 saw the export of portfolio capital and the migration of labor. Over the last 20 years, the main vehicle of international economic involvement has been direct investment. Perhaps we are now at the beginning of a new period, in which firms will increasingly export a package of services, comprising knowledge, loan capital, and human skills, rather than own productive facilities. The era of the multinational consultancy firm or agency selling capital services may have begun.

PART FOUR   International Economic
Interdependence and
Monetary Reform

National Economic Policy
in an Interdependent World Economy

RICHARD N. COOPER

*Richard N. Cooper, a professor of economics on leave from Yale
University, is undersecretary for economic affairs at the U.S. Department of State. In this essay, originally published in the June
1967 issue of the* Yale Law Journal, *he considers the implications
of increased economic interdependence for policy making in the
industrial nations.*

DURING THE PAST DECADE, there has been a strong trend toward
economic interdependence among the industrial countries. This
growing interdependence makes the successful pursuit of national economic objectives much more difficult. Broadly speaking,
increasing interdependence complicates the pursuit of national
objectives in three ways. First, it increases the number and
magnitude of the disturbances to which each country's balance
of payments is subjected, and this in turn diverts policy attention and instruments of policy to the restoration of external
balance. Second, it slows down the process by which national
authorities, each acting on its own, are able to reach their domestic objectives. Third, the response to greater integration can
involve the community of nations in counteracting motions which
leave all countries worse off than they need be. These difficulties
are in turn complicated by the fact that the objective of greater
economic integration involves international agreements which

reduce the number of policy instruments available to national authorities for pursuit of their economic objectives. This article touches on all of these facets of higher economic interdependence among industrial nations, both as a fact and as an objective, but its principal focus is on the third complication—the process of mutually damaging competition among national policies.

There can be little doubt about the great growth in international economic interdependence over the last two decades. Import quotas in industrial countries have been virtually abolished on trade in manufactured products, tariffs have been reduced, and transportation costs have fallen relative to the value of goods. At the same time, the accumulation of capital and the spread of technology have made national economies more similar in their basic characteristics of production; comparative cost differences have apparently narrowed, suggesting that imports can be replaced by domestic production with less loss in national income than heretofore. Whether a country imports a particular good or exports it thus becomes less dependent on the basic characteristics of the economy, more dependent on historical development and on relatively accidental and transitory features of recent investment decisions at home and abroad. An invention in one country may lead to production there for export, but the new product will relatively quickly be produced abroad—or supplanted by a still newer product—and possibly even exported to the original innovating country.

Monetary disturbances, too, are likely to be much more quickly translated into changes in the volume of exports and imports than they were formerly. Under fixed exchange rates, greater than average monetary inflation in one country will invite a more rapid deterioration in the balance on goods and services than was true in the past.

Enlargement of the decision-making domain of the world's great producing firms results in the rapid movement of capital and technical knowledge across national frontiers, thereby contributing to the narrowing of comparative cost differences; but their activity will also quicken the speed with which trade adjusts to new sales opportunities because they have direct knowledge of foreign markets and access to distribution channels.

Finally, as financial markets become more closely integrated, relatively small differences in yields on securities will induce large flows of funds between countries. Banks will increasingly number "foreign" firms among their prime customers; the advantages of inexpensive credit to firms in countries with ample savings and well-functioning financial markets, such as the United States, will be shared increasingly with firms elsewhere.

All of these changes in the characteristics of the international economy during the past decade—and it should be emphasized that economic integration is still far from complete—are crucial to the functioning of the international payments system and the autonomy which it permits to national economic policy formation. These changes mean that in normal periods prospective imbalances in international payments—imbalances which would arise if countries did not respond to reduce them or did not adjust policy measures to forestall them—are likely to be more frequent and of larger amplitude than they have been in the past. "Disturbances" arising from new innovations, from generous wage settlements leading to price increases, and from excess or deficient domestic demand will affect the balance of payments more perceptibly. Whether or not imbalances also last longer depends upon the relationship among the "disturbances"; if they are well distributed among countries and tend equally toward deficit or surplus, the duration of prospective imbalances may well be less than in the past; otherwise it may be longer.

These changes suggest that balance-of-payments difficulties are likely to be more common in the future, and that they will worsen as the structural changes continue in their recent trend. By the same token, however, correction of imbalances in international payments should be easier in the future. Trade flows will respond more sharply to given small "disturbances"; but they should also respond more quickly to policy measures designed to influence them. If a small relative increase in the price level will lead a national economy into greater balance-of-payments difficulties than heretofore, a relatively small decrease should undo the difficulties. Similarly, international capital flows will respond more rapidly to small differences in national credit conditions; but small differences in national credit conditions directed to correcting the imbalance can induce equilibrating flows of capital. Thus if the national authorities can recognize disturbances early, are willing to use some of the tools at their disposal for correcting imbalances in international payments, and act reasonably quickly in doing so, then the increased sensitivity of international payments to various disturbances need cause no undue difficulty—provided that policy instruments are properly chosen and adequately coordinated among countries.

ECONOMIC OBJECTIVES AND POLICY INSTRUMENTS

A well-known proposition in the theory of economic policy requires that the number of policy instruments be at least as great as the number of objectives (target variables) if all objectives are to be achieved. If the number of instruments is fewer than the number of targets, it will not be possible to reach all of the targets; in that case, at least some targets must be given up, and the authorities must choose among them.

A simple example can illustrate the need to have at least as many instruments as targets. Suppose the government of an isolated country has two economic objectives: it would like to assure full employment of its labor force at all times, and it would like its national product to grow at a specified rate each year. It can vary the overall size of the budget deficit or surplus (fiscal policy) to assure full employment. But full employment of resources can be met with a variety of combinations of investment, consumption, and government expenditure. Without some other instrument, the desired growth rate cannot be assured. If, however, investment leads to more growth, then monetary policy and fiscal policy together can be manipulated to achieve the two objectives. The higher the growth rate desired, the lower should be the rate of interest. Fiscal policy can then be adjusted to assure full employment. This very simple model apparently influenced thinking in the early years of the Kennedy Administration.

Viewing economic policy as a problem in specifying targets and finding sufficient instruments to reach them helps to illuminate many policy problems confronting national authorities. The objective of greater economic integration has led many officials to reject both flexible exchange rates and frequent variations in fixed exchange rates as instruments for maintaining balance-of-payments equilibrium. A number of other instruments of policy have been ruled out by international agreement on the same grounds, or to avoid a round of retaliation and counter-retaliation that would leave all countries worse off than they were at the outset. Most types of export subsidies, tariff discrimination among countries, increases in tariffs, and discriminatory exchange regulations fall into this category. A number of provisions of the General Agreement on Tariffs and Trade (GATT) are devoted to these exclusions and prohibitions; with specified exceptions, such as the formation of customs unions or free-trade areas, trade discrimination is proscribed. So are many types of export subsidies and discrimination in domestic taxation between home and foreign goods. The articles of Agreement of the International Monetary Fund (IMF) make similar prohibitions with respect to currency arrangements. The extensive use of these measures in the past, especially in the 1930's, led to widespread retaliation and mutual recriminations, and they acquired a bad name among outward-looking officials. But the price of international rules of good behavior as set forth in the GATT and the IMF Articles has been a reduction in the range of instruments available to national policymakers.

Some usable policy instruments may be used, as a practical matter, only within a limited range. In the United States, changes in the discount rate of the Federal Reserve System and (since 1962) deliberate deficits or surpluses in the government budget are both regarded as legitimate tools of economic policy; but in normal times, the public is not likely to countenance a discount rate of 20 per cent or a budget deficit of $50 billion. These exceed the range of acceptability; policy instruments have "boundary conditions." In the abnormal situations when such limits become operative, they withdrew an instrument from use. Sometimes these limits are not fully known until they are tested; then we discover that we have more targets (or fewer instruments) than were previously apparent.

It goes without saying that to be attainable, economic objectives must be consistent. If they are not consistent, no number of policy instruments will be sufficient. One illustration in the forefront of discussion in most industrial countries involves the relationship between employment and price stability. Given the institution of private collective bargaining, is the target of "full employment" (4 per cent unemployment in the United States, under 2 per cent in the United Kingdom, each by its own standards and definitions) consistent with "price stability," defined, say, as stability in the consumer price index? Many economists would find a conflict.

This kind of inconsistency can perhaps be overcome by developing new policy instruments.[1] Another kind of inconsistency, especially important to national economies linked through international trade and capital movements, cannot be eliminated through the development of new instruments. Examples are objectives regarding the balance of payments or the trade balance. Since one country's trade surplus is another country's trade deficit, it is impossible for all countries to succeed in running trade surpluses. The same is true for balance of payments, taking into account capital movements. If there are n countries, only $n-1$ of them can succeed in achieving their independent balance of payments targets; at least one must accept defeat or else fail to target values for its trade position and its balance-of-payments position, thereby acting as an international residual. It has been suggested that the United States played this role until the late 1950's, by taking a relatively passive position toward its payments position after the termination of Marshall Plan aid.

The requirement of consistency is not merely theoretical. In 1962, for instance, all of the major industrial countries wanted simultaneously to improve their payments positions on current account. While mutual success was not logically impossible in this case, it did imply a correspondingly sharp deterioration in the current account position of the less developed countries taken together, which in turn would require ample financing from the industrial countries in the form of grants or loans. No such increase in capital movements was targeted. Thus national targets were inconsistent.

THE SPEED OF ADJUSTMENT

In summary, successful economic policy requires an adequate number of policy instruments for the number of economic ob-

1. These new instruments would involve shifting the trade-off between unemployment and price inflation—called the Phillips Curve—enough to make simultaneous attainment of the two objectives feasible. This is the thrust of "incomes policies."

jectives, and it requires that these objectives be consistent with one another. If either of these conditions fails, policymakers are bound to be frustrated in their efforts. Before turning to how these frustrations become manifest, however, one other point should be made: growing interdependence can slow down greatly the process by which independently acting national authorities reach their economic objectives, even when all the targets are consistent and there are sufficient policy instruments at hand to reach them. Thus in practice nations may find themselves further from their objectives than would be true with less interdependence.

High interdependence slows the speed of adjustment to disturbances if national policyholders do not take the interdependence into account. This is because the economic authorities in different countries may be working at cross-purposes. An investment boom in one country may raise interest rates both at home and, by attracting internationally mobile funds, in neighboring countries. The first country may temporarily welcome the high interest rates to help curb the boom and may also tighten fiscal policy to keep inflationary pressures in check. But the other countries may fear that higher interest rates will deter investment at home and take steps to lower interest rates. Unless this monetary relaxation is taken into account in framing fiscal policy in the first country, its authorities will find that fiscal policy has not been sufficiently contractionary. But more contractionary fiscal policy will tend to hold up interest rates, so that the monetary authorities in the neighboring countries will find they have only been partially successful in lowering their rates. Even if in the end the whole process settles to a point where the various national authorities are satisfied, it will have taken longer than if there had been close coordination between the authorities in the several countries involved. The greater the interactions between countries, the longer convergence will take if countries act on their own.

Sometimes, of course, actions in a neighboring country can reinforce those taken at home. If in the above example the domestic investment boom transmitted inflationary pressures to a neighboring country through enlarged imports, then contractionary fiscal policy there would complement contractionary fiscal policy at home. But in this case failure to take into account the interactions betwen the two countries may lead to over-correction and excessive unemployment. This will arise if the authorities in each country decide how much they have to act when acting alone to restore equilibrium; then when both groups act, the total effect will be excessive.

If policy decisions are truly decentralized among nations, in the sense that the authorities in each nation pursue only their own objectives with their own instruments without taking into account the interactions with other countries, then the more interdependent the international economy is, the less successful countries are likely to be in reaching and maintaining their economic objectives. This is due to the greater impact of domestic measures on foreign economies, calling forth correspondingly greater offsetting responses which in turn affect the first country. Under these circumstances, countries must either reconcile themselves to prolonged delays in reaching their objectives or they must coordinate their policies more closely with those of other nations.

It has of course long been true that small countries must watch closely economic developments and policies in their larger neighbors, and they would take these developments into account. For the Netherlands, forecasting German GNP and German economic policies is a critical component to forecasting Dutch GNP. But as economies grow more interdependent, the importance of two-way interactions increases, so that economically large countries such as Britain, Germany, and even the United States must increasingly take into account developments and policies abroad.

INTERNATIONAL COMPETITION IN ECONOMIC POLICY

In an interdependent economy, governments do not have full control over the instrument variables needed to influence the trade balance or the balance of payments. Each government can affect the domestic interest rate in an attempt to influence international capital movements or can set tariffs on imports and subsidies on exports to influence the trade balance. But success in influencing capital movements or trade flows depends on what other countries are doing. It is interest rate differentials, not the absolute level of interest rates, which induce the movement of capital. And it is domestic tariffs less foreign subsidies which influence the level of imports. There are many instruments of economic policy for which relative differences affect international transactions, but where the absolute value may continue to exert a strong influence on purely domestic decisions. This is true, for example, not only of short- and long-term interest rates, but also of liberal tax benefits to investment, generous depreciation allowances, lax regulation of corporate activities, and a host of other measures designed to influence corporate location. It is also true of foreign trade: generous credit arrangements or credit-risk guarantees for exports may encourage total exports without improving the trade balance if other countries are pursuing similar measures.

This feature of policy instruments—that the absolute level of the instrument may have important effects domestically, but that only the level relative to that in other countries influences the balance of trade or payments—raises the question: Where do the values of these instruments finally settle? International capital movements between two otherwise isolated countries will presumably be roughly the same whether interests rates are at 7 per cent in one and 5 per cent in the other or at 4 per cent in the first country and 2 per cent in the second. In each case, the differential is two percentage points. But what determines whether "community" interest rates settle at the higher level or the lower one? The effects on other objectives may be very different. Economic growth will be inhibited more in the first case than in the second.

This would be of secondary importance if all countries had many policy instruments at their disposal. Each country could compensate for any deleterious effects on domestic objectives arising from the value of instruments determined predominantly by the community as a whole. But, as we already noted, the number of instruments and the range of values they can assume are often sharply limited by tradition or law. Indeed, it is highly likely that at any point in time a country will have at its disposal only the minimum number of policy instruments that it needs to satisfy important domestic political demands. Policy instruments affect the welfare of particular members of the community as well as national economic objectives, so their use will be resisted. Public expectation is that certain measures, while theoretically conceivable, will in practice not be used. Any attempt to invoke them therefore meets stiff resistance.

The values which policy instruments take on in the community of nations, and the process by which those values are reached, are therefore of strong interest to the individual nations. They may not have sufficient domestic flexibility to offset the damaging effects of policy instruments which are forced to an inappropriate level by international competition among governments. As a result, greater international integration can force choices among national objectives which otherwise would all be attainable.

There are occasions in which most or even all members of the international community will find themselves worse off. The competitive devaluations and tariff wars of the interwar period offer the most striking examples; many of the proscriptions in the GATT and the IMF Articles of Agreement are designed to avoid a repetition of those events.

But competition among policies was not thereby banished on all fronts. For example, interest rates shot upward in 1965 and 1966 to levels one to two percentage points higher than those which had prevailed in most countries in 1964. Some of the increases were designed to curb domestic demand; others were defensive, to limit capital outflow. Even after domestic economies had cooled down, it took a dramatic meeting of finance ministers at Checquers, England, in early 1967, to reverse the process. Four other types of policy instruments having these characteristics have been used in the effort to strengthen the balance of payments of various countries: restrictions on government procurement, government-sponsored export promotion, tax incentives to domestic investment, and changes in domestic tax structure. The United States, faced with large payments deficits during the early sixties, made or considered moves in all of these areas; but in each case there was ample precedent abroad for doing so.

Government purchases for government use are specifically excluded from coverage by the GATT rules governing international trade. The result is that a conspicuously small proportion of government purchases, by any government, is from foreign suppliers who compete with domestic producers. In the United States, the Buy American provision—which since 1954 officially gives preferential treatment of 6 to 12 per cent (in addition to tariffs) to domestic over foreign competitors for the government's custom—has existed since the 1930's. But in 1962 a number of government agencies, including most importantly the Department of Defense, raised the preference accorded to domestic suppliers as high as 50 per cent. Foreign aid expenditures by the American government are even more restricted. Starting with development loans in 1959, such expenditures were tied increasingly to purchases in the United States, until by 1965 only a limited class of expenditures was not so tied, regardless of the price advantages offered by foreign suppliers.

The government procurement practices of other countries are more difficult to document, since most governments do not require open bidding on government purchases with well-publicized preferences for domestic producers, such as those found in the Buy American provisions. Many countries follow the practice of tying foreign assistance, either by law or by skillful selection of projects and recipient countries, to purchases from the donor country. This is as true for those donors with fully employed economies as for those with excess capacity and unemployment —even though tying is far less effective in the former case, and merely stimulates additional imports—and it is as true for donor countries in balance-of-payments surplus as for those in deficit. Canada, Japan, and the United Kingdom tie the bulk of their foreign assistance, and France ties some expenditures. France and the Netherlands give virtually all of their foreign assistance to colonial or former colonial areas, where de facto aid-tying takes place through long-established trading firms. German aid often originates with requests from prospective exporters who have found projects in recipient countries eligible for foreign assistance by German criteria.

Many of these practices, of course, arise not only from balance-of-payments considerations but also from protectionist sentiment. Domestic producers apply strong political pressures on their governments to buy at home—the more so when the goods are to be "given away." But weakness in the balance of payments

often strengthens their arguments and increases public acceptability of such restrictive measures.

Government activities are not solely restrictive of trade. On
the contrary, a second range of practices involves all kinds of
schemes, except direct subsidies proscribed by GATT, to promote exports of goods and services. Governments sponsor trade
fairs, product exhibitions, and other advertisements for the products of their exporters; they insure commercial and so-called non-
commercial risks involved in exporting; and they often help to
finance exports directly. No major industrial trading nation can
be found without a government or government-sponsored agency
for insuring and/or extending credit for exports. Some countries,
such as France and Italy, give especially favorable treatment to
export paper in their banking systems or at their central banks.
And export credit is often exempt from general credit limitations to restrict domestic demand. All of these measures really
subsidize exports, although it is often impossible to identify the
amount of the subsidy to any particular sale.

The United States established the U.S. Travel Service in 1961
to attract foreign tourists to the United States. European governments have been aiding tourism much longer, and each year
spend substantial amounts for the purpose of attracting foreign
tourists. Moreover, expenditure for tourist promotion has been
growing rapidly, doubling every two to four years. In addition
to straightforward publicity, most European countries subsidize
the hotel industry either through preferential tax treatment or
through low-interest or government-guaranteed loans. In most
countries, these programs date from the late fifties or the early
sixties.

Subsidies to domestic investment is the third area in which
governments have moved to improve their international payments positions. Investment subsidies for manufacturing and
agriculture improve the competitiveness of a country's products
in world markets. Some countries give direct tax incentives to
new investment in plant and equipment, such as the investment
tax credit of 7 per cent adopted by the United States in 1962 and
the 30 per cent investment allowance in the United Kingdom (in
early 1966, the latter was also converted into a direct grant of
20 per cent of expenditures on new plant and equipment). Japan

permits greatly accelerated depreciation of assets. . . .

Under a regime of fixed exchange rates, government subsidy for domestic investment is similar to a devaluation of the currency in that it improves the cost competitiveness both of the country's export products and of its products which compete with imports.

Subsidies to investment are obviously motivated by considerations extending well beyond the balance of payments; economic growth has become a target of economic policy in its own right, partly for political and strategic reasons (arising in part from the "economic race" with the Soviet Bloc), partly because rising standards of living are universally desired. But balance-of-payments considerations do play an important role in the decision to inaugurate investment incentives. Britain for years has emphasized the need to enlarge and improve its capital stock to compete more effectively in world markets. And former U.S. Secretary of the Treasury Douglas Dillon, testifying on behalf of the U.S. investment tax credit in 1962, argued that the measure was required "if U.S. business firms are to be placed on substantially equal footing with their foreign competitors in this respect. It is essential," he said, "to our competitive position in markets both here at home and abroad, that American industry be put on the same basis as foreign industry. Unless this is done, increased imports and decreased exports will unnecessarily add to the burden of our balance of payments deficit."[2]

Changes in the structure of domestic taxation, and in particular the "mix" between direct and indirect taxes, constitute a fourth area in which governments have moved, or have been tempted to move, to improve their national trade positions. GATT rules prohibiting export subsidies have been interpreted to preclude remission of direct taxes on exports but to permit remission of indirect taxes. Thus taxes on the corporate profits arising from export cannot be rebated, but manufacturers' excise taxes or turnover taxes can. Similarly, countries are permitted to levy indirect taxes, but not direct taxes, on imports. Because of this asymmetry in border tax adjustment, it is possible under fixed exchange rates for a country to stimulate exports and im-

---

2. *Hearings on H.R. 10650 Before the Senate Committee on Finance,* 87th Cong., 2nd Sess., pt. 1 (1962), p. 83.

pede imports by shifting its tax structure from direct taxes to indirect taxes, provided that direct taxes affect prices.

The GATT rule is based on the classical economic assumption that indirect taxes are shifted entirely to the purchaser, while direct taxes are not shifted at all, being absorbed entirely (in the case of the corporate profits) by the firm. Recent work in the field of public finance suggests, however, that there may be much less difference in the price effects of, say, corporate profits taxes and manufacturers' excise taxes than was once thought to be the case.[3] To the extent that indirect taxes are partially absorbed by the producer, or that profits taxes are partially shifted forward to the consumer, the GATT rules regarding border treatment of national taxes allow some "subsidy" to exports and a country can improve its trade position by switching from corporate profits taxes to excise or turnover taxes.

Some countries have made tax changes in this direction, and others have ben urged to do so. Sweden reduced its income tax and imposed a general sales tax in 1960; in mid-1964, Italy reduced payroll taxes (which are not rebatable) and, to recoup the revenue, increased turnover taxes (which are rebatable). The German government in 1967 approved a change from a turnover to a value-added tax which will improve the export competitiveness of German products;[4] and Britain has been periodically urged to increase its indirect taxes and lower the direct corporate taxes, although a special committee set up to examine the matter rejected the proposed change.[5] Similar changes have been proposed for the United States.

Once again, many considerations have influenced these proposals; in some cases, there may be powerful arguments for making the change regardless of the effects on the balance of payments. But it is interesting to note that these proposals have

3. M. Krzyzaniak and R. Musgrave, *The Shifting of the Corporation Income Tax* (Baltimore: Johns Hopkins Press, 1963), chaps. 6,8; J. A. Stockfish, "On the Obsolescence of Incidence," *Public Finance* 14 (1959): 125–48.

4. Because rebates under the turnover tax, due to complications in calculating the exact burden of the tax on each commodity, are lower than the values or rebates—and import levies—that would be permissible under the GATT rules.

5. Report of the *Committee on Turnover Taxation*, Cmnd. No. 2300 (1964).

come alive only since the late 1950's, as international competition has stiffened, and that improvement in the trade balance is often mentioned explicitly as an important reason for making the change. The Committee for Economic Development has stated, for example, that "a major advantage of a general excise tax [over a corporate profits tax] is that it would tend to improve the ability of the United States to compete with others in world markets," and it goes on to argue that the United States must "equalize" its tax structure with that of the Common Market as tariffs between the two trading areas are reduced.[6]

All of these policy measures have a common characteristic. Taken by one country alone, each represents a concealed devaluation of the currency, at least with respect to a selected class of transactions. But, like devaluation, these measures are effective only if other countries do not respond in kind. To each country, tying foreign aid and giving preference to domestic producers in government procurement may appear to offer a means to improve the balance of payments; and, indeed, in the short run it may do so. But if all countries follow the same practices, the benefit to each is much reduced and some countries will have their payments positions worsened as a result. In the meantime, the total real value of foreign aid has been reduced by reliance on high-cost suppliers, and inefficient production has been fostered.

The same thing is true of the other measures discussed. General adoption of export promotion schemes and government-sponsored tourist publicity will surely have a much greater effect on total level of world exports and tourism than on the payments position of any one country, since the measures will largely cancel one another and leave only residual effects on the balance of payments. Similarly, if all countries adopt special tax incentives for domestic investment, the net improvement in competitiveness—which depends as much on incentives abroad as on those at home—will be haphazard and unpredictable. The principal effect may well be not on any one country's balance-of-payments position but on the total investment and the rate of

6. Committee for Economic Development, *Reducing Tax Rates for Production and Growth* (New York, 1962), pp. 39–40.

growth in the world economy at large—so long as these effects are not nullified by a competitive rise in long-term interest rates! Finally, an effort to raise exports and impede imports through changes in domestic tax structure may have little overall effect on foreign trade and leave countries with tax structures which many would prefer not to have.

At any point in time there are often cogent and persuasive arguments for introducing one or more of these measures to improve the balance of payments. If other countries did not respond in kind, the desired improvement would be forthcoming. But if other countries act likewise, the measures largely cancel out. Not only is the purpose of the move nullified, but all countries may find themselves worse off in terms of their other objectives. As a rule, individual countries cannot act unilaterally without inviting reaction. If they are successful, they are quickly emulated by their neighbors, so that the initial gains are transitory at best. Countries often must act in self-defense, in response to the behavior of their trading partners. This is particularly so when measures to reduce one country's deficit do not reduce the surpluses of the surplus countries but increase the deficit of another deficit country or move countries in balance into deficit. These third countries then feel compelled to respond defensively and their actions in turn increase the deficit of the initial country. Moreover, many of the measures thus taken are difficult to reverse —countries do not readily contract export credit programs or lengthen the periods of depreciation allowable for tax purposes.

Today there is little blatant competition among policies, such as the round of tariff increases in the late twenties and the competitive depreciations of the early thirties. But more subtle and sophisticated methods can substitute, albeit imperfectly, for currency depreciation. Taken in sequence by different countries, these measures produce a kind of ratchet effect. We then have a series of competitive depreciations in disguise.

In this case it is balance-of-payments difficulties, actual or feared, which give rise to the undesirable competition in policies. Competition for the location of industry can also weaken economic policy in the area of regulation and taxation, due to the mobility of business. To attract new firms or to keep the firms they have, local authorities may eschew tax or regulatory measures which in the view of the authorities would benefit the community as a whole, but for the possibility of driving away investment.

National governments have not yet engaged in a scramble to adjust their policies to be most attractive to foreign-owned business firms; on the contrary, a number of countries are concerned about the amount of foreign control already present. Differences in taxation and other measures relating to business activity do, however, affect international corporate location, and some beginnings of national competition for this location can be seen. Luxembourg liberalized its depreciation allowances and offered an investment allowance in 1962 in what appeared to be a deliberate move to attract foreign investment for operations throughout the European Common Market. Belgium and the Swiss cantons have also adopted tax and other features designed to attract foreign enterprise.[7]

IN SUMMARY

In a highly integrated economic area which surpasses in size the jurisdiction of governments, each group of policymakers is subject to such strong interactions with the surrounding area that the constraints on its actions become very severe. Indeed, in the hypothetically limiting case, these constraints determine entirely the course of action each jurisdiction must take. The region— or the nation—in a highly integrated economy becomes analogous to the perfect competitor—or at best the oligopolist—in a market economy. The range of choice it has, consistent with economic survival, is very small; for the most part, it simply adapts its behavior to stimuli from outside. Awareness of the high interactions will eventually inhibit action.

A. C. Pigou and John Maynard Keynes pointed out long ago that the sum of individual decisions by consumers and producers may not always be optimal for society as a whole (and hence for its members), even though its members may be acting individu-

7. Furthermore, the relaxation in France's tough policy on foreign investment may have been dictated in large measure by the prospect of losing investment to other members of the European Economic Community which would nonetheless have free access to the French market.

ally on entirely rational grounds.[8] Some kind of collective action is therefore required to produce an optimal outcome.

The same can be true among nations, or among regions within a nation, if the interactions among their decisions are sufficiently strong. One jurisdiction gropes for new instruments in an attempt to improve its position. If it succeeds, others follow and there is a competition in policies which defeats everyone's objectives and in fact can even lead all participants away from their national or local objectives, like the members of a crowd rising to their tiptoes to see a parade better but in the end merely standing uncomfortably on their tiptoes.

An invisible hand seems to be working in economic policy as well as in the market place. Competition in the market place is alleged to lead to the most efficient allocation of resources. Whatever the merits of this claim, we can be much less confident that competition among policies will be optimal. Governments seek many ends, not the efficient allocation of resources alone; and the process of policy competition can certainly thwart some of those objectives.

Existing rules of international behavior as set forth in GATT and in the IMF Agreement do limit the use of direct and straightforward means of policy competition such as open export subsidies and multiple exchange rates, and they therefore slow the process of policy competition since the more subtle and sophisticated methods—loopholes in GATT and the IMF Agreement—usually involve strong domestic considerations which delay their implementation. But existing rules do not fully accomplish the aim of preventing self-defeating policy competition and of freeing domestic policy measures to pursue largely domestic objectives. Moreover, the pressures on domestic policy are likely to become greater as the world economy becomes more interdependent. Freedom of action in economic policy formation can be lost through the need for each country to compete in policies with its competitors in commerce.

To minimize adverse effects from this competition, countries can coordinate closely their national economic policies, attempt-

8. A. C. Pigou, *The Economics of Welfare* (London: Macmillan, 1932). This was also the central underlying message of J. M. Keynes, *General Theory of Employment, Interest, and Money* (London: Macmillan, 1936).

ing to define and reach an optimum combination of policies for the community as a whole. This route involves extensive "internationalization" of the process of economic policymaking, transferring this governmental function to the larger integrated area.

Alternatively, countries can attempt to remove the major source of pressure on their actions—deleterious effects on their international payments positions—by providing each country with ample liquidity to finance any deficit and allowing it to go its own way. Or this goal can be accomplished by reversing the process of economic integration, artificially breaking down or reducing the numerous economic links between countries. While some movement can be seen on all three of these fronts, actions in the United States and Europe in the mid-sixties seemed dangerously pointed toward the third alternative.

International Reserves, Money, and Global Inflation

H. ROBERT HELLER

H. Robert Heller, chief of the Financial Studies Division of the Research Department of the International Monetary Fund, examines the relationships between international reserves, national monetary aggregates, and world inflation. His essay was first published in the March 1976 issue of Finance and Development.

To WHAT EXTENT did the increase in international reserves help to precipitate the world-wide monetary expansion that was an important cause of world-wide inflation in the early 1970s? To consider international monetary factors from this angle should not imply that they were exclusively responsible for global inflationary forces. Other factors played important roles: autonomous supply changes, some of them triggered by bad harvests or declining fish catches; the exercise of newly found monopoly power on behalf of producers; and increasing aggregate demand due to population and real income increases. Furthermore, it should be recognized that the monetary changes that will be analyzed here were often the result of fiscal policy actions.

There does, however, appear to exist a link between changes in international reserves and changes in world prices. Changes in global international reserves have both a direct and an indirect impact on the world money supply, and these changes in the world money supply in turn influence the world-wide rate of inflation.

Three basic factors determine the changes in a nation's money supply: changes in the international component of the monetary base, that is, international reserves; changes in the domestic monetary base components; and changes in the monetary base multiplier. The acquisition of new international reserves will have a direct impact on a nation's money supply by expanding the monetary base. An increase in the international reserves held may also have an indirect impact on the money supply if the monetary authorities feel that the increase in international liquidity has eased their reserve constraint so that more expansionary domestic monetary policies may be pursued. These increases in the monetary aggregates will in turn have an impact on national inflation rates. The channels through which such monetary changes are translated into prices changes are many and varied, and have been the subject of extensive discussion.

The world monetary expansion of the early 1970s triggered a sharp increase in the demand for internationally traded commodities, because the rise in international reserves had eliminated or substantially reduced foreign exchange constraint in many countries. Consequently, the global trade sector became the leading sector in the recent inflation. The sudden rise in the prices of internationally traded goods was a significant factor in making the recent inflation a truly world-wide phenomenon.

WHY RESERVES EXPANDED

Between 1950 and 1969, international reserves grew at an average annual rate of 2.7 per cent (Table 1). From the beginning of 1970 to the end of 1972, they increased from SDR (Special Drawing Rights) 78 billion to SDR 146 billion; of this, increases in foreign exchange reserves accounted for SDR 67 billion—almost the entire addition to reserves during that period.

Since SDR 59 billion of this increase can be identified as a growth of U.S. dollar reserves, it has been argued that an excessive monetary expansion in the United States was the main cause of the increase in world liquidity and the ensuing world-wide inflation. However, there is not much convincing evidence to support this notion. In fact, during 1970–72, the increase in the money supply of the United States was more moderate than in any other industrial country.

Instead, a shift by U.S. and foreign private entities out of dollars and into other currencies led to an excessive expansion of global liquidity in the early 1970s. Between the end of 1965 and 1969, private foreign entities had increased their liquid assets in the United States from $11.5 billion to $28.2 billion. But as the inflation rate in the United States accelerated somewhat during the late 1960s, the real returns on these financial assets fell. In addition, the growing volume of U.S. liquid foreign liabilities resulted in a questioning of the future external stability of the dollar and, in particular, the convertibility of the dollar into gold. Consequently, foreign private entities—in particular foreign commercial banks—shifted out of dollars and into other currencies. Between the end of 1969 and the end of 1971, U.S. liquid liabilities to private foreigners decreased from $28.2 billion to $15.1 billion.

There is also reason to believe that U.S. corporations and individuals correctly anticipated the dollar devaluations of 1971 and 1973 and moved substantial funds into currencies that were likely to appreciate. For instance, U.S. commercial banks more than doubled their foreign assets from $6.5 billion at the end of 1969 to $13.6 billion at the end of 1972, while their foreign liabilities actually decreased from $32.5 billion to $26.0 billion during the same period.

THE EURO-CURRENCY MARKET

At the same time the size of the Euro-currency market continued to grow. The U.S. dollar component of the Euro-currency market, however, decreased from 81.3 per cent of total liabilities in December 1969 to 72.4 per cent by December 1971. The net dollar positions of the Euro-currency banks decreased from $1.43 billion to $0.75 billion over the same period, while their net

TABLE 1. *International Reserves*

End of Period	Amount in Billions of U.S. Dollars	SDRs	Annual Growth Rate (in per cent) U.S. Dollars	SDRs
1950–59	57.7	57.7	2.3	2.3
1960–69	78.1	78.1	3.1	3.1
1970	92.4	92.4	18.4	18.4
1971	130.3	120.0	41.0	29.9
1972	158.1	145.6	21.3	21.3
1973	181.8	150.7	15.0	3.5
1974	218.0	178.1	19.9	18.1

SOURCE: IMF, *International Financial Statistics.*

positions in other Euro-currencies increased from $0.06 billion to $1.65 billion. It stands to reason that this shift in the currency composition of the Euro-market was indicative of the expected exchange rate movements.

The Euro-currency market might also have played a role in international reserve expansion in the early 1970s. If central banks in the rest of the world place their funds in the Euro-currency market, an additional multiple deposit expansion may result, which is unregulated and outside the traditional scope of monetary policy.

It appears, then, that the expansion in the volume of international reserves held by foreign central banks in the early 1970s was not due to an excessive monetary expansion in the United States but to a decrease in the private demand for dollars.

As some private households, banks, and firms shifted their assets from dollars to other currencies, they forced central banks in the rest of the world to purchase these dollars at the agreed-on parity of their own currency. These central banks, in return, issued their own currency or other central bank liabilities to the depositors of dollars and added the dollars to their foreign exchange reserves. This process led to a multiple expansion of the global money supply, as the amount of high-powered central bank money increased.

Because reserves are a component of the monetary base, one might expect that the relationship between reserve changes and changes in the monetary aggregate is direct and instantaneous. However, changes in international reserves are only one factor determining the changes in a nation's money supply. Central banks have the option of offsetting the changes in the external component of base money by changing the domestic elements of the monetary base. Changes in reserve requirements, discount policies, and other monetary instruments may also be used to neutralize the effects of autonomous changes in the external component of the monetary base. Furthermore, it takes time for the impact of a change in a monetary base component—such as a change in international reserves—to be fully reflected in changes in the monetary aggregates. The money multiplier does not operate instantaneously. It is dependent on the interaction between many decision-making units, and a considerable amount of time may pass until final portfolio equilibrium is attained by all relevant units.

Investigations covering the 126 Fund member countries for the period 1951–74 indicates a significant lagged relationship between percentage changes in the value of global reserves and the growth rate of the world money supply.[1] Estimates using both annual and quarterly data indicate an average lag of approximately one year in this relationship between global resrves and money. The results show that changes in international reserves can explain slightly more than half the variation in the world money stock actually observed.

EFFECT OF RESERVE CHANGES ON PRICES

The second link in the chain connecting reserve changes to price changes is the relationship between changes in the monetary aggregates and changes in the price level. That this relationship exists on a national basis has been well established in economic investigations covering a wide variety of countries. Our data permit us to test this relationship for the first time on a global basis. Data limitations made it necessary to restrict ourselves to tests of the simple hypothesis that there is a direct relationship between the percentage changes in the global money supply and the rate of global inflation. Through regression techniques we estimated the lag structure and determined an average lag of approximately one and a half years in the relationship between money and prices.

It may well be that velocity changes account for part of this lagged price response to changes in the monetary aggregates. As the world money supply increases, the velocity of circulation may well decrease at first. Therefore, the impact of the monetary changes on the price variable will be experienced only after the velocity of circulation has returned to its normal value.

It is tempting to add the mean lag of one year established in the relationship between reserves and money and the mean lag of approximately one and a half years in the relationship between money and consumer prices, and to conclude that a lag of of approximately one and a half years in the relationship between reserve changes and world price changes. Direct estimates of

1. See H. Robert Heller, "International Reserves and World-Wide Inflation," *Staff Papers* (March 1976).

the length of the lag between reserve and price changes indicate an average lag of three to four years in this relationship, emphasizing the variability of the lagged response.

THE DIRECTION OF CAUSATION

On the basis that an increase in the global price level will increase the demand for nominal reserves as countries want to restore the real value of their international reserve holdings, it can be argued that reserve changes do not cause price changes but vice versa. To test the validity of this alternative hypothesis we estimated an equation that incorporated percentage changes in international reserves both as leading and lagging variables. It was found that only the coefficient for reserve changes leading price changes by two periods is statistically significant. On the other hand, none of the reserve coefficients lagging behind the price changes are significantly different from zero. It is also noteworthy that the sum of the regression coefficients with reserve changes leading the price change is equal to 1.08, indicating that an increase in international reserves by 1 percentage point will eventually be reflected in a price change of slightly more than 1 per cent. In contrast, the sum of the coefficients for reserve changes lagging behind prices changes is equal to 0.01, as one might expect if reserves are not influenced by the monetary aggregates. On the basis of this evidence we may conclude that reserve changes do indeed cause price changes rather than the other way around.

EFFECTS ON STRUCTURE OF WORLD INFLATION

International reserves have often acted as a constraint on economic expansion. However, in the years 1970–72 each of the industrial and more developed countries registered an increase in international reserves (with the sole exceptions of the United States and South Africa). Even among the less developed nations only a few experienced reserve losses, with most countries making substantial reserve gains. The industrial countries as a group increased their international reserves by 92 per cent, and the less developed countries increased theirs by 106 per cent during the first three years of the 1970s.

These substantial reserve gains had a particular influence on commercial policy. Between 1970 and 1972, out of a total of 111 countries, the number of nations having restrictions on current account transactions decreased from 73 to 58. Other countries substantially reduced their import restrictions. The response by importers was not surprising: in the years 1970–72 imports increased by an average annual rate of 12 per cent in real terms. The plentiful supplies of international reserves fueled this worldwide import boom. However, it is clear that this rate of real increase was not sustainable at constant prices. The index of world import prices almost doubled, from 100 to 195 in the 1970–74 period, with most of the increase coming in the last two years of this period.

A further factor contributing to the inflation in the prices of traded goods was that many international prices are quoted in dollars. Given the declining value of the dollar itself, many commodity prices looked very attractive indeed to foreign buyers, and therefore the demand for commodities increased.

The sharp increases in international reserves during the years 1970–72 consequently had an effect on the structure of world prices, and here the relationship between prices of traded and nontraded commodities is particularly interesting. As there is no adequate price index of nontrade goods, the world-wide consumer price index can be used as an indicator of general price developments, while the world export and import price indices are indicative of price developments in the traded goods sector.

Since World War II, prices of internationally traded goods have shown a marked stability and have generally exercised a restraining influence on domestic price developments. Only minor

TABLE 2. *Percentage Changes in World Prices*

Year	Consumer Prices	Export Prices	Import Prices
Average 1950–59	3.5	1.2	0.5
Average 1960–69	4.4	0.6	0.6
1970	6.2	6.4	5.3
1971	5.9	4.0	6.0
1972	5.9	8.7	6.6
1973	9.6	24.8	24.8
1974	15.1	43.3	38.3

SOURCE: IMF Data Fund.

changes in world trade prices occurred between 1950 and 1969. It is one of the hallmarks of the recent world-wide inflation that this historical tendency has been reversed. Table 2 shows that increases in consumer prices exceeded price increases in traded commodities during the 1950s and 1960s, while in the years since 1972 the rate of price change of traded goods was greater than the changes in the consumer price index.

In virtually all earlier inflationary episodes, an excessive expansion of the domestic component of the monetary base was responsible for the creation of inflationary pressures, but during the recent inflation the high rate of expansion of the international reserve component of the monetary base played a decisive role.

A SYSTEMATIC RELATIONSHIP

Under fixed exchange rates there is then a systematic relationship between changes in world-wide international reserves and the rate of world-wide inflation. Changes in the world money supply serve as the crucial link in this relationship.

The evidence examined shows that changes in global international reserves have a significant impact on the aggregate world money supply and that there is an average lag of about one year in this relationship. There also exists a relationship between changes in the world money stock and changes in world prices. The evidence indicates a mean lag of approximately one and a half years in this relationship.

Estimates relating changes in global international reserves directly to changes in world consumer prices found a significant lagged relationship between these two crucial variables. The mean length of the lag was determined to be three to four years. All these lags are averages of distributed lag relationships. The standard errors vary between one-half and three years, which indicate that there is considerable variability in the estimated lag structure.

It was also found that the sharp increase in international reserves that helped to trigger the world-wide inflation of the early 1970s had an effect on the structure of the recent inflation. The increase in international means of payments in the hands of individual countries led to a world trade boom that resulted in a significant increase in the prices of internationally traded commodities. In contrast to the experience after World War II, the international sector represented an intensifying rather than mitigating inflationary influence since 1972.

While an increase in the U.S. dollar component of international reserves was the proximate cause of their increase in the early 1970s, there is little evidence that a more excessive monetary expansion in the United States than in other countries was responsible for this. Instead, a private shift from dollar into other currencies resulted in an expansion of the volume of foreign exchange reserves in the form of U.S. dollars.

The expansion in international reserves played a crucial role in the recent worldwide inflation. The large increases in the world monetary aggregates created the framework for translating what might have been sectoral price increases into a world-wide inflationary surge. Had the same real changes taken place within a framework of monetary restraint, the outcome would probably have been different.

It should also be noted that the conceptual framework of this analysis and the empirical data base pertain to the period of largely fixed exchange rates. Under such a fixed exchange rate system monetary impulses are transmitted between countries and it is difficult for any individual nation to isolate itself from foreign monetary developments. We might expect that the introduction of widespread floating will result in a greater independence of countries to pursue appropriate anti-inflationary policies and that countries willing to take the appropriate policy actions might insulate themselves more successfully from international inflationary pressures than was possible under the fixed rate system.

Although the volume of international reserves in existence has no direct effect on price levels, the changes in national monetary aggregates that accompany changes in international reserves do have a significant lagged impact on national and international price developments—unless national monetary authorities take appropriate actions to neutralize these induced monetary changes. An alternative would be a better control over international liquidity creation, so that the aggregate volume of international reserves may be expanded to avoid excess demand and inflation as well as economic stagnation and deflation in the world.

Reforming International Monetary Relations: An Analysis

TOM DE VRIES

Tom de Vries has been alternate executive director of the International Monetary Fund for Cyprus, Israel, the Netherlands, Romania, and Yugoslavia since 1969. In this essay, he briefly reviews the main events since the demise of the fixed exchange rate system and interprets the actions taken at the Jamaica Conference in January 1976.

THE TERM *international monetary relations* describes the present situation better than *international monetary system,* because no agreed comprehensive system of coherent rules exists any longer. Fundamentally, this is the result of the fact that the major changes in international financial relations over the past few years have come about through the breakdown of the old system and not as a result of its conscious reform. This occurred when the authorities, forced by circumstances, ceased to observe particular rules without wanting to bring about the results that flowed from their action. The advent of flexible exchange rates in 1973 is a telling case in point. In the face of overwhelming pressures from speculators, it became impossible for the authorities to maintain support of their exchange rates under the existing rules for intervention. Such intervention at times involved the purchase of currencies by the authorities to the tune of several billions of dollars within a single day, sometimes within a single hour. They were thus forced to cease their intervention. Floating exchange rates were the unwanted result.

EARLY WARNINGS

The fact that fundamental changes in international monetary arrangements have come about through breakdown rather than through reform is disturbing. One unsatisfactory result is that no agreed conception exists of how the new system is to be operated, for instance of the criteria by which to judge the exchange rate policies of a country which has adopted managed floating. Another, more general, disturbing feature is that we observe similar trends in other fields, for example in the decline in real terms of official funds available for development assistance, and the slow movement toward European economic integration. There is thus for the moment a general low tide in international cooperation, whose fundamental causes are inadequately understood.

The developments in international financial relations are the more striking since the tensions that had ben emerging in the system and the causes of its instability had been fully analyzed. Moreover, a large measure of agreement on necessary remedial action had been achieved both in the academic community and in official circles.

In the academic field the first warning, together with a detailed remedy, came as early as 1960 from Robert Triffin in his book *Gold and the Dollar Crisis*. In the ensuing discussion, the academic community reached a large degree of consensus around 1964 on what should be done, when on the initiative of Fritz Machlup 32 economists produced a report entitled *International Monetary Arrangements: The Problem of Choice*, published by the International Finance Section of Princeton University. And after the Smithsonian agreement of December 1971 had temporarily patched up the par value system, a large measure of agreement on remedial action was reached in official circles in the summer of 1972. This was contained in a report by the executive directors of the International Monetary Fund—based on an imaginative first draft from its economic counsellor, J. J. Polak—entitled *Reform of the International Monetary System*.

THE SHORTCOMINGS

What then were the shortcomings of the system? First, the process designed to maintain international payments equilibrium —the adjustment process—was found to function less and less effectively. For the most part this was due to a tendency toward increased rigidity of exchange rates under the Bretton Woods par value system, a rigidity that went far beyond what had originally been envisaged. "In the future, the external value of sterling shall conform to its internal value as set by our own domestic policies, and not the other way round," Lord Keynes, one of the founding fathers of the Fund, had emphasized in a speech in the House of Lords on May 23, 1944. In fact, over time, the system evolved in a very different direction. This was mainly the result of the fact that adjustable par values and free international capital movements are incompatible, since the combination leads to unmanageable currency speculation. Yet capital movements were freed. The result was rigid exchange rates and hence the disappearance of an adequate adjustment mechanism for international payments.

Second, in the Bretton Woods system itself there was no practical provision for an increase of international liquidity. However, given the central position of the dollar, many countries found it convenient to add easily usable, interest-earning dollar balances to their monetary reserves instead of gold. This made additions to international liquidity possible but dependent on the U.S. balance-of-payments position, and on the decisions of individual countries to hold on to their dollars rather than to convert them into gold. Both these elements were completely unrelated to the need of the world economy for liquidity, and moreover were beyond any general control. In addition, the volume of international liquidity was influenced by changes in the monetary gold stock. These changes were dependent on the caprice of gold production and Soviet gold sales on the one hand, and private demand for gold on the other, factors equally unrelated to the need for liquidity and equally outside rational monetary control. Thus international control over international liquidity was lacking.

The third problem, related to the second, was the absence of an internationally managed reserve asset. This not only hampered international control over international liquidity, but also implied that the savings involved in the accumulation of monetary reserves flowed to the world's richest country, the United States, which provided the new official liquidity in the form of dollar deposits. These reserve arrangements, called the gold-exchange or gold-dollar standard, were moreover prone to a well-known instability as a consequence of the continued accumulation of short-term debt by the reserve center. This led to the downfall of the pound in 1931 and to that of the dollar in 1971, exactly 40 years later.

ACTION TAKEN

The international community responded by solving the easiest of the three problems which had arisen, namely the need for an international reserve asset, by the creation of more paper money. Agreement was reached in 1968 on arrangements which permitted the creation in the Fund of an international reserve asset called special drawing rights, SDRs for short.

However, on the two other points the international community adamantly refused to take any meaningful remedial action. The two pillars on which a reformed international monetary system was to be constructed were "fixed exchange rates and the established price of gold," as the ministers of the Group of Ten put it in 1964 and repeated over the next few years. Yet it is precisely on these two points, and on these two points only, that the Jamaica agreement contains fundamental changes as far as the system is concerned. The fact that the agreement mainly recognizes and legalizes the changes that had already evolved spontaneously does not alter this fundamental truth.

It is a rather puzzling fact that the Committee of Twenty, charged to produce an outline for a comprehensive reform of the system by the governors of the Fund, hardly ever discussed the exchange rate system, even though the par value system broke down during the course of its deliberations and the world moved from fixed to flexible exchange rates under its very eyes. In fact, three weeks after the final collapse of the par value system in March 1973, the committee reiterated its conviction that the reformed system should be based on some resurrected par value system. And as late as June 1974, Sir Jeremy Morse, chairman of the "Bureau" of the Committee of Twenty and of its deputies, stated that the system described in the outline of reform which the committee had produced "is to be based upon stable but adjustable par values and is to be equipped with intervention and convertibility arrangements which do not belong to widespread floating." It is evident from the same speech that in mid-1974 Jeremy Morse still believed in the return to some par value system. Others still cherish that hope today. One cannot help being struck by the curious parallel between this continuing hope for a return to par values in the 1970s, and the equally unrealistic wish to return to gold in the 1930s on which the World Economic Conference of 1933 foundered.

In the light of these conditions, what is the significance of the agreements finally completed at Jamaica?

EXCHANGE RATES

Much energy has already been expended on penetrating analyses of the language of the proposed new Article IV of the Fund's charter entitled "Obligations Regarding Exchange Arrangements." I feel it a duty to sound a note of warning here. Article IV is a Franco-American compromise between two opposing points of view. Even though the legal style of the original text has been greatly improved with the help of the Fund's general counsel, Joseph Gold, the language basically conceals differences instead of revealing agreement. It is, of course, possible—and most certainly to be desired—that future developments and negotiations will bring about a greater degree of consensus on the world's exchange rate regime. Since Article IV is rather verbose, passages will then no doubt be found on which to base these future agreements. But the process cannot be reversed. Exegesis of the language of Article IV will not reveal the nature of these much-needed future agreements, which unfortunately do not yet exist.

This is not to say that for the immediate future Article IV does not do a number of important things. First, it legalizes the present rather varied exchange rate regimes, applied by the member countries. Each Fund member will be entitled to have the exchange arrangement of its choice, as long as it does not prevent effective balance of payments adjustment.

Second, the Article abolishes the par value system, and in addition it creates a barrier against its reintroduction. "The Fund may determine by an 85 percent majority . . . that international economic conditions permit the introduction of a widespread system of exchange arrangements based on stable but adjustable par values." Please note (1) the par values may under these circumstances be "introduced," which clearly means that they do not exist beforehand; (2) that the introduction must be "widespread"; (3) that an 85 per cent majority is required, which gives the United States, with 20 per cent of the voting power, a veto; and (4) that U.S. assent to such an introduction of par values will be further discouraged by the fact that the convertibility obligations of Article VIII have been left untouched. This means that difficult negotiations on the question of convertibility would no doubt have to precede the introduction of stable but adjustable par values.

GOLD

The second basic problem facing the system is the absence of international control over international liquidity. On this score the Jamaica agreement offers no solution. Indeed, it seems to have made such control—national or international—more difficult to achieve than before.

The Interim Committee concentrated its attention in this field almost exclusively on the role of gold. The present Articles of Agreement of the Fund forbid monetary authorities from buying gold at a price higher than the official one. As the gold price on the free market continued to rise after official intervention on the gold market was halted in March 1968—in a way rather similar to the suspension of official intervention on the exchange markets—the gold holdings of the monetary authorities, in effect, became unusable. However, as a practical matter one could not indefinitely prohibit central banks from dealing at a realistic price in a commodity of which they possessed huge quantities. Thus the real question became whether the prohibition would be either lifted in a way that would enhance the monetary role of gold, or under such rules and safeguards as would ensure its phasing out as a monetary instrument, so as to increase the possibilities of international control over international liquidity.

On August 30, 1975, the finance ministers of the United States, France, the Federal Republic of Germany, the United Kingdom, and Japan, meeting on the U.S. presidential yacht *Sequoia,* agreed to abolish the official price of gold. This would permit monetary authorities to engage in gold transactions at any price they see fit. It was further agreed to eliminate all obligations to use gold in transactions with the Fund, and that the Fund would sell one-third of its gold holdings. One-sixth would be "restituted" at the old official price to all Fund members in proportion to quotas and another sixth would be sold on the market with the profits going to the developing countries, mainly via a Trust Fund. Moreover, the countries in the Group of Ten (industrialized nations) agreed to certain arrangements, outside the Fund Articles but to which other Fund members may adhere, of which the three essential paragraphs are as follows:

1. That there be no action to peg the price of gold.
2. That the total stock of gold now in the hands of the Fund and the monetary authorities of the Group of Ten will not be increased.
. . .
5. That each party agree that these arrangements will be reviewed by the participants at the end of two years and then continued, modified, or terminated. Any party to these arrangements may terminate adherence to them after the initial two-year period.

In essence, these arrangements were identical to the agreement reached among the ministers of the European Common Market at Zeist in the Netherlands in the spring of 1974.

The question of pegging or stabilizing the price of gold is decisive for its future monetary role. Without official intervention the gold price is likely to fluctuate sharply, as during the past years, just like the price of other commodities. But this very price instability makes gold unusable as a monetary asset. There are only seven central banks that have large gold holdings. Their governors know each other well and have a tradition of close and cordial cooperation. If two of them were to conclude a gold transaction between them in a volatile market, the likelihood is that after a few months, one governor would have realized a sizable profit at the expense of the other. This is in clear conflict to their normal working relationships. Or, to put the matter in a more analytical way, it is not the business of central banks to engage in speculative commodity transactions. Without official stabilization of the gold price, gold is unsuitable as a monetary asset, and gold transactions are to be expected only in emergencies.

Whatever objections one might raise against the gold agreement, such as the huge unwarranted increase in international liquidity and the extremely unequal distribution of gold profits, its no-pegging provision would have speeded up the phasing out of the gold's monetary role but for paragraph 5, binding countries to adhere to those provisions for two years only.

The result of these agreements is an immediate rise in the price at which monetary authorities can deal in gold with one another, and freedom to peg the price or to reduce the price fluctuations after two years, unless the United States succeeds in prevailing upon the European authorities to refrain from such action.

What this means is that the outlook for gold in the next few years is uncertain. This uncertainty about such a key element of the system underlines once again the interim character of the Jamaica agreements; they do not introduce a new monetary system in a meaningful sense. Nevertheless important decisions were reached. The demonetization of gold, desired by the United States, has been avoided by the European countries, and when in need, they can use gold at a vastly increased price, and as a competitor to the dollar. On the other hand, the United States got practically everything it wanted in the field of the exchange rate regime. This is the political deal that was struck at Jamaica.

The developing countries obtained an increase in their voting power in the Fund, an increase in the resources of the Fund from SDR 29 billion to SDR 39 billion and an immediate liberalization of the regular tranche policies in anticipation of that increase, an easing of the rules concerning the granting of compensatory financing when countries dependent on a few staple commodities experience a sudden fall in export earnings, and a Trust Fund granting loans on concessional terms for the poorest among them.

LIQUIDITY CONTROL AND THE SDR

The Interim Committee of the Fund's Board of Governors did not discuss convertibility, or its milder form of asset settlement, which had occupied so much of the time of its predecessor—the Committee of Twenty. As noted, these reforms worked out by the Committee of Twenty were designed for a fixed-rate system. Little relevant thought has been given to the question of how to control the volume of reserve currencies used as monetary reserves under a flexible exchange rate system.

In a world in which most non-oil producers have to worry about borrowing to cover their current account deficits, the inconvertible dollar has become the international money *par excellence* in spite of much comment to the contrary. This hampers the control over international liquidity, which is rendered even more difficult by the fact that part of the official borrowing leads to a raise in liquidity. Moreover, the sharp movements in the gold price lead to dramatic movements in the total volume of international liquidity. It has been argued that in spite of these difficulties countries can to some extent approach their desired level of reserves by movements of the exchange rate. But there are other, far more powerful considerations, such as the effect on trade, that countries have in mind when managing their exchange rate.

We are thus further away than ever from international control over international liquidity. There can be no doubt that this is at least contributing to the difficulties in fighting world-wide inflation. Liquidity control is possible only if countries are willing to accept rather strict rules regarding the composition of their monetary reserves, which affect their holdings of both currencies and gold. Full control may well require depositing reserve currencies and gold with the Fund in return for SDRs. But enabling authority to achieve this goal—technically through a so-called substitution account—does not form part of the proposed amendment of the Fund's Articles. Indeed, rather than concentrating monetary gold in the Fund, where it is out of sight and does not circulate, the Fund is selling part of its gold to members. And there are no rules about reserve currencies. In these circumstances, the phrase about "making the special drawing right the principal reserve asset in the international monetary system" (Article VIII, Section 7) has a rather hollow tone.

Apart from reaching the agreements described on exchange rates and gold, while leaving the control over liquidity to another day, the Jamaica conference reached final agreement on a comprehensive amendment of the Fund's Articles, which will simplify, streamline, and update the operations of the Fund. While these amendments are of great importance for the daily work of the Fund, and although they provide, in many instances, enabling authority which will make it easier for the Fund to adapt its operations to changing circumstances, these amendments do not significantly affect the monetary system as such. The principle of self-amendment by a vote of the Board of Governors, even with a highly qualified majority, has continued to be rejected—rightly so, in my opinion.

The conclusion is that the Jamaica agreement mainly legalizes the situation that had evolved in practice. This is true both with regard to exchange rates and to gold, for central banks had started using gold at near-market prices as collateral for loans. Hence, the implementation of the new amendments will bring little additional change that is fundamental to the international monetary system. But they do provide a basis for constructive future action.

THE TASKS AHEAD

Since the change in the exchange rate regime came about as a result of breakdown, not of reform, not only are there no rules on how to operate the new flexible exchange rate regime, but also an agreed philosophy on which to base such rules is lacking.

Under the amendments the Fund is to "exercise firm surveillance over the exchange rate policies of members." This opens the possibility for important and most constructive action by the Fund. Such surveillance can only be meaningful against the backdrop of an agreed conception of proper policies. It will therefore be a most important task for the Fund in the next year or two to develop and reach agreement on such a conception concerning exchange rate policies. In this way, practical rules concerning the new exchange rate regime would be developed on the basis of experience now being obtained.

But the task will not be easy. Some countries, especially the United States, believe that exchange rates should be left to "market forces." I find this view not altogether easy to understand, since the authorities themselves, through their monetary policy, are a most important market force on the short-term money market, whose conditions directly influence the exchange market.

Many other countries consider the exchange rate an important instrument of economic policy, and therefore have "managed" it when it was floating. The rather large changes in the exchange rates between major currencies within a short period, which in a number of cases were clearly inappropriate when related to the fundamental economic situation, have reinforced this view. In either case, Fund surveillance will have to include both monetary and exchange rate policies.

Thus the Jamaica agreement provides an important starting point for further progress in the field of exchange rates. The other main task for the next few years will be to prepare the ground for eventual control over liquidity creation in the form of reserve currencies and gold. Only then could the SDR resume its place as the symbol of more rational monetary arrangements.

A most significant fact has been that through the turmoil of the past years, the need for cooperation instead of unilateral action, let alone economic warfare, has been universally recognized. The Fund has been accepted, as a matter of course, as the main center for such cooperation. If the monetary system has fallen into ill health for the moment, the Fund as the center of international monetary cooperation has come through the vast changes in full vigor and ready to act more effectively than before under its amended charter.

The Benefits and Costs of an International Monetary Nonsystem

JOHN WILLIAMSON

John Williamson, a former adviser to the International Monetary Fund, is professor of economics at the University of Warwick. His proposals for internationally supervised managed floating contained in this essay were published, together with other statements, in the Princeton Essays in International Finance.

THE SIGNIFICANCE of the agreements reached in Jamaica in January 1976 is that they make provision for legalizing the existing nonsystem governing international monetary relations. In place of the explicitly specified and reasonably coherent sets of rights and obligations that constituted the Bretton Woods system, which more or less functioned until August 1971, or the comprehensively redesigned successor system sought by the Committee of Twenty (C-20), the world is to function on the basis of a set of conventions and practices that have evolved out of a mixture of custom and crisis.

The formal international obligations that remain in the monetary field are minimal. Countries that have accepted the International Monetary Fund's (IMF) Article VIII—broadly speaking, the developed countries and some of the oil exporters—are obligated to maintain current-account convertibility; members of the Special Drawing Account must still accept SDRs at a well-defined price when designated to do so by the IMF; all IMF members must permit the use of their currencies in IMF drawings; and those in debt must still repay their debts. Beyond this, however, countries are in large measure free to do as they please. They can impose capital controls if they so desire but cannot be forced to do so. They are not limited in the size of the reserves they can hold, as under a reserve-indicator system, or in the composition of their reserves, which can be held in SDRs, gold, or currencies (in the issuing country or in the Euromarkets). They can accept gold or currencies if they want to, at a price of their own choosing, but they are not compelled to accept or surrender either at a particular price, or at any price (i.e., there is no asset settlement). They can peg their currencies if they want to, to anything they choose except gold—to any other currency, a composite of several currencies, including the basket SDR, or by mutual pegging, as in the European snake. They can do so within any margins they choose, and they can change the peg gradually, as under the crawling peg, or by large steps, as under the adjustable peg, apparently without the need for explicit Fund endorsement as was previously necessary under Article IV.5. Or they can let their currencies float, intervening as and when they please, subject only to the rather weak restraints on aggressive intervention provided by the IMF Guidelines adopted in June 1974.

All this is a far cry from Bretton Woods or the ambitions of the C-20. But that is not to say that it is worse. A written constitution has the advantage of providing an explicitly endorsed framework of rules within which to resolve disagreements according to agreed procedures. But if the rules themselves are such as to compel inefficiency or provoke disagreements, an unwritten constitution may well prove preferable. An evaluation of the existing non-system therefore requires enumeration of particular benefits and costs in comparison with defined alternative sets of arrangements.

A first benefit of present arrangements concerns the exchange-rate regime. A central fact of international monetary life is that the development of capital mobility has rendered the continued use of the adjustable peg impracticable. The reason is fundamental: under capital mobility, exchange markets can be in equilibrium only if all existing stocks of the several currencies are willingly held, which requires either that the stocks themselves be adjusted according to the gold-standard "rules of the game" or that the expected yields of different currencies be adjusted in order to satisfy the conditions of asset-market equilibrium.

Governments show no signs of being willing to play the gold-standard game, for the compelling reason that it disrupts internal stabilization policy. And expected yields, which consist of their own interest rates plus expected rates of currency appreciation, cannot always adjust, because acceptable interest-rate differentials cannot offset anticipations of discrete changes in exchange rates, and exchange rates cannot always be allowed to adjust without making a mockery of the very idea of a par-value system. Hence, as capital mobility develops, the adjustable peg is bound to generate a series of ever more disruptive crises—as, indeed, it did from the early 1960s to March 1973. This basic inadequacy of the Bretton Woods system was the principal reason for its collapse.[1] Nevertheless, only three weeks after the collapse of the adjustable peg and the move to generalized floating in March 1973, the C-20 decided that the reformed system was to be based on a resurrected adjustable peg.

The first and overwhelming benefit of existing arrangements, in comparison with both the Bretton Woods system and C-20 aspirations, is therefore that they make no attempt to force countries to revert to the adjustable peg and do not envisage any such attempt in the future, unless 85 per cent of the IMF membership are prepared to vote for such a reversion, which is an eventuality that can safely be disregarded. Instead, they allow the maintenance of the system of generalized managed floating that replaced the adjustable peg, and this provides the viable crisis-proof adjustment mechanism that the Bretton Woods system lacked.

The adoption of managed floating has also defused the most potent sources of controversy in international monetary relations. In particular, the problem of distributing the obligation of initiating necessary adjustments is no longer the explosive issue that it was during the 1960s or was perceived to be in the C-20, where it underlay the major controversies surrounding the U.S. proposal for a reserve-indicator system and the European insistence on asset settlement. There are two reasons. First, the economic burden of undertaking adjustment is no longer associated with the act of taking the initiative, as it was when adjustment was to be effected by deflation or inflation at a fixed exchange rate. Second, the act of changing the exchange rate no longer requires a formal initiative, with its implications for national prestige, as it did under the par-value system. Another important way in which floating has defused past controversies is that the

1. This case is argued in some detail in my forthcoming book, *The Failure of World Monetary Reform, 1971–74* (London: Nelson, 1977), chap. 3.

rest of the world is no longer obliged to follow U.S. monetary policy, as it was under the *de facto* dollar standard spawned by the Bretton Woods system in the late 1960s.

A second benefit of existing arrangements is one that it is sad but nonetheless realistic to record as an advantage: the fact that perpetuation of the *status quo* is diplomatically undemanding. Countries are not at present favorably disposed to undertake formal commitments, even if these involve no sacrifice of national interests, unless there is a rather immediate gain to be realized.

The obverse of this second benefit is that current diplomatic tranquility is bought at the cost of possible tension in the future. Without a set of rules governing national behavior in the international arena, there is an ever-present possibility that inevitable differences in national interests will provoke international conflict. There is also a strong case for wanting to see rules (and, indeed, practices) that are broadly symmetrical as between countries, as the C-20 sought. Differences per se can foster grievances: even where differences imply both advantages and disadvantages that may seem reasonably balanced to an impartial observer, it is only to be expected that countries will focus attention on the disadvantages to themselves and the advantages to others.

In addition to this political disadvantage of existing arrangements, a series of economic costs attach to the present nonsystem in comparison with a reformed system of the general character sought by the C-20.

The first relates to the degree of volatility that exchange rates have exhibited during the period of floating. It is an established historical fact that exchange-rate variations have been pronounced under floating and have exceeded those under the par-value system on just about any measure, despite the occurrence of substantial central-bank intervention designed to smooth rate fluctuations. These movements have often been reversed, rather than always being explicable as prompt adaptations of rates to changes in underlying conditions. It seems doubtful whether the agreement reached at Rambouillet and endorsed at Jamaica to "act to counter disorderly market conditions or erratic fluctuations in exchange rates" will substantially change this situation. Just how costly this exchange-rate volatility is in impeding international transactions is very much open to question, but it strains credulity to imagine that it does not have any antitrade bias at all.

The second economic cost of existing arrangements is the total lack of control over the volume of international liquidity, which arises from the absence of asset settlement, the unconstrained freedom to place reserves in Euromarkets, and possibly also from fluctuations in the value of gold reserves that may result from variations in the gold price. It can be argued that variations in the foreign-exchange component of reserves are unlikely to be a major disruptive force, inasmuch as floating gives countries individually far more power to avoid major unintended reserve accumulations or losses than the par-value system did, and the danger of a major general surfeit or shortage of reserves emerging and provoking global inflation or deflation is therefore substantially reduced. However, no such reassurance exists so far as the gold component of reserves is concerned. The Jamaica Agreement gives central banks the freedom to trade gold among themselves at mutually agreeable prices. If it transpires that a willing buyer at a near-market price can always be found when a central bank wishes to sell (which is a possibility, though perhaps not a probability), the Jamaica Agreement may reverse the de facto demonetization of gold that occurred in August 1971. If gold is thus effectively remonetized, any new speculative bubble in the gold market would increase the value of gold reserves, and countries in general could find their reserves carried far above their optimal level. The fact that exchange rates were floating would then do nothing to prevent a competitive scramble to dispose of excess reserves, with inflationary consequences or even attempts at inconsistent intervention.

The third unsatisfactory economic aspect of the present situation, at least in the eyes of many, is the maldistribution of the seigniorage that results from reserve creation. With the present elastic supply of reserves, it seems unlikely that sufficient reserve stringency could develop to convince the necessary 85 per cent of the IMF membership that new SDR allocations are called for. Seigniorage will therefore continue to be distributed arbitrarily to reserve centers and perhaps to gold holders, rather than on the agreed basis reflected in the distribution of SDR allocations.

A fourth aspect concerns the continued asymmetry in the position of the U.S. dollar, which has been aggravated rather than ameliorated by the switch to managed floating, inasmuch as the asymmetry formerly consisted of U.S. inability to influence the exchange rate of the dollar within the margins, and the margins have now been extended from 2¼ per cent to infinity. (The United States always had the right to change the par value of the dollar; she was merely reluctant to exercise it, for reasons that were understandable under the adjustable peg.) It is conceivable that the ability of other countries to manipulate exchange rates so as to contribute to stabilization policy, and the inability of the United States to defend herself against manipulation, will lead to a significant intensification of the problem of demand management in the United States.

There are other reasons for fearing the weakness of existing defenses against the pursuit of aggressive payments policies. It is true that the Guidelines for Floating provide some defense against overtly aggressive policies, but the defenses are weak ones. The speed with which the industrialized countries have passed the oil deficit on to the primary producers is a worrying example of what can happen when sharp conflicts of national interests over payments objectives exist and there are no effective international constraints on the pursuit of national self-interest.

None of these costs is of comparable importance to the benefit of having a workable exchange-rate regime in place of the adjustable peg. Yet collectively they are important enough to make it worthwhile considering whether it is possible to devise arrangements that might reduce those costs without reintroducing the brittleness of the adjustable peg. In my view, there is reason to suppose that this would be technically feasible. The key need is for an exchange-rate regime that retains the flexibility of managed floating but also embodies an official and agreed view as to what rates ought to be, to provide a fulcrum for international management. The "reference-rate proposal" suggests precisely this. It envisages the negotiation of an agreed structure of reference rates that would be regularly revised at prespecified intervals. It only forbids countries to intervene to push rates away from their reference rates, rather than compelling them to intervene to hold the rate close to a particular rate, which is the obligation that creates the one-way options that are the fatal weakness of the adjustable peg.[2]

Adoption of this proposal, which is a natural evolution from the IMF's existing Guideline 3, might go a considerable way toward alleviating the first, fourth, and fifth of the economic costs of the present nonsystem, enumerated above, and would lay a foundation for possible subsequent introduction of asset settlement, which is an essential condition for establishing control of international liquidity and permitting future reserve growth to take the form of SDRs. (There would of course remain other problems, such as that of securing control of reserve placements in the Euromarkets and, if gold proves as popular with central bankers as its friends believe it will, of bringing the gold price under control to the extent needed to prevent any new speculative bubble from having disruptive effects on international liquidity.)

Desirable as such developments may be, the chance of their occurring cannot be rated very high, if only because existing arrangements seem unlikely to generate those crises which are apparently a precondition for the achievement of international agreements. That means that the existing nonsystem is likely to persist without major change for some time. The Jamaica Agreement is helpful in adapting the IMF Articles so as to enable the Fund legally to play its modest but useful role in organizing get-togethers where the international financial establishment can rub shoulders with one another and thereby wear down their nationalistic edges, and in serving in a fire-brigade role to keep the developing countries from disaster.

The Fund's ability to fulfill the latter task has been aided by most of the specific agreements endorsed at Jamaica—those relating to the increase in quotas and the temporary increase in the size of tranches, the liberalization of the Compensatory Financing Facility, and the establishment of the Trust Fund to be financed by sale of part of the IMF's redundant gold stock. On the other

2. The proposal is that of Wilfred Ethier and Arthur I. Bloomfield, "Managing the Managed Float," *Essays in International Finance*, No. 112 International Finance Section, Department of Economics, Princeton University, and has been discussed in Chapter 9 of my forthcoming book as well as in my paper, "The Future Exchange Rate Regime," *Banca Nazionale del Lavoro Quarterly Review* June 1975.

hand, the unprincipled decision to increase international liquidity by "restituting" a part of the IMF's gold without any pretense of first establishing a need for increased liquidity is a graphic demonstration of just how far the ideal of purposive international management has been eroded. The lesson of the train of events that culminated in Jamaica is, however, that purposive international management is rather less critical in the monetary sphere than in many other aspects of international economic relations. Hence, it will be no bad thing if, as now seems to be the trend, the monetary component of international economic diplomacy greatly recedes in importance.

Monetary Arrangements in the European Common Market[1]

BELA BALASSA

In this essay, originally published in the December 1976 issue of the Banca Nazionale del Lavoro Quarterly Review, *the editor reports on the deliberations of a group of experts concerning the possibilities for improved monetary arrangements among the common market countries.*

INTRODUCTION

THE JAMAICA AGREEMENT essentially grants every country the freedom to determine—and to modify—its own exchange rate system. It thus confirms a situation characterized by a wide variety of national arrangements, which include pegging currency values to the special drawing rights (SDRs) or to a major currency as well as joint and individual floating.

This situation has given rise to considerable uncertainty as regards trade and capital transactions. Uncertainties are aggravated by exchange rate fluctuations that much exceed in amplitude variations in purchasing power relationships. An example is provided by the relationship of the French franc and the U.S. dollar. The average monthly exchange rate between the two currencies declined from 5.51 in December 1971 to 4.10 in June 1973, increased to 5.10 in January 1974, fell to 4.04 in June 1975, and rose again to 4.92 in August 1976, while the purchasing power ratio between the franc and the dollar hardly varied by more than 3 per cent. More recently, the value of the Italian lira and

1. This paper was drawn up by Bela Balassa, following discussions in the Villa Pamphili group on Economic Integration. Apart from the repporteur, the group consists of Lord Cromer, Geoffrey Denton, Armin Gutowski, Norbert Kloten, Alexandre Lamfalussy, Giovanni Magnifico, Conrad Oort, Andrew Shonfield, Robert Triffin, Pierre Uri, J. Van Ypersele.

The paper has been broadly agreed to by the members of the group acting in a private capacity. Individual members naturally do not necessarily subscribe to every particular point.

the British pound in terms of SDRs fell by 17.6 per cent and 11.0 per cent, respectively, over a three-month period.[2] The wide variability of exchange rates may be explained by short-term inelasticities in trade, leading to perverse changes in the trade balance; by speculative capital movements and by expectations as regards inflation rates that may be self-fulfilling and give rise to cumulative movements in exchange rates and in domestic prices. Action taken by a country that intends to derive advantages in export markets by accelerating a decline, or resisting an increase, in the value of its currency may also contribute to exchange rate variability.

The increased instability of foreign trade and payments associated with present exchange rate arrangements has been widely criticized, and suggestions have been made for measures to be taken to reduce its amplitude.[3] At the same time, given the differing interest of the individual countries and the varying importance of foreign trade in their national economies, the chances for an international agreement on such measures are slim, at least for some time to come. There is a greater chance for reaching an agreement on measures aimed at reducing instability within a group of countries which carry out much of their trade with each other and whose domestic economic activities are intimately linked by their mutual trade. These conditions are fulfilled in the European Common Market where intra-area trade accounts for more than one-half of total trade and, in view of the elimination of internal tariffs, domestic activities and intra-area trade are closely interconnected.

Greater stability in financial arrangements among the European Communities (EC) countries would reduce uncertainty in their mutual trade and investment and contribute to harmonious economic development in the European area. But, establishing an area of greater stability is also in the interest of other nations, and especially African and Middle Eastern countries that carry out

2. The relevant periods are December 1975 to March 1976 for the lira and February 1976 to May 1976 for the pound.
3. Cf. e.g., the essays by Edward M. Bernstein, Richard N. Cooper, Nurul Islam, Charles P. Kindleberger, Fritz Machlup, Robert V. Roosa, Robert Triffin, and John Williamson, in "Reflections on Jamaica," *Essays in International Finance*, No. 115, International Finance Section, Department of Economics, Princeton University, April 1976.

a large part of their foreign trade with Western Europe.

The high, and rising, degree of economic interdependence of the EC countries further points to the Common Market increasingly assuming the characteristics of an optimum currency area. However, experience has confirmed the views that the integration of national monetary and fiscal policies is a precondition for currency unification. In the absence of policy integration, currency unification remains a distant goal. Yet, in view of the advantages of optimum currency areas, this goal should be considered in devising measures to be applied in the more immediate future.

The objectives of lessening uncertainty in trade and payments within the European area and strengthening the European integration process can be served in a variety of ways. Alternative solutions include adopting a market-oriented or a policy-oriented approach, when the former would give emphasis to the establishment of a parallel currency and the latter would concentrate on the coordination of the economic policies of the member countries. Given the constraints under which the countries of the European Common Market operate, an intermediate solution is proposed here. This would entail adopting a three-pronged approach to include establishing rules for exchange rate adjustment, making steps for harmonizing national economic policies, and creating a parallel currency, the Europa. As it will become apparent, actions in these three areas are interdependent and would reinforce each other.

EXCHANGE RATE ADJUSTMENTS IN THE EUROPEAN AREA

Since the publication of the Werner Report in October 1970, discussions on monetary arrangements in the European Common Market have largely focused on the snake, an arrangement under which participating countries agree to maintain their exchange rates within a band of 2¼ per cent around the central cross-rates. While originally intended as an instrument of monetary integration through a gradual narrowing of fluctuations among the currencies of the EC member countries, the snake has in fact become a device for the joint floating of certain EC and non-EC currencies. At present, the snake combines the German mark and the currencies of several smaller countries whose economies are close-ly linked. Apart from small adjustments, since the establishment of the snake in April 1972 parity has been maintained between the German mark and the currencies of the Benelux countries that carry out about two-fifths of their trade with Germany and with each other. After a temporary absence, Denmark has also rejoined the snake, although the proportion of its trade with Germany and the Benelux countries is somewhat smaller. Finally, Norway and Sweden, who also carry out a substantial proportion of their trade with the EC countries, have joined the snake al-though they are not members of the Common Market. In turn, among the larger countries, Italy and the United Kingdom left the snake soon after its establishment while France was absent between January 1974 and July 1975, and left the snake again in March 1976. A lower degree of dependence on intra-EC trade, divergences in economic performance and differences in nation-al economic policies have often been invoked to explain these developments. Another important factor has been the strict con-ditions imposed on the participating countries by the arrange-ments under which the snake has operated.

The resulting divergence in the national economies of countries inside and outside the snake would be aggravated if actions aimed at furthering monetary integration were limited to coun-tries participating in the snake. Such a two-tier system would further contribute to divergences in policies, with adverse effects on the individual countries.

At the same time, given the interdependence of the national economies of the Common Market countries, actions taken in regard to the exchange rate by any of them will necessarily affect all others. Recognizing this interdependence makes ad-justments in exchange rates, whether in the form of changing the central rate or through floating, a matter of common con-cern. Accordingly, there is need for agreement on rules to be applied in regard to exchange rate adjustments.

It is suggested here that countries establish a "target zone" for their currencies, agreed upon jointly with the other member countries.[4] The target zone would be reviewed periodically and

4. A proposal to this effect was first made by C. J. Oort in a talk de-livered at The Royal Institute of International Affairs on June 18, 1976.

adjustment made when conditions so require. Such adjustments would take place in small steps, in the form of a "crawling zone," rather than in large jumps. The target zone would be initially set in terms of effective exchange rates, i.e., with respect to average changes in currency values weighted by trade shares. Eventually, however, the target zone should be defined in relation to the average movement of the participating currencies by linking it to the proposed parallel currency, the Europa (see below). Also initially the countries would not have the obligation to stay within their target zone, but would be expected to refrain from domestic policies and interventions in foreign exchange markets that would accelerate movements bringing their currency values outside the zone. In turn, they would be permitted to accentuate changes that bring their currency back to the target zone and will have in this the support of the other participating countries.

The establishment of a target zone and acting according to the described rules would be a condition for having access to financing from the European Monetary Co-operation Fund and benefiting from the support of the other member countries. At the same time, in order to make lending by the European Monetary Co-operation Fund a credible instrument to induce countries to behave according to the agreed-upon rules, it would be necessary to increase the credit facilities of the Fund. Lack of access to the Fund would not be a deterrent, however, to excessive devaluation or to a country refraining from revaluation. It is hoped that in such instances the consensus of opinion within the Common Market would be sufficient to induce the country in question to take appropriate action. Should this not be the case, the country could be obliged to lend its excess accumulation of member country currencies to the European Monetary Co-operation Fund. In extreme cases, the other member countries may also consider invoking escape clauses under the Rome Treaty.

Agreement on the establishment and the modification of target zones should be based on a thorough review of the situation in the individual countries at the Community level. This is preferable to relying on automatic rules based on a particular quanti-

---

Oort's proposal draws on guidelines for floating established by the IMF in June 1975, which have not been implemented.

tative indicator. Thus, it would be inappropriate to use reserve changes as the only indicator as it has been suggested. For one thing, reserve changes may be the result of temporary variations in the capital account; for another, there is a danger that even small variations in reserves would lead to speculative flows that would, in turn, trigger an exchange rate adjustment. Nor can one rely solely on indices of relative costs and prices that are subject to statistical problems and take no account of changes in service items, such as tourism, and in the capital account.

The proposed arrangements are compatible with some countries taking stricter obligations, such as maintaining present exchange rate margins in the framework of the snake. Enlarging these margins would not be desirable, since it would reduce stability in transactions among countries in question. However exchange rate changes and temporary floating would be allowed. At the same time, the snake countries would have a common target zone.

While permitting a choice among alternative arrangements, the application of the proposed rules would lead to greater stability in exchange markets among Community currencies. At the same time, consultations cannot be limited to actions concerning exchange rates. In fact, taking account of its effects on the national economies of the partner countries, reliance on exchange rate adjustment may often appear to be less desirable than changes in domestic policies or financing the deficit.

Recognizing the interaction of policy measures that may be used in the event of disequilibria would, in turn, require making lending by the European Monetary Co-operation Fund contingent on agreement on the measures to be taken in a particular situation. This, indeed, appears to be necessary in order to induce surplus countries to agree to a substantial increase in the size of the Fund that would be needed to make possible the operation of the proposed rules on exchange rate adjustment.

At a subsequent stage, member countries would assume the obligations to take appropriate policy measures aimed at remaining within the target zone. Eventually, the scope of common decision-making would also be increased and, if and when conditions warrant, the target zones would be narrowed.

STEPS TOWARDS POLICY COORDINATION

Thus far, we have considered the need for coordinated action to deal with disequilibria as they arise. While such coordination would have an *ex post* character, the objective of avoiding the emergence of disequilibria would call for *ex ante* coordination. The necessity of *ex ante* policy coordination also follows from the interdependence of the national economic policies of the EC countries. This fact is well-understood by the smaller member countries but it is only beginning to be recognized by the larger countries. Yet, the difference between the two groups of countries relates more to the speed of adjustment than to the ultimate effects of the policies applied.

The smaller countries have long recognized the limitations economic interdependence imposes on their scope of action. For one thing, the effectiveness of monetary and fiscal policies is severely circumscribed by the spillover in the form of higher imports and lower exports. For another, exchange rate changes will have immediate effects on domestic prices. Thus, for the smaller countries, purchasing power parity relationships hold even in the short run; domestic prices and exchange rates will adjust in a parallel fashion, irrespective of whether the initial change originated in domestic policies or in exchange rate adjustments.

The larger countries are less exposed to foreign trade, and hence experience a smaller spillover in the form of exports and imports following the application of expansionary policies, as well as smaller changes in domestic prices following an exchange rate adjustment. However, the greater freedom of action of the larger countries should not be overstated. This is because with the increased interdependence of the national economies of the EC countries, the length of the period of adjustment is shortening and, in the absence of barriers to intra-area trade, the indirect effects of actions taken by the larger countries reduce the effectiveness of these actions.

Thus expansionary policies will have a limited impact on domestic activity, even in the case of the larger countries. And, while a devaluation can be used to correct the resulting balance-of-payments disequilibrium, this will further exacerbate the inflationary repercussions of the expansion. At the end, real economic variables may have been little affected while the country has set in motion an inflationary spiral that is difficult to control.

For similar reasons, under free trade and capital mobility over-devaluation or the failure to revalue would not have lasting effects on the level of domestic economic activity because of imported inflation. At the same time, temporary benefits to one country involve losses to its partners. Now, since any country can play the game, it is in the interest of all member countries to agree on policy coordination in order to avoid temporary resource shifts and the creation of inflationary pressures that are not easily reversible.

In the context of medium-term programming over the last decade emphasis was given to agreeing on targets for economic growth, unemployment, and inflation in the Common Market countries without however providing for the coordination of policy measures necessary to attain these objectives. Thus, target setting has become an empty exercise as demonstrated by persistent deviations from the targets.[5] A more appropriate approach is to agree on targets for policy measures. In this connection, the question arises what kind of policies need to be coordinated. Extreme solutions derive from "monetarist" and "fiscalist" approaches.

While criticizing the policy-coordination approach, the authors of the All Saints' Day Manifesto, published in the November 1, 1975, issue of the *Economist*, effectively call for the coordination of monetary policies by proposing that national governments adopt noninflationary monetary targets. This recommendation appears to be based on the premise that one can rely on monetary policy alone and that inflation could be eliminated forever at a relatively moderate cost. By contrast, the new Cambridge School claims primacy for fiscal policies and suggests that government budgetary deficits are fully translated into balance-of-payments deficits.[6] This presumes that the private savings-and-

5. Cf. Bela Balassa, "Planning and Programming in the European Common Market," *European Economic Review*, October 1973.

6. Cf. e.g., R. J. Ball, T. Burns, and J. S. E. Laury, "The Role of Ex-

investment balance is not affected by fiscal policy and assigns a passive role to monetary policy.

The All Saints' Day Manifesto represents an extreme version of monetarist views. Thus, while the claim that maintaining unemployment at its "natural" level is compatible with any rate of inflation originated with U.S. monetarists, they do recognize that adjustment to a zero rate of inflation is a long process which would involve a considerable economic cost. Nor can it be assumed that adjustment to a zero rate of inflation would proceed smoothly, without being disturbed by internal or external shocks. Political developments in France and Italy and the drought in the summer of 1976 provide examples of internal shocks. In turn, the oil crisis, the U.S. recession, and the sudden increase of import demand for food on the part of the Communist parties have originated outside of the Community. Such shocks, whether internal or external, interfere with the adjustment process or disturb an equilibrium once established. Thus, rather than the postulated once-for-all adjustment to price stability, policies would need to be adopted to deal with recurrent shocks. A singleminded persistence in pursuing the objective of a zero rate of inflation would, then involve a cost in the form of unemployment and the underutilization of resources whenever a particular shock has had inflationary repercussions.

At the same time, apart from their being subject to different internal shocks, external shocks will have different effects on the individual member countries, depending on their economic structure, the bargaining power of various economic agents, and the political decision-making process. The balance-of-payments effects of the oil crisis, for example, varied from country to country depending on their reliance on imported oil, and policy reactions to this shock in the form of oil price adjustments and oil conservation measures also varied.

Also, reliance on monetary policy alone would effectively mean using a single instrument to pursue several, in part, conflicting objectives, such as price stability and full employment. And the monetarist approach assumes that a budgetary deficit will affect economic activity to its full extent if financed through money

change Rate Changes in Balance of Payments Adjustment—the United Kingdom Case," *Economic Journal* 87 (March 1977): 1–29.

creation and will have no effect at all if financed through borrowing in financial markets.

By contrast, according to the new Cambridge school, a government budgetary deficit will have identical effects on the savings-investment process and on the balance of payments, irrespective of the mode of financing. This approach attributes a passive behavior to private investors who are assumed to make their savings and investment decisions independently of the government deficit. Nor would these decisions be affected by changes in economic variables the budget deficit would engender. In assuming the irrelevance of government borrowing for private investment and savings decisions, the Cambridge approach neglects the possibility of "crowding out" private investors. It also disregards the effects of changes in the trade balance on the budget balance and fails to take account of monetary variables.

Nor can one assume that in the absence of money creation change in public and private spending will be fully offsetting as presumed by the monetarist approach. At any rate, the monetarist approach takes an essentially long-run view, while for policy-making the medium run is relevant. In fact, in the presence of continuing shocks, one cannot even speak of a long-run adjustment process, but rather of a succession of medium runs.

Although empirical evidence is far from conclusive, it would appear that in the medium run both monetary and fiscal policies matter.[7] And while they are not necessarily equally suitable to pursue particular objectives, monetary and fiscal policies are complementary in their economic effects.

These considerations point to the need for the coordination of monetary and fiscal policies in the European Common Market. Coordination would take the form of agreeing on targets for the relevant policy measures, such as the rate of monetary expansion, the size of the deficit in the public sector, and the method of

7. In experimenting with several macro-models in a recent paper Modigliani and Ando have found that in the United States over a 2 to 3 year horizon economic activity is affected by monetary policy, accompanied by a neutral fiscal stance as well as by fiscal policy, combined with neutrality in the monetary field. In fact, the effects of fiscal policy appeared to be somewhat greater. Franco Modigliani and Albert Ando, "Impacts of Fiscal Action on Aggregate Income: The Monetarist Controversy—The Theory and the Evidence," mimeo, 1975).

financing this deficit. As suggested in the Marjolin report, there is also need for coordinating the monetary measures used in carrying out particular policies.[8]

Given differences in the economic structure of the individual countries, however, it would be inappropriate to aim at identical policy targets. Also, the targets should be determined in terms of a range rather than a single figure. With the judicious choice of the targets, then, the scope for conflict in the determination of exchange rates may be reduced and advances can be made in the process of European economic integration.

Establishing and implementing targets for monetary and fiscal policies should be made a precondition for lending by the European Monetary Co-operation Fund and for mutual support by the EEC member countries. At the same time, it would be desirable to increase the relative importance of long-term credits. Long-term credits would contribute to more rapid economic growth in the Common Market by accelerating the structural transformation of the national economies of the member countries; they are also necessary to remedy structural imbalances in the Common Market countries that may be intensified as a result of the coordination of monetary, fiscal, and exchange rate policies. While the increased application of structural policy measures, in particular regional policy, becomes necessary to offset the possible adverse effects of the coordination of monetary, fiscal, and exchange rate policies, financing structural transformation from Community funds should be made contingent on the coordination of these policies. In this way, a *quid pro quo* is created in the application of measures that further economic integration in the Community.

ESTABLISHING A PARALLEL CURRENCY, THE EUROPA

Progress towards European integration would also require a unified capital market on a scale that can finance European industry. Such financing is especially necessary in the technological-

---

8. Rapport du Groupe de Reflexion, "Union Economique et Monétaire 1980," Commission des Communautés Européennes, 8 mars 1975. Cf. also Ronald I. McKinnon, "On Securing a Common Monetary Policy in Europe," *Banca Nazionale del Lavoro Quarterly Review*, March 1973.

ly sophisticated industries, such as aircraft, computer, and electronics, where its absence has been one of the obstacles to the development of European transnational firms that could fully utilize economies of scale and effectively compete with their American counterparts.

Denominating capital market transactions in terms of a parallel currency unit, the Europa, would serve the objective of establishing a unified capital market that would have a breadth national capital markets do not possess. It would thus permit achieving economies of scale in financial transactions, leading to a reduction in differences between interest rates paid by borrowers and received by lenders, and contribute to greater competition and efficiency in financial markets. The Europa would also offer an alternative to the U.S. dollar whose use in transactions among the Common Market countries has been objected to on several grounds. Apart from the seigniorage accruing to the issuer, the objections pertain to the use of the currency of a nonmember country accounting for only one-sixteenth of Common Market trade in intra-EC transactions; the impact of fluctuations in its value vis-à-vis member country currencies on these transactions; and the resulting effects of United States monetary policy on the national economies of the member countries.

The Europa would further offer advantages in denominating trade transactions among the Common Market countries as well as with countries that have strong trade ties with the Community. The increased use of the Europa in financial and in trade transactions, in turn, would make it attractive for use as a unit of account by transnational corporations that carry out the bulk of their activities in the European area.

The Europa could be employed as a unit of account in capital market transactions, in trade transactions, in the operations of transnational corporations, and in transactions between member country governments and with the Community without it being a means of payment. Such an alternative would, however, involve additional transaction costs associated with conversion into national currencies and it would not permit holding working balances in terms of the Europa, although this is desirable for carrying out international trade denominated in Europas. Further advantages can be derived therefore if the Europa is used as a means of payments. Using the Europa as a means of payments would also be necessary for it becoming an intervention and reserve currency. The performance of these functions would, in turn, require devising rules on the issue of the Europa, with attention given to the need to maintain equilibrium in foreign exchange markets.

Initially, issuing the Europa as a parallel currency would involve exchanging national currency reserves for Europas in a proportion and according to a timing to be agreed upon. This could take place in the framework of the European Monetary Co-operation Fund that would thus assume certain central banking functions. At the same time, increasing the resources of the Fund would make it possible to perform the functions described in connection with exchange rate adjustments.

The Europa would also eventually become a *numéraire* in which exchange rates of member country currencies are defined. It would finally provide the basis for the establishment of a common European currency if and when the necessary political and economic conditions are fulfilled.

In short, the Europa would serve a variety of functions in the private and in the public domain: (a) it would be used as a contractual unit of account, a means settlement, and a medium for holding working balances in private international transactions, capital and current; (b) it would be used in transactions between member country governments and the Community; (c) it would become a reserve and an intervention currency; and (d) it would serve as a *numéraire* in defining national exchange rates.

In order to appropriately fulfill these functions, the Europa should conform to certain criteria: it should be attractive for current and capital transactions; its use should discourage speculation; and it should be acceptable to national governments and to Common Market institutions. These criteria will be employed in evaluating alternative definitions below.

The authors of the All Saints' Day Manifesto proposed "the launching of a parallel European money of constant purchasing power . . . that would circulate along with the existing national currencies." While such a fully indexed currency would be attractive to lenders, it would be unattractive to borrowers. Also, it would be unacceptable to national governments as they would run the risk of wholesale shifts from national currencies to the Europa whenever real interest rates on obligations denominated in national currencies became negative. Negative real interest rates were often observed in the past and may also recur in the future, especially in regard to short-term securities, the market for which is greatly affected by the state of the business cycle and by monetary policy. In the event of negative real interest rates on short-term securities denominated in national currencies, large shifts out of these currencies could be avoided only if the nominal interest rate on the Europa was negative, which is hardly practicable. Nor do financial markets require obligations to be fully or even partially indexed. In the United States even the few bonds with variable interest rates issued during the period of rapid inflation in 1974–75 lost their attraction since and no new issue has been floated. Also, maturities have been lengthening in the Euro-dollar market. Bonds exceeding a maturity of 10 years were sold in early 1976 and it has been reported that a 15-year bond is now feasible. At any rate, indexing and the introduction of the Europa are independent from each other and serve different objectives. Thus, purely on the basis of Occam's razor principle, one should not burden the launching of the Europa with the extraneous requirement of indexing that would also encounter practical difficulties in the choice of the appropriate index number.

An alternative solution would be to link the Europa to the strongest Community currency. Under one variant, the value of the Europa would change parallel with the strongest currency *ab initio* (i.e., from the time of the Europa's establishment). This alternative is open to the objection that at any point of time the value of the Europa would be determined by past changes in the values of national currencies. Also, there would be a risk of speculation whenever a national currency would be expected to appreciate vis-à-vis the strongest currency *ab initio*, and hence the Europa. Last but not least, this alternative would be identified in the public mind as linking the Europa to the German mark, given the fact that Germany has had the lowest rate of inflation and it is likely to continue to do so for some time to come.

Linking the Europa to the strongest currency *pro tempore*

would eliminate the risk of speculation as the value of the Europa would always rise in proportion with that of the currency (currencies) which appreciate or appreciate the most at any particular point of time. And the cumulative change in the value of the Europa would not equal that of any single member currency, unless that currency never depreciated compared to the others. This has not been the case in the recent past and cannot be expected to occur in the future. In this connection, the experience of the last few years is of interest. If we take December 1971 as a basis and adjust the hypothetical European parallel currency in quarterly intervals in proportion with the appreciation of whichever currency appreciated the most during that quarter, by August 1976 its value would have increased by 43.6 per cent as compared to the SDR and 52.4 per cent as compared to the U.S. dollar while the relevant figures are 22.0 and 29.3 per cent for the German mark and 0.2 and 6.2 per cent for the French franc. The results were due to the fact that the French franc appreciated vis-à-vis the German mark between December 1971 and the third quarter of 1972, between the first and third quarters of 1974, and again between the fourth quarter of 1974 and the second quarter of 1975, and it depreciated in the remaining periods.

The continuation of these tendencies would make the value of the Europa to increase relative to all EC currencies and, most likely, against any other. It has been suggested that in this respect we would return to a situation existing in earlier times when national currencies showed a tendency to depreciate over time vis-à-vis an international or parallel currency. This international currency was first gold, subsequently the pound sterling, and until recently the U.S. dollar. There is an important difference, however, between the two cases. While the earlier predominance of international currencies was the result of the free play of market forces, the value of the Europa would have to be maintained artificially so as to avoid depreciation vis-à-vis the strongest currency. Such support would entail the Community providing Europas to all comers in exchange for national currencies and bearing the burden of the exchange rate risk. Also, it would be difficult to establish forward markets in the Europa so defined which is necessary for the functioning of capital markets.

Similar objections apply to introducing asymmetry in formulations based on a basket of currencies and to linking the value of the Europa to currencies that adopt narrower margins vis-à-vis each other. In the first case, the value of the average currency basket would increase when a participating currency appreciates but it would not decrease when a participating currency depreciates. In turn, the second formulation, used today by the Kredietbank of Luxembourg, that is by far the largest issuer of bonds denominated in terms of a composite unit, would in practice mean linking the value of the Europa to the snake currencies.

This conclusion follows, since in defining depreciation and appreciation in relative terms, asymmetrical adjustments in the value of the currency basket would make it equivalent to the strongest currency *pro tempore*, since at any point of time the value of the basket would change in the same proportion as the currency which appreciates or appreciates the most. At the same time, any other definition of depreciation and appreciation would introduce an element of arbitrariness. In turn, as we have seen, the snake itself presently consists of the German mark and the currencies of small countries linked to it. Thus, albeit to a lesser extent, this alternative is open to objections evoked in connection with the strongest currency *ab initio* formula.

Another alternative, put forward by Robert Triffin,[9] would involve defining the Europa as equivalent, at any point of time, to whichever currency has remained the most stable in terms of a weighted average of all member currencies. A similar formulation underlies the European Payments Union unit of account and the European unit of account originally used by the Kredietbank to denominate bond issues, both of which reflect Triffin's contribution. The choice of the most stable currency would appear to avoid fluctuations in the value of the Europa resulting from changes in a single currency which is out of line with others. This is not necessarily the case, however. With the depreciation of the British pound and the Italian lira in the first half of 1976, for example, the currencies of the countries participating in the snake would have provided the basis for determining the value of the Europa until the floating of the French franc, when the

9. "The Community and the Disruption of the World Monetary System," *Banca Nazionale del Lavoro Quarterly Review*, March 1975.

latter became the "center of gravity" between the snake currencies on the one hand and the depreciating pound and the lira on the other.

Thus, changes in the value of a single currency may affect the value of the Europa under this definition since, with the average changing, there may be a shift from one currency to another in terms of stability vis-à-vis this average. The possibility of such shifts, in turn, would create uncertainty in financial markets. At the same time, the formula of the stablest currency may not be easily comprehensible to the public.

The simplest solution would seem to be to define the Europa as a weighted average of the currencies of the EC member countries. This is the formula utilized by the official European Unit of Account, with weights assigned to the currencies of the individual EC countries on the basis of their gross national products and external trade as of June 28, 1974. The weights have been changed subsequently in accordance with the appreciation and the depreciation of the constituent currencies, resulting in an increase (decrease) in the share of appreciating (depreciating) currencies in the currency basket. The European Unit of Account offers advantages for trade transactions among the Common Market countries as it provides a pivot for national currencies. But, with inflation rates differing among the member countries, the dispersion of currency values around the EUA is bound to increase. It has been suggested that this fact would reduce the attractiveness of the European Unit of Account as a store of value in favor of the stronger currencies and explains the relative lack of success in capital markets of bond issues using the basket formula. Also, surplus countries may be reluctant to lend in terms of a unit that has a tendency to depreciate in terms of their own currencies. Finally, it is feared that there is a danger of speculative flights from the Europa.

It may be assumed, however, that differences in changes of currency values over time would be offset by interest rate differentials. Thus, interest rates on obligations denominated in terms of the Europa would tend to be lower than on obligations denominated in national currencies that tend to depreciate relative to the Europa and higher than for currencies that tend to appreciate. Furthermore, while speculation may be possible for short-term funds denominated in Europas, this will hardly be the case for long-term funds. And, there is no reason to assume that the possibility of speculation would increase due to the introduction of the Europa. At the same time, emphasis should be given to the need for the acceptance of the Europa in the financial markets that can alone ensure its widespread use. This objective can be furthered by modifying legislation so as to admit the holding of obligations denominated in the Europa in portfolios of banks and insurance companies.

The International Monetary System of the Year 2000

ROBERT TRIFFIN

Recent events have, if anything, increased the relevance of this essay by Robert Triffin, Frederick William Beinecke Professor of Economics at Yale University. It was published in 1972 in a volume edited by Jagdish N. Bhagwati under the title Economics and World Order, *from the 1970's to the 1990's.*

SAFE LONG-RUN FORECASTS

The safest prediction to make is that the world will not stand still. The international monetary field is dominated, as are all other aspects of human life, by the iron law of evolution and exhibits the same persistent struggle of man to control his physical environment rather than be controlled by it. This basic trend is often frustrated, slowed-down, or even reversed in the short run by man's inability to organize collective decision-making and to adjust outworn legal institutions and habits of mind to the new challenges, needs, and opportunities that confront him. In the longer run, however, conservatives are invariably defeated in their attempts to stop the clock of evolution, reactionaries in their efforts to set it back, and radicals in their hopes to jump into a future unrelated to the past that nurtures evolutionary growth. The tensions and crises springing from such misguided policies eventually result in their failure and reversal. Major evolutionary changes have indeed emerged most often from the failure, rather than from the success, of deliberately chosen government policies.

Future forecasts and policy advice should thus be derived from an examination of historical trends rather than from purely rational and abstract considerations taking no account of the constraints imposed upon us by the building materials inherited from the past and presently available to construct the future. Such a methodological approach suggests five steps in the past, present, and future evolution of the international monetary system.

From International Commodity Moneys to National Credit Moneys and International Commodity Reserves · This first stage in the modern evolution of the international monetary system was initiated long ago, but its major strides were taken in the nineteenth century and were completed during the early years of the 1930's world depression. Commodity moneys—in the form of gold and silver coins—still accounted for about two-thirds or more of the world monetary circulation in 1815, and more than half toward the middle of the nineteenth century, but only about one-seventh in 1913, and none by 1933. Their place was, by then, taken everywhere by subsidiary coinage—with a commodity value far inferior to its monetary value—and, overwhelmingly, by paper currency and bank deposits. Man-made money has long replaced commodity money in every country, the world over.

As distinct from commodity money, however, man-made money has little or no intrinsic value and normally circulates only within the national borders of the country in which it is issued. When payment has to be made abroad, the issuing national institutions must redeem their currency liabilities in a form acceptable to the foreign payee. Conversely, when a resident receives payment from abroad, the national issuing institutions must stand ready to convert into the national currency payments tendered from abroad in a form acceptable to them.

Since foreign payments and receipts do not balance exactly from day to day, month to month, or even year to year, national issuing institutions are led to accumulate so-called international monetary reserves in order to prevent—or keep within bounds—any undesirable fluctuations in the external value of the national currency. No specific agreement was ever negotiated internationally as to what should be regarded as international monetary reserves, acceptable to all countries in exchange for their respective national currencies. In the absence of such agreement commodity moneys—silver or gold alone—retained as international payments and reserves media the role which they were gradually losing as national payments media.

Such international reserves were initially held directly by each issuing bank, particularly as long as paper money issues—currency and deposits—remained for a considerable time legally convertible at the discretion of the holders into gold and/or silver coins for national as well as for international payments. This international reserve function, however, was gradually concentrated in the hands of a single national monetary authority (treasury or central bank), as each country found it desirable to assert some centralized control over the national money supply in order to avoid inflationary excesses by—and bankruptcies of—private banking firms and to use such centralized controls as a powerful instrument of national economic policy.

By 1933 international commodity moneys—gold and silver—had totally disappeared from actual circulation in the public and had been replaced everywhere by national credit money in the form of bank currency and deposits. The issuing deposit banks held most or all of their cash reserves aaginst their deposit obligations in the form of national claims—currency and deposits—against the country's central bank. Central banks, however, held international reserves—primarily in the form of gold—against their national monetary obligations to deposit banks and to the public. This process can be described for short as the substitution of the "gold-reserve standard" for the "gold-money standard" of former days.

From International Commodity Reserves to International Credit Reserves · The second stage of the international monetary voyage was the displacement of commodity money by man-made money in the international reserve system as well as in national monetary circulation in the public.

This second stage was initiated with the gradual substitution of the "gold-exchange reserve standard" for the previous pure "gold-reserve standard." It began moderately in the nineteenth century by the introduction of such a system in the colonies or dependent territories of the colonial powers. Local currency was issued by a "currency board" which held its own reserve funds, not in gold, but in the national currency of the so-called mother country (primarily the United Kingdom, the United States, and France). The system expanded vastly in the aftermath of the First World War, as most countries of the world began to accumulate a growing portion of their international monetary reserves in the form of short-term sterling and dollar claims alongside gold metal. It reached its first peak in 1928, foreign exchange reserves accounting in that year for about 24 per cent of world monetary reserves as against 15 per cent in 1913.

The devaluation of the pound (1931) and the dollar (1933) led to a temporary collapse of the system, but the trend away from commodity reserves toward man-made reserves was soon resumed and greatly accelerated during and after the Second World War. By mid-1969 gold reserves had dropped to about 51 per cent and foreign exchange holdings had risen to 41 per cent of world monetary reserves. A new form of man-made credit reserves made up the remaining 8 per cent: international credit claims on the International Monetary Fund (IMF).

There can be little doubt that this trend will continue at an accelerated pace in future years and that gold will ultimately lose its international reserve role, as it has long lost its role already as a circulating currency. Past trends, as well as economic analysis, suggest that the international reserve pool should grow at an annual rate of from 3 to 5 or 6 per cent a year in order to sustain feasible expansion of world trade and production. Even the lowest of these estimates would require reserve increases of more than $120 billion over the next 32 years—from $76.5 billion at the end of 1968 to nearly $200 billion by the year 2000. Gold reserves, on the other hand—including IMF and BIS (Bank of International Settlements) gold holdings—have grown by less than $16 billion over the last comparable span of 32 years, by less than $0.8 billion over the last 10 years, and have even declined by about $2.3 billion over the last 4 years. Barring a considerable increase in its official price—adamantly and, to my mind, rightly opposed by official as well as academic opinion—gold cannot be expected to provide more than an insignificant fraction, at best, of the needed reserve increases of future years.

The March 1968 two-tier gold market decision of the former gold-pool countries and the 1969 Amendment of the IMF Articles of Agreement contemplate indeed a total cessation—at least for the time being—of gold purchases by central banks from the market and the creation of a new reserve asset in the form of Special Drawing Rights (SDRs) on the IMF to the tune of $9.5 billion over the next three years.

These past trends and official intentions are all the more likely to persist in the future as they are strongly supported by rational arguments about the role of monetary reserves and by statistical evidence about the supply and demand of gold metal.

The need for monetary reserves is clearly related to the growth of world trade and production and of the international reserves required to preserve the international convertibility of the growing amounts of national currencies needed to sustain an expanding volume of production and exchange transactions. It is equally clearly, totally unrelated to the hazards governing the residual amount of monetary gold available to the monetary authorities, when private, industrial, artistic, hoarding, and speculative demand—at $35 an ounce, or any other price—is deducted from the total supplies coming to the market that are determined by gold mining and refining profitability, the latter being influenced in turn by the hazards of new gold field discoveries, of technological mining and refining innovations, of wage, interest, and taxation costs in the gold producing countries, etc.

Any rational management of world reserves and money must obviously lead to the ultimate discarding of the gold crutch that in the past eased, but constrained, the difficult task of reaching agreement on the objectives and means of the world reserve system. Man-made credit reserves will continue to displace and will eventually replace gold reserves, just as man-made credit money has long replaced gold money in every national monetary system, the world over.

From Spontaneously Held Credit Reserves to Negotiated Credit Reserves · Man-made reserves, however, are inevitably credit reserves, and the central banks that hold such reserves are in fact using their money-printing press to finance the policies of the debtor countries.

This did not concern them unduly as long as the amounts of financing involved were relatively small and the borrowing reserve-center countries (primarily the United States and the United Kingdom) highly solvent and liquid. Purchases and retention of foreign exchange holdings under the traditional "gold-exchange standards" were spontaneously decided by the creditor central banks, motivated by their own interest in maximizing their earnings and confident that such holdings could be freely converted into gold any time they decided to liquidate them.

All these props of the traditional gold-exchange standard were unviable in the long run and have by now been fully knocked out of the system. The credibility of the gold-conversion obligation assumed by the reserve centers could not survive indefinitely the persistent piling-up of gold-convertible indebtedness up to amounts far in excess of their total gold holdings. This stage has long been reached by Britain, whose pound sterling never regained fully its world role after the 1930 devaluation, but became mostly the regional settlements and reserve currency of the sterling bloc or area, bolstered for many years by exchange controls and experiencing two further devaluations in 1949 and in 1967. The U.S. dollar became, in practice, the sole full-fledged reserve currency of the world, following the Second World War. Liquid liabilities to foreigners began to exceed the gross gold reserves of the United States in the early months of 1960 and reached by mid-1969 the huge total of $39 billion—of which $10.2 billion, plus $4.7 billion were non-liquid liabilities to foreign official agencies and $1.0 billion to the IMF—while the total U.S. gold stock had fallen to little more than $11 billion and other U.S. reserve assets to $4.9 billion. It had long become clear that any large-scale exercise of the gold-conversion rights of foreign dollar holders could no longer be met from the declining U.S. gold stocks and would trigger in effect a formal suspension of gold payments and/or a devaluation of the dollar.

The reality of this threat—and of a repetition of the 1931 collapse of the gold-exchange standard—was brought home to the officials by the brief flare-up of gold prices to more than $40 an ounce in the London market in October 1960. Continuous consultation betwen the monetary authorities of the so-called Group of Ten major financial powers and of other IMF members succeeded in warding off this danger but have already modified out of all recognition the functioning of the traditional gold-exchange standard, transforming it in effect into a "negotiated credit reserves standard." By mid-1969 traditional reserve assets—i.e., gold and "liquid" dollar and sterling reserve balances—had dropped from $63.6 billion at the end of 1964 to less than $49.4 billion, while "negotiated" credit reserves had risen from $6.5 billion to

$26.7 billion. Gold reserves had contracted by $1.9 billion and liquid unnegotiated dollars and sterling holdings by $12.3 billion over the last 4½ years. Negotiated foreign exchange holdings, on the other hand, had risen by $26.2 billion, as a result of IMF operations, of the continuous expansion of so-called swap agreements between central banks, of the conversion of liquid U.S. obligations into "Roosa bonds," etc., of the various Basle agreements in defense of sterling, and of the semi-consolidation of U.K. liabilities to the monetary authorities of the overseas sterling area countries.

Toward a Centralized International Credit Reserves System · This motley of agreements and salvage operations performs two essential functions. They are designed, first of all, to avoid a brutal collapse in the basic components of the international reserve pool, i.e., the massive liquidation of sterling and dollar reserve balances and large-scale transfers of gold from official reserves to the private gold market. They have also been used to increase world reserves by credit operations in the face of the drying up of new gold supplies to the monetary authorities.

The shortcomings of the methods used to achieve these results are however, increasingly obvious. They entail, first of all, extremely precarious forms of financing, subject to continuous negotiation and renegotiation of short-term or medium-term credits whose actual liquidation would in fact provoke widespread defaults by the debtors. This feeds a speculative climate prompting destabilizing movements of funds which further aggravate the tensions and risks inherent in such an absurd system of reserve creation.

A second, and even greater, defect is the disproportionate political power conferred thereby to major creditor and reserve-debtor countries to distort the normal functioning of the so-called adjustment mechanism. Creditor countries are legally entitled to decide whether to finance persistent deficits of the reserve-debtor countries and to switch at any time such financing from one country to another—converting, for instance, their sterling holdings into dollar holdings, or vice-versa—or to extract from them, in repayment of previously as well as of currently accumulated claims, huge amounts of gold, far in excess of new world supplies and even of the debtor countries' outstanding gold stocks. The reserve debtors, on the other hand—i.e., the United Kingdom and, primarily today, the United States—can use the threat of default and their enormous economic and political power to force weaker countries to finance their continuing deficits. As of June 1969, their net indebtedness to foreign central banks and the IMF totalled more than $28 billion, i.e., about half of the gross monetary reserves of all the other countries of the world taken together. The SDR Agreement itself—essential as it is for the rationalization of the reserve-creating process—allots, largely as potential gifts, to these two most capitalized countries of the world well over a third of future SDR creation, as against less than a fourth for the more than eighty poorer countries of the developing Third World.

The future evolution and reforms of the international monetary system should cure these various shortcomings through the centralization and joint management of international reserves.

1. First of all, international monetary reserves should be held exclusively in the form of truly international reserve assets with the IMF—or a similar institution—rather than in gold or metal or in the national currencies of so-called reserve centers. (Working balances needed for daily stabilization interventions in the exchange market will undoubtedly continue for a while to be held in such currencies, but should ultimately be held also in the form of reserve deposits with the IMF.)

2. Secondly, the overall volume of such reserves should be jointly determined and adjusted to the reserve requirements of the potential expansion of world trade and production, so as to minimize inflationary and deflationary pressures on the world economy. Reserve creation—and destruction—should no longer be abandoned to the hazards of gold production and private demand, of balance-of-payments fluctuations of the reserve center countries, nor of the decision—spontaneous or enforced from outside—of individual reserve-holding countries to extend reserve credits to one country rather than another, and to switch or liquidate them at any time. The reserves held by any country with the IMF should remain fully liquid for the settlement of balance-of-payments deficits, but not for any other purposes unrelated to their basic economic functions. No country should be

forced to accumulate more reserves than it wishes, at the cost of inflating its own economy. It could, at any time, stop this accumulation by modifying its own internal or external policies, but not by imposing policy changes upon other countries through unilaterally decided switches in the composition of its reserve assets from one currency into another or into gold.

3. The lending power inevitably entailed by reserve accumulation would thus be exercised and managed through collective decisions of the international community itself, rather than through the unilateral, and often mutually conflicting decisions of several scores of supposedly independent countries. Such a centralized reserve system would, moreover, be free to use such lending power for long-term, as well as for short-term, investments, without running any risk of illiquidity. Any withdrawals of deposits by the deficit countries would necessarily be matched by equivalent increases in the deposits of the surplus countries, as long as the centralized institution included as members all countries of the world. The IMF could indeed hold the bulk of its assets in any form acceptable to its members, up to and including long-term loans and investments, "consols" carrying no fixed repayment obligations, or even straight grants if it so decided.

It is inconceivable that this lending power could long continue to be used—as contemplated in the present SDR agreement—for the automatic distribution of reserve assets among all members, in accordance with any arbitrary allocation formula, irrespective of the soundness of their national policies and of their acceptability to prospective lenders, i.e., to the member countries with net surpluses in their overall balance of payments. The countries that decide jointly on the amounts of reserves to be created in the future will also wish to decide jointly how the counterpart lending power should be used. They will wish to have it used for jointly agreed purposes and policies, rather than for the blind underwriting of national policies on which they have not been consulted and with which they may at times strongly disagree. Such purposes should clearly include the normal stabilization operations of the IMF and those now covered by swap agreements and by the IMF "General Arrangements to Borrow." They should extend further to the indirect financing of development loans, through purchases of such obligations as those now issued by the International Bank for Reconstruction and Development, the International Development Association, etc. They could even be directed toward the financing activities of the United Nations, the programs of the World Health Organization, etc.

In brief, the collective creation of international reserves required to sustain the growth of world trade and production should be put at the service of collectively agreed purposes, even though they can hardly be expected to finance more than a fraction of them and although other sources of financing will remain necessary to satisfy recognized needs.

From Centralized Reserve Creation to Centralized Money Creation · The centralization of reserve creation might logically lead to the centralization of money creation itself, and the adoption of a single circulating—as well as reserve—currency for the world as a whole.

Such a crowning achievement should indeed be within reach if the twin goals of exchange freedom and stability, so often affirmed even by the most nationalistic policy makers, were to be taken at face value. The merger of national currencies into a single world currency would, of course, require national sovereign states to accept collectively decided monetary disciplines and to relinquish their "sovereign right" to the use of their national money-printing press. Identical—and indeed stiffer —disciplines and renunciations of sovereignty would, however, be equally entailed in their firm and irrevocable adherence to free and stable exchange rates. The more expansionist countries would be forced, willy nilly, to bring their rate of monetary expansion in line with that of other countries, in order to avoid continued reserve losses that would otherwise make it impossible for them, in the end, to preserve free and stable exchange rates.

The harmonization of national policies is indeed as indispensable to the maintenance of exchange rate stability and the absence of exchange restrictions as it would be to the merger of national currencies into a single currency.

The recent advocacy of more flexibility in the exchange rates system—"wider bands" or "crawling pegs"—is indeed inspired by this observation and by the crises triggered over recent years by the undue postponement of needed exchange rate readjustments among major trading countries.

The substitution of a centralized reserve system for the present gold-exchange reserve system would remove major obstacles to such readjustments for the so-called reserve currencies, i.e., the pound, sterling, and primarily the U.S. dollar. A system of universally and constantly fluctuating exchange rates, however, would be as unrealistic and undesirable as a system of universally and permanently stable exchange rates. The former would be justified only if we were forced to resign ourselves to the universal and constant failure of more desirable harmonization policies, while the second is prematurely predicated on the universal and uninterrupted success of such policies.

Neither assumption fits the variety of conditions influencing the failure, or success, of harmonization policies. Some countries are closely linked by intensive trade and capital relations, making them highly interdependent on one another and incapable of pursuing successfully disparate national monetary policies. Full recognition of this   interdependency may prompt greater and more successful efforts at policy harmonization among them than would be acceptable and feasible, at this stage, on a world-wide scale, between countries less closely linked together not only economically, but geographically and historically.

Looking toward the year 2000, one should certainly anticipate full economic, monetary, and even policital unification within emerging regional groups of countries such as, for instance, the European Economic Community and the countries of Central America.

World-wide monetary union or even exchange rate stability are less likely to prove feasible and successful, even by the year 2000. The maximum that I would dare hope for, in this respect, is that exchange rates among regional monetary areas far wider than the present national states will be operationally recognized as a matter of collective interest, calling for collective, rather than unilateral, decisions.

The first step in this direction is already embodied in the IMF Articles of Agreement. Except for an initial change of no more than 10 per cent, a country cannot change its par value unless the Fund concurs that it has become incompatible with "fundamental equilibrium." A similar procedure should be adopted in order to bar the maintenance of a par value which has, in the view of a majority of Fund members, become incompatible with fundamental equilibrium.

The evidence on which such a decision could be reached might be derived primarily from the evolution of a country's monetary reserves level. For instance, excessive or persistent reserve losses or gains could be regarded as a *prima facie* presumption of fundamental disequilibrium, entailing an undue export inflationary or deflationary pressures by the country concerned to other Fund members. Such a country should then be required to consult with the Fund to determine whether this presumption should, or not, be reversed by other evidence—such as, for instance, abnormal capital movements—and which changes in its policies and/or exchange rates should be called for in order to restore fundamental equilibrium with the least possible damage to it and to other members.

If these consultations failed to produce agreement between the country concerned and the Fund, or if the country's authorities found themselves unable to carry out the agreements arrived at, the Fund would of course be powerless to enforce and implement the changes which it deemed desirable in the country's internal policies. It could, however, if it wished, decide to protect its members against the continued exportation of inflation or deflation to them, by enjoining the monetary authorities of the country concerned from further sales—or purchases—of foreign exchange from the market. That is to say, if fundamental equilibrium cannot, in fact, be restored by agreed internal policy measures, the country in disequilibrium must alow the market itself to bring its external accounts into balance. It should no longer be allowed to perpetuate its deficits—or surpluses—by preventing its currency from depreciating—or appreciating—in the market.

Needless to say, this description is only a highly simplified outline of a procedure which may be modified substantially in its application. Transitional measures may ease and smooth it out over time. For instance, further market interventions might not be entirely prohibited but might be limited instead either in actual amounts, per month or per quarter, or to the extent necessary to limit market changes in exchange rates to an agreed "rate of crawl."

Let us note, finally, that this proposed "fork" or reserve changes already applies in effect to the countries in persistent deficits. Reserve losses and depletion will indeed force them to let their rate depreciate on the market if they cannot reach agreement with the Fund on the policy measure needed to obtain assistance from it. All that I foresee here is the extension to surplus countries of restraints symmetrical to those which the facts of life already impose upon the deficit countries.

UNPREDICTABLE SHORT-TERM MEANDERS

The long-run evolution confidently described above on the basis of economic rationality and historical trends may, however, proceed more or less smoothly and rapidly, depending on the understanding or resistance which it encounters on the part of the national authorities among which international agreements will have been hammered out.

Two major issues may call for brief comments in this respect: the speed with which gold, on the one hand, and reserve currencies, on the other, may make room for the centralized reserve system of the future.

The Future of Gold · Irrational as it is, the survival of gold in the international monetary system is historically understandable, as the by-product of the lack of international agreement on any generally acceptable reserve instrument. The only practical alternative to gold—or other forms of commodity reserves—is credit reserves. Credit reserves, however, cannot be made generally acceptable and transferable for balance-of-payments settlements in the absence of previous international agreement as to their amounts, their beneficiaries, the purpose which they finance, and the guarantees and other conditions applicable to them.

Such agreement had never been reached in fact, or even seriously attempted, before the recent adoption of the SDR Amendment to the Fund's Articles of Agreement. Sterling, and later the dollar, had emerged *de facto* as supplementary reserve instruments, but only under the assumption—later, and inevitably, disproved—that they could easily be converted at any time into gold without danger of exchange losses.

Gold still retains its attraction, today, as an imagined alternative to the acceptance of a satellite "dollar area" status by other theoretically sovereign countries. Yet, the evolution of events since the March 1968 two-tier gold decision should have dispelled this illusion. The real alternative to an international credit reserves system is no longer gold, but the dollar itself in the short-run, followed sooner or later by a relapse into trade and exchange restrictions and exchange rate instability.

In the short-run, overall surplus countries are faced with the alternative of accumulating dollars—either as central bank reserves or through the Euro-dollar market—or to let their currency appreciate in relation not only to the dollar but to the other currencies which are kept at par with the dollar. This provides a most unhealthy incentive to the U.S. authorities to let other countries worry about the persistent balance-of-payments deficits of the United States. If they accept the responsibility of keeping the dollar stable in terms of their currency—as most have done up to now—they will in fact help finance the U.S. deficits. If they refuse such financing, their currency will appreciate and this will help decrease or wipe out the overvaluation of the dollar and the undercompetitiveness of U.S. producers in international trade.

In both cases, official gold prices will remain stable in terms of dollars. Most speculators wrongly assumed, until March 1968, that the ending of official interventions in the gold market would drive gold prices far above their official level. This might be true in the long run, since current gold production in the non-Communist world (about $1.4 billion per year) hardly exceeds any longer the sum of traditional, persistent hoarding demand (about $200 million to $300 million a year?), as distinguished from speculative demand, plus fast-rising industrial and artistic demand, running in the first quarter of 1969 at about $1.1 billion a year, and bound to rise further in future years. There is little doubt that market demand will soon and increasingly exceed production if gold prices remained at $35 an ounce, while all other prices continued to rise, even at relatively moderate rates, over future years. This should normally force gold prices up, but the process may be considerably delayed by disgorging from the huge private hoards accumulated in recent years (more than $5 billion since the end of 1964 and nearly $12 billion since 1949) and/or from official reserve hoards (about $41 billion in mid-1969) which full acceptance of SDRs or other credit reserve instruments might transform into surplus stocks, no longer needed or attractive as reserves for the monetary authorities.

Yet, although less and less likely as of now, an increase in gold prices cannot be totally ruled out if the persistence of U.S. deficits finally induces major surplus countries to stop their accumulation of dollars, and even to try to liquidate their dollar holdings on the market if the U.S. Treasury suspended formally its gold payments to official dollar holders. For the reasons indicated above, however, this would merely postpone temporarily, rather than arrest permanently, the historical trend and rational evolution from gold reserves to man-made credit reserves. There can be little doubt that, over the long run, monetary authorities will wish to put international reserves at the service of broad economic objectives and policies, rather than at the service of gold price stability. Once a reasonable alternative to gold has been found workable, they will have no more reason to stabilize the price of gold—a foreign commodity to most of them—than that of ivory, salt, or any other commodity.

The Future of Reserve Currencies · The centralized reserve system envisaged above will ultimately take the place of the present reserve currencies—primarily sterling and the dollar—as well as of gold. This transition should be eased by the adoption of an "International Conversion Account," proposed under various names by private economists[1] and unanimously endorsed by the Joint Economic Subcommittee of Congress on International Exchange and Payments in their *Report* of September 1968. Outstanding reserve currency stocks would be taken over by such an account, in exchange for the new centralized credit reserves on the IMF. The obligation of the reserve-debtor countries would be thereby transformed into long-term debt, or even "consols," whose actual reimbursement could be spread over a long period of years, and/or—even better—geared to the stabilization inter-ventions of the IMF.

Again, protracted lack of agreement on some such solution may

[1] Such as Fritz Machlup, Harry G. Johnson, Robert Mundell, E. M. Bernstein, James Tobin, myself, and others.

well spell a continued drift into a *de facto* inconvertible dollar area system, bound to explode sooner or later into exchange restrictions and exchange rate instability. It is unlikely, however, that all countries would resign themselves indefinitely to abandon to one country alone the actual management of an international credit-reserves system. I have little doubt that the trend outlined above will continue to assert itself and prevail in fact, well before we, or our children, reach the year 2000.

CONCLUDING REMARK

The past history of the international monetary system strongly supports—and, indeed, largely inspires—the long-term forecast ventured in this paper. It also inspires considerable pessimism, however, as to the likelihood of an orderly evolution, effectively oriented by our so-called monetary and political leaders. They have been led by events far more often than they have shown themselves willing and able to lead them. The major changes in the international monetary system have, nearly invariably, been misunderstood and resisted by bureaucrats and officials. They have come, in most cases, as the by-products of the failures of official policies and of the resulting crises of the system, rather than as the planned outcome of official intentions and pronouncements.

If the past must be taken as a guide to the future, the long-run evolution forecast in the first part of this paper will be the meandering one which I refused to predict in its second part. Man, however, is not totally a prisoner of his past. He can influence— if not determine—his future if he understands the evolutionary forces which may help carry him to success, but which will defeat him if he obstinately tries to ignore them.